PORTUGAL

Contents

Original text by Tony Kelly
Updated by Kerry Christiani

Edited, designed and produced by AA Publishing, a trading name of AA Media Limited, whose registered office is Fanum House, Basing View, Basingstoke, Hampshire RG21 4EA.
Registered number 06112600.

The content of this book is believed to be accurate at the time of printing. Due to its nature the content is likely to vary or change and the publisher is not responsible for such change and accordingly is not responsible for the consequences of any reliance by the reader on information that has changed. Any rights that are given to consumers under applicable law are not affected. Opinions expressed are for guidance only and are those of the assessor based on their experience at the time of review and may differ from the reader's opinions based on their subsequent experience.

Published in the United States by AAA Publishing, 1000 AAA Drive, Heathrow, Florida 32746-5063.
Published in the United Kingdom by AA Publishing.

ISBN 978-1-59508-509-2

Cover design and binding style by permission of AA Publishing
Color separation by AA Digital Department
Printed and bound in China by Leo Paper Products

A04749
Maps in this title produced from mapping © MAIRDUMONT / Falk Verlag 2012 (except p185)
Transport map © Communicarta Ltd, UK

The Magazine

A great holiday is more than just lying on a beach or shopping till you drop – to really get the most from your trip you need to know what makes the place tick. The Magazine provides an entertaining overview to some of the social, cultural and natural elements that make up the unique quality of this engaging country.

21st-century PORTUGAL

Visit Portugal today and you are just as likely to hang out in a trendy lounge bar, play on some of Europe's best golf courses or shop in the chic Chiado quarter of Lisbon as you are to sit on a beach or watch a religious procession.

Portugal in the 21st century is changing fast. This dynamism can be partly traced to entering the European Economic Community (EEC, now the European Union (EU)) in 1986, when Portugal broke with its more traditional past. Since then, it has adopted the euro as currency (in 2002), hosted Europe's biggest football competition (Euro 2004) and enjoyed several years as one of Europe's fastest-growing economies. All this, despite having the longest working hours in the EU (apart from the UK) with some of its lowest salaries.

Economic Woes

In the latter half of the decade, with crippling public debt and low productivity and growth in the light of the global recession, the country's economic tides changed. In 2011, there was widespread opposition to the proposed austerity measures to tackle the budget deficit, which included tax increases and cuts in pensions, salaries and unemployment benefits. Faced with a struggling economy, Portugal followed Greece and Ireland and was the third country to receive a bail-out (€78 billion) from the EU and the International Monetary Fund. At the time of writing, Portugal had committed to cutting its deficit to three per cent of GDP by 2013.

Bright Future

Portugal, its current economic troubles aside, has progressed rapidly over the past few decades, its state-of-the-art airports and railway stations annually welcoming 13 million people. For much of the 20th century, Portugal was inaccessible for the average traveller, and even in 1985, there was just one motorway running between Porto and Lisbon, and very few ways of exploring further afield. Today, there are dozens of new roads opening up the interior and linking previously inaccessible regions with Lisbon and Spain.

The staging of Expo'98 in Lisbon (➤ 58–59) on the 500th anniversary of Vasco da Gama's epic journey to India unleashed a building boom in Lisbon, bringing about new bridges, Metro lines, skyscrapers and malls; Euro 2004 also meant vast sums spent on new stadia and upgrading hotels. The most recent example of Portugal's wide-scale urban regeneration is the vibrant city of Guimarães (➤ 93) in northern Portugal, Europe's Capital of Culture 2012. Once famous as a textile-manufacturing hub, today Guimarães is getting a new lease of life, with a growing crop of

Vasco da Gama bridge at Parque das Nações in Lisbon
Page 5: The fishing fleet at Albufeira

design-oriented restaurants, artists' studios and cultural centres giving the UNESCO-listed city a new buzz and energy.

Breaking with the Past

The first seeds for this intense period of change came with the Carnation Revolution of 1974, when the people of Lisbon ended over 40 years of dictatorship under António Salazar by stuffing carnations down the barrels of soldiers' guns. At the same time, the end of the colonial wars and giving independence to their former African colonies brought thousands of Angolans, Cape Verdeans and Mozambicans to Lisbon, creating a vibrant, racially diverse, tolerant city.

> "Catholic priests are no longer seen as the guardians of public morality in Portugal"

During the 1980s, Portugal moved into the European mainstream, and some of its more entrenched traditions began to wane; the influence of the Catholic church, for example, is declining and, although over 84 per cent of the population declared themselves Catholic in the 2001 census and religious festivals are as popular as ever, Sunday attendance at church is low. Catholic priests are no longer seen as the guardians of public morality, and contraception is widely available. Unmarried sex is not taboo and homosexuality is more widely accepted.

Portuguese Heroes

Portugal is also making more impact outside of its borders. Novelist José Saramago won the Nobel Prize for Literature in 1998; Paula Rego is an internationally feted artist whose painting of Germaine Greer hangs in the National Portrait Gallery, London; and Álvaro Siza Vieira is a Pritzker Prize-winning architect. Cristiano Ronaldo and former player Luis Figo rate among the world's best footballers, and coach José Mourinho has won the Champions League, and also coached FC Porto, England's Chelsea and Italy's Internazionale. At the time of writing, he is the manager of Real Madrid.

SPEAKING PORTUGUESE

Today, the population of Portugal stands at around 10.7 million, with a further three million citizens living abroad. Portuguese is spoken by more than 200 million people worldwide and is the official language of five African nations, as well as Brazil in South America (in fact, in May 2008, parliament controversially voted to bring the spelling of "Portuguese" in its home country in line with that in Brazil). This makes Portuguese the world's seventh most spoken language and more common than French.

Portugal in a glass
PORT AND WINE

It is many years since Portugal's wine industry has been just about port and Matheus Rosé. Inspired by indigenous grape varieties and helped by a warm sunny climate, winemakers are now making rich, smooth red wines and crisp, fresh whites that compete with other quality wine regions.

It takes grit to make wine in much of the country. Many of the vines grow on sharp, heat-baked schist rocks that can only be cared for by hand because of steep slopes that sit at around 700m (2,297ft) above sea level. Nowhere is this more evident than the beautiful Douro Valley (➤ 176–79) in the north of Portugal, which has long been famous for its production of grapes destined for port and is the oldest demarcated wine region in the world. Today, it is also producing well-structured, powerful red wines that have deservedly been getting more and more international attention – perfect for pairing with a rich steak sauce.

The mild and sunny Portuguese climate creates the perfect conditions for winegrowers

Fruity Reds and Crisp Whites

Heading further south, halfway between Porto and Lisbon, the pretty Beiras region produces the full-bodied reds of the Dão and the fruity reds of Bairrada. Further still, between Lisbon and the Algarve, the Alentejo is probably Portugal's fastest-growing wine region, with new producers bringing in fresh ideas and outside investment.

> "Alentejo is probably the fastest-growing wine region in the country"

White-wine lovers shouldn't dismiss the vibrant, slightly sparkling Vinho Verde that comes from northwest Portugal. It has managed to shake off much of its old-fashioned image in recent years, and is the perfect aperitif; order it on a shaded terrace in the hot sunshine, or pair it with an appetizer of grilled sardines.

Port – Perfect Anytime

While the vineyards of Portugal develop, port still remains the symbol of the local drinks industry and is a drink to be enjoyed at any time – a white port and tonic as an aperitif or an aged tawny with chocolate cake.

Wine has been made in the 100km (62-mile) stretch of the Douro Valley since Roman times, but the origins of port lie in the 17th century, when British traders, cut off from their supplies of claret by wars with France, developed a taste for strong Portuguese wines. The Methuen Treaty of 1703 lowered the duty on Portuguese wine coming into Britain in return for concessions for British textile merchants in Portugal. Unfortunately, the wines did not travel well, so the port shippers began adding brandy to fortify them during their voyage. Port was born, along with the names (Croft, Dow and Taylor) that still control much of the trade.

VISITING THE PORT HOUSES

Both the Douro vineyards and Vila Nova de Gaia are UNESCO World Heritage Sites, and a new wine tourism movement in both areas has meant that many port houses open for visitors, plus there are a variety of car, boat and train trips that can take you out to explore the terraced vines. The town of Porto (➤ 80–83) is a perfect weekend destination, with its narrow winding streets and large handsome squares. Climbing to the highest point of Porto, you get a beautiful view over the river to Vila Nova de Gaia (➤ 84–85), with the neon signs for famous names of port flashing like a tiny Hollywood Hills. Over in Gaia itself, there are increasing numbers of wine bars and restaurants opening up, and extensive restoration work has been done on the waterfront. Some of the best port houses to visit include Ramos Pinto and Taylor's (➤ 85). For a wide range of ports by the glass, visit the Solar do Vinho do Porto (➤ 72) in Lisbon where there are more than 300 varieties to choose from.

STYLES OF PORT

White: Dry or sweet, and served chilled as an aperitif.

Pink: Light and fruity style of port designed to appeal to younger drinkers.

Ruby: Dark, full-bodied and fruity.

Tawny: Amber-coloured, aged in wood for 10 years or more.

Colheita: Complex, spicy, single-harvest tawny aged for at least seven years.

Late Bottled Vintage (LBV): Smooth and light-bodied port from a single-harvest wine aged in wood for four to six years.

Vintage: In exceptional years, a vintage may be declared and the very best wine will be transferred into bottles after two years in the cask. It will age in the bottle for at least 10 years, developing a dark colour, a heady aroma and a crusty sediment. Vintage port should be decanted before being served, and unlike other ports, it needs to be consumed within a day of being opened.

The grapes – usually Tinta Roriz and Touriga Nacional – are harvested by hand in autumn, and crushed in stone vats or (more usually) fermented in steel tanks. After two days, the fermentation process is stopped by the addition of grape spirit and the wine is transferred into wooden casks (known as pipes). The following spring, the casks are taken to mature in the port lodges at Vila Nova de Gaia (➤ 84–85). Since the construction of several dams, traditional *barcos rabelos* (➤ 84) can no longer travel along the Douro. Today, trucks are often used to transport the casks from the *quintas* (farms) to the lodges in Vila Nova de Gaia, which has led to the emergence of smaller houses that sell direct from the Douro.

A few of the famous port lodges lining the river bank in Vila Nova de Gaia

Nautical NATION

On the edge of the Atlantic and at odds for much of its history with Spain, its only land neighbour, the coastline defines Portugal's identity as a seafaring nation, and its influence is seen in everything from architecture to food.

The Age of Discovery

The Portuguese like to look back to the golden age when their explorers sailed uncharted waters in search of new lands. The greatest of all these heroes is Henry the Navigator (1394–1460, ➤ 80, 156), Grand Master of the Order of Christ and architect of the *descobrimentos* (discoveries).

Henry took part in the capture of Ceuta on the Moroccan coast in 1415, but never sailed again, retiring instead to Sagres (➤ 156–157) where he established a school of navigation to train the nation's best minds. Here, new forms of navigational instruments were developed and a design for a new type of ship, the caravel, a cross between a traditional Douro cargo boat and an Arab dhow. The caravel revolutionized sea travel. Its triangular sails allowed sailors to take advantage of side winds and travel much faster and were used by Columbus (1451–1506) in voyages to the New World.

Great Explorers

During Henry's lifetime, Madeira and the Azores were "discovered" and the explorer Gil Eanes rounded the Cape Bojador in West Africa – believed at the time to be the end of the known world, beyond which were thought to lurk sea monsters and unknown perils.

The holy grail was the discovery of a sea route to India by Vasco da Gama in 1498, which allowed Portugal to control the trade of oriental spices, silks and carpets that crossed Asia, and establish colonies in Angola and Mozambique as well as trading posts in Goa, Timor and Macau. The Vasco da Gama bridge in Lisbon is a fitting tribute to the great man; it crosses the Rio Tejo and at 17.2km (10.7 miles) is the longest bridge in Europe.

A statue of Henry the Navigator in Lagos

Fishing boats at Setúbal harbour, representing one of Portugal's major industries

In the meantime, Pedro Álvares Cabral had found Brazil, awarded to Portugal under the 1494 Treaty of Tordesillas, which divided the known world thus far into Spanish and Portuguese spheres of influence. The country's naval influence declined during the 17th century as the Dutch and English fleets grew in strength, particularly in the trade with the East Indies and Asia, although Portugal's last overseas colony, Macau, was handed back to China only in 1999.

Portuguese Fishing Industry

In the 20th century, Portugal still had one of the world's largest fishing fleets and cod fishing off the coast of North American and Canada became

PORTUGAL'S GREAT VOYAGES OF DISCOVERY

1419 Madeira
1427 The Azores
1460 Cape Verde
1482 Diego Cão reaches the mouth of the Congo, leading to the Portuguese conquest of Angola.
1488 Bartolomeu Dias rounds the Cape of Good Hope, South Africa.
1498 Vasco da Gama discovers a sea route to India.
1500 Pedro Álvares Cabral discovers Brazil.
1519 –1522 Fernão de Magalhães (Ferdinand Magellan) leads the first circumnavigation of the world. He dies en route and the journey is completed under the leadership of Juan Sebastián del Cano.
1572 Luís Vaz de Camões' epic poem, *Os Lusíadas* (The Lusiads), is first published, evoking the Age of Discovery with tales of distant lands.

To learn more about Portugal's relationship with the sea, visit the Museu de Marinha in Belém (➤ 48), which is devoted to Portugal's maritime history.

Padrão das Descobrimentos, Lisbon, built to commemorate Portugal's great explorers

the driving force of the Portuguese economy, with elaborate ceremonies held to wave the men off on fishing voyages. In recent years, however, the Portuguese fishing fleet has declined due to overfishing, and stringent rules aimed at conserving the world's deep-sea fish stocks. However, fishing is still an important industry and brightly coloured wooden boats remain a familiar sight in ports like Peniche and Nazaré (➤ 27) on the west coast, and Lagos (➤ 165) and Olhão in the Algarve.

These days, the sea is yielding a different but still lucrative harvest, as hordes of tourists are attracted to the superb beaches of the Algarve, Costa de Lisboa, Costa de Prata and Costa Verde. In one maritime area, Portugal in still leading the world – just off the northern coast, in Agucadoura, the world's first commercial wave farm opened in October 2008. Unfortunately, it was shut down in early 2009 when the financial crisis hit. Plans are still in the pipeline for a second 26-machine farm.

MANUELINE ART

King Dom Manuel I is known as Manuel the Fortunate as it was during his reign (1495–1521) that the sea route to India was discovered, bringing riches to Portugal in the form of spices, ivory and gold. The king has lent his name to a uniquely Portuguese version of late Gothic architecture, inspired both by the florid forms of Indian art and by the discoveries themselves. The most typical symbols of Manueline art are the armillary sphere (a navigational device consisting of a celestial globe with the earth at the centre, which became the emblem of Manuel I), the cross of the Order of Christ, seafaring imagery such as anchors and knotted ropes, and exotic fauna and flora from the newly discovered lands. The finest examples of Manueline art are the monastery and tower at Belém (➤ 47), the cloisters and unfinished chapels of the abbey at Batalha (➤ 112–113) and the windows of the Convento de Cristo at Tomar (➤ 116–117).

POUSADAS and *Solares*

A Portuguese guest house is a great way to experience local traditions. Choose between *pousadas* (historic buildings converted into atmospheric hotels) and *solares*, usually former manor houses now upmarket family-run B&Bs.

On 19 April 1942, the first *pousada* opened in the border town of Elvas to cater for travellers from Spain. The price of a double room was 80 escudos (€0.40). The *pousadas* were state-run inns along the lines of the Spanish *paradores*, offering simple hospitality and regional cuisine, and were the brainchild of the minister for popular culture and tourism, António Ferro. "At the current time, nearly all construction in Europe is intended for war," he said at the opening ceremony. "Our *pousadas* will be fortresses of peace, refuges of grace and quiet."

Pousadas Today

Seventy years later, there are 40 *pousadas* in Portugal, but they are no longer state-owned. All of them are housed in historic buildings, such as a restored castle in Óbidos (➤ 124) or Estremoz (➤ 144), or situated in places of natural beauty (a village house in Monsanto, ➤ 122) or Marvão (➤ 143), or both (a monastery in Évora, ➤ 143, or Beja, ➤ 144).

Convento dos Lóios is a 15th-century monastery converted into a *pousada* in Évora

Perhaps the finest of all the *pousadas* is Pousada de Santa Marinha (➤ 97), a beautifully converted 12th-century Augustinian monastery overlooking the historic city of Guimarães. The bedrooms are in former monks' cells around the cloisters, with gorgeous tile-lined stairways and corridors filled with antiques. By contrast, the simple *pousada* at Ourém (➤ 123), just outside Fátima, is a tasteful modern conversion of a group of medieval houses attractively set in the centre of the walled village.

António Ferro wanted the *pousadas* to be "small hotels where people could feel at home". For Ferro, rustic furniture and local crafts were part of the experience, which was summed up as unostentatious comfort.

Ironically, as levels of service rise ever higher in response to customer demands, the *pousadas* are in danger of moving away from their roots and Ferro's ambition to make guests feel truly at home: "If a guest walks into one of our *pousadas* and feels as if he has returned to his own house, then we will have achieved what we were striving for."

Solares de Portugal

For a home-from-home experience, you could stay in a Portuguese family *solar*. This is hardly a low-key option, as many *solares* are manor houses converted into guest houses where you will be warmly welcomed, have the chance to brush up your Portuguese and sample home cooking at its best.

The Count of Calheiros, president of the Solares de Portugal (➤ 35), has been welcoming guests to his ancestral home (Paço de Calheiros, tel: 258 947 164, www.pacodecalheiros.com) since 1985. The house, built in the 17th century, stands at the end of an avenue of magnolia trees with a stone fountain in the yard. Chestnut ceilings are weighed down with chandeliers, and family portraits hang on the walls. The chapel has a carved 17th-century altarpiece and a vault where the last count is buried. The old stables have been turned into apartments and there is a swimming pool and tennis court in the grounds. From the terrace, there

The elegant and comfortable interior of the Pousada Flor da Rosa in Crato

Many *pousadas* are converted historic buildings, such as this castle in Palmela

are views over the vineyards to Ponte de Lima, the headquarters of Solares de Portugal and the town with the largest concentration of manor houses in the scheme.

A few hours east in Trás-os-Montes (➤ 76), Brazilian artist Maria Francisca Pessanha introduces visitors to Solar das Arcas (tel: 278 400 010, www.solardasarcas.com), a 17th-century mansion built for the descendants of a Genoese navigator who arrived in Portugal in the 14th century at the invitation of Dom Dinis. The library has shelves of antique books. The apartments have wooden furniture, granite fireplaces and Maria Francisca's modern art on the walls. From your room, the only sounds you can hear are church bells and horses' hooves on the village street. The Pessanhas offer guests their own wine and home-cured sausages, and advice on walking, cycling and horse-riding in the area.

"From your room, the only sounds you can hear are church bells and horses' hooves"

Solares de Portugal offers around 100 properties, from manor houses and country estates to rustic farmhouses and cottages. Most are in the Minho, but others are scattered across Portugal, right down to the Alentejo and the Algarve. Most are in quiet rural locations and many have swimming pools. However, what makes this experience really special is that guests enjoy a real insight into Portuguese family life.

Useful Addresses

- Pousadas de Portugal, Rua Soares de Passos 3, Alto de Santo Amaro, 1300-314 Lisbon, tel: 218 442 001, www.pousadas.pt (➤ 35).
- Solares de Portugal, Praça da República 4990, Ponte de Lima, Lisbon, tel: 258 741 672, www.solaresdeportugal.pt (➤ 35).

ON THE TILES
The art of *Azulejos*

If a single image defines Portuguese style, it is the *azulejo* tile. You see them at stations, churches and shops, palaces and backstreet bars, and covering entire buildings in Lisbon.

Azulejos are not unique to Portugal, but it is perhaps here that they have achieved their finest expression. Similar glazed and painted tiles are found across the Arab world and in the Spanish region of Andalucía, from where *azulejos* originally came.

The name probably derives from an Arabic phrase meaning "azure polished stone" and they were first introduced to Portugal in the late 15th century when Manuel I imported Hispano-Arabic tiles from Seville for his royal palace at Sintra (➤ 60).

Early Tiles
These early tiles were called *alicatados* and were made of monochrome pieces of glazed earthenware that were cut into shapes or separated by strips to form mosaic-like geometric patterns.

The Majolica technique was introduced from Italy during the 16th century. This involved coating the clay in a layer of white enamel onto

WHERE TO SEE AZULEJOS

- Museu Nacional do Azulejo, Lisbon (➤ 65)
- Palácio Nacional de Sintra (➤ 60)
- Sé Velha, Coimbra (➤ 108)
- Igreja dos Lóios, Évora (➤ 133)
- Igreja de Nossa Senhora da Consolação, Elvas (➤ 141)
- Museu Regional, Beja (➤ 142)

which the artist could paint directly. In the 17th century, the fashion was for *tapetes* (carpet tiles), painted blue and yellow and resembling Moorish tapestries and rugs.

Mass Production

The first mass-production tile factory was set up after the 1755 earthquake in Lisbon, which also saw the development of the familiar blue-and-white tiles, heavily influenced by Chinese porcelain.

The custom of covering entire house- and shopfronts with *azulejos* began in Lisbon during the mid-19th century and came from Brazil, where Portuguese settlers used it as a way of keeping out the tropical rain. Today, *azulejos* continue to be a popular decoration, brightening up patios and courtyards, parks and gardens, and several of Lisbon's Metro stations.

Left: Cloisters of the Sé (Cathedral), Porto. Right: Jardim Zoológico de Lisboa, Lisbon

FADO Lisbon's urban blues

You may not have heard of *fado* before, but even first-timers are struck by how this melancholy, bittersweet music evokes the worldwide tradition of folk and blues music, telling stories of destiny, love, death and despair.

A traditional *fado* evening can be dramatic – all eyes are on the musicians, one with a *guitarra* (a Portuguese guitar like a mandolin), the other with a *viola* (acoustic Spanish guitar). There is silence as a woman dressed in black rises to sing. She sings of love and death, of triumph and tragedy, of destiny and *fado* (fate). Above all she sings of *saudade,* that Portuguese notion best translated as a longing for that which has been lost, from a broken love affair to the days when Portugal was a great seafaring nation.

Fado Clubs

There are singers today who are renewing *fado* and finding new audiences both in Portugal and internationally, but a lot of musicians are happily stuck in their old, pleasurable ways. *Fado* is a great night out – although watch out for being overcharged for meals at some events – but mainly the music is taken very seriously, and the *fado* clubs in Lisbon are wonderful places to go. For the most authentic experience, try the backstreet cellar clubs of Alfama. At A Baiúca in Alfama, *fado* performances are neighbourly affairs. In the low-lit restaurant, locals give heartfelt renditions

THE ORIGIN OF *FADO*

Fado has its origins in the working-class *bairros*, or neighbourhoods, of Lisbon in the early 19th century where it was played in taverns and brothels. In the 1920s, the first *casas de fado* opened, with professional singers making records and putting on shows for tourists. It is only now that *fado* is making a comeback among young Portuguese as a genuine art form. It is melancholy, dramatic and heart-wrenching – think of the blues born in the poor neighbourhoods of America. All female *fadistas* wear a black shawl in memory of Maria Severa (1820–46), the first great *fado* singer, whose scandalous affair with a bullfighter and tragically early death are the subject of many songs.

A traditional *fado* singer in a restaurant in Lisbon

of *fado vadio* (spontaneous or amateur *fado*) to a captive audience. A few streets away, guitarist Mário Pacheco plays every night in his intimate, vaulted surrounds of Clube de Fado, one of Lisbon's top-drawer *fado* clubs. These places have a minimum charge but beyond that there is little commercialism and most of the customers are Portuguese. Outside of Lisbon, the other *fado* centre is in Coimbra, where it is usually sung by men wearing academic robes in the city's streets and squares.

For a more spontaneous experience, head for bars and clubs where house musicians play *fado vadio,* but any one can turn up to sing. In Bairro Alto, Adega do Ribatejo is popular.

Modern *Fado*

Other modern singers include Ramana Vieira (American Portuguese), and Lisbon native Raquel Tavares, who won the biggest song contest dedicated to *fado* in Portugal, Grande Noite Do Fado, and sings regularly at Bacalhau de Molho, one of the most famous houses in Lisbon.

LISBON'S *FADO* CLUBS

- A Baiúca, Rua de São Miguel 20, tel: 218 867 284, www.fadovadioabaiuca.com
- Adega do Ribatejo, Rua do Diário do Notícias 23, tel: 213 468 343
- Adega Machado, Rua do Norte 91, tel: 213 224 640, www.adegamachado.web.pt
- Bacalhau de Molho, Casa de Linhares Restaurante, Beco dos Armazens do Linho 2, tel: 218 865 088, www.casadelinhares.com
- Clube de Fado, Rua São João da Praça 94, tel: 218 852 704, www.clube-de-fado.com
- Parreirinha de Alfama, Beco de Espírito Santo 1, tel: 218 868 209

BEYOND THE BEACHES

Portugal has 960km (600 miles) of beaches, but a few days exploring the interior will reveal traditional villages, vast acres of cork trees and breathtaking mountain ranges that offer excellent walking, hiking and adventure sports.

The highest mountains in Portugal – known as *Terra Fria* (Cold Lands) – are concentrated in the north and east and have a climate often described as "nine months of winter and three months of hell". Until fairly recently, these regions were very difficult to reach, but a new highway from Porto to Bragança has opened up the route to northern Spain, which passes through many of them. Today, you can easily reach the spectacular Douro Valley (➤ 176–179), with its terraced vineyards and craggy peaks that cover 250,000ha (617,763 acres), the bleakly beautiful Trás-os-Montes (➤ 76) and Serra da Estrela (➤ 119–120), the highest range in Portugal.

For a gentler experience, explore the Peneda-Gerês ranges (➤ 91–92) in Vinho Verde, a stunning national park that has several camping sites, beautiful waterfalls and plenty of activities, including walking trails.

Behind the Mountains

In Trás-os-Montes (which translates literally as Behind the Mountains, giving you some idea of how cut off the region has been), cars and tractors are replacing horse-carts and bullock-ploughs, and the emigrants who abandoned the area for lack of work opportunities are returning to build chic new houses *(casas de emigrante)* with the money they have made in France, Germany, Luxembourg and the USA, bringing with them cosmopolitan values and a taste for fast food.

However, the sense of other-worldliness has not entirely left Trás-os-Montes, making it fascinating to explore. Until recently, when people were ill, they used folk remedies or consulted the local witch. The winter solstice is still marked by masked dancers running through the village with cowbells round their waists in a ritual that dates to pagan times.

Vines growing on the terraced slopes in the Douro Valley

Tranquil scenery in Parque Nacional da Peneda-Gerês

As you move further down the country, the mountains may lose a little height, but that doesn't mean you can't find excellent walking and exploring opportunities. Near Lisbon, check out the dinosaur footprints near the village of Bairro in the Serras de Aire natural park, the oldest of their kind in the world, while children will love the many donkeys that live around here. Limestone is the dominant rock in both the Serras de Aire and Candeeiros natural park, and you can visit the dramatic caves and gullies.

For beach lovers who want a day off from the Algarve coast, there are a couple of very good walking opportunities in Serra de Monchique (➤ 154–155). This low-lying mountain range is within an hour's drive of the coast and is blanketed with cork, chestnut and eucalyptus trees.

INTO THE WILD

Some of the wildest parts of Trás-os-Montes are in the Parque Natural de Montesinho, between Bragança and the Spanish border. The heather-clad uplands rise to 1,480m (4,855ft) while the lower slopes support chestnut and holm oak. Golden eagles hover above the hills, wolves hide in the forests, and at weekends the local farmers go hunting for partridge, deer and wild boar. At least 90 villages are scattered about the park, with horseshoe-shaped dovecotes and slate-roofed houses where the oxen sleep downstairs and a granite staircase leads to the living quarters above.

The village of Rio de Onor, right on the border, is half-Spanish, half-Portuguese. The only sign that you are crossing from one country to another is a stone block marked with the letters "E" (España) and "P" (Portugal) and the change to a tarmac road on the Spanish side. A study by the Portuguese anthropologist António Jorge Dias in 1953 found that the people of Rio de Onor lived a communal existence, sharing land and cattle with their Spanish neighbours quite independently of the State and speaking a dialect common to them both, Rionorês. Although the village has become depopulated in recent years, some of these traditions still survive.

Trás-os-Montes Folk Traditions

To find out more about Trás-os-Montes folk traditions, visit the local museums in Bragança (➤ 94–95) and Miranda do Douro (➤ 95).

Portuguese PASSIONS

There is probably a festival going on somewhere in Portugal every day of the year. Outside these celebrations, Portuguese culture is full of drama, from the national obsession of football to the traditional spectacle of running with the bulls.

Festa!

Nothing quite matches the colour and spectacle of a Portuguese *festa*. Every town and village has its own saint's day, marked by religious processions, music, dancing and parades. Many of these festivals combine Christian and pagan elements, and all provide an excuse for partying, drinking, flirting and fireworks.

The biggest of the year centre around Holy Week in March or April, when there are candlelit processions. Another excellent entertainment is the Festa de São João in June for the summer solstice in Porto (➤ 80–83) and Vila Nova de Gaia (➤ 84–85) where the streets on either side of the River Douro are full of people hitting each other on the head with leeks or plastic hammers, and fireworks are set off over the city late into the night. Food plays an important part in almost all Portuguese festivals, with tiny stalls set up along the roads selling grilled sardines and sweet treats.

Left: Traditional costume of Costa Verde. Right: Festival of Tabuleiros, Tomar

Football... the Beautiful Game

There are plenty of secular pleasures to enjoy in Portugal as well, and football is the true modern-day obsession. Football has been played in the country since the 19th century, and the main competition is the Portuguese Liga. This highly popular league usually comes down to a play-off between the red Benfica and the green Sporting (➤ 74), both Lisbon teams, and both national and former European champions, and FC Porto.

Portugal hosted the UEFA European Football Championships in 2004 for which new stadia were built all over the country and the host nation managed to make the final, losing to Greece. Portugal reached the FIFA World Cup semi-finals in 2006, when Germany defeated them 3–1.

Best Annual Festivals

Carnival (Feb/Mar): Masked dances, fancy-dress and processions mark the arrival of Lent. The Loulé (➤ 163) and Elvas (➤ 140–41) parades are especially colourful.

Holy Week (Mar/Apr): Torchlit processions of hooded and barefoot penitents on the Thursday and Friday before Easter in Braga (➤ 88–89).

Festa das Cruzes (first weekend in May): A country fair in Barcelos (➤ 94), with processions of crosses along flower-strewn streets.

Festas dos Santos Populares (12–29 Jun): Three weeks of merrymaking takes place in Lisbon (➤ 41–74) to mark the feasts of the "popular saints". On 12 June, the *bairros* of Lisbon are decorated and people pour into Alfama to eat grilled sardines at tables set up on the street.

Festa de São João (23–24 Jun): Bonfires and fireworks mark the summer solstice in Porto (➤ 80–83) with a regatta on the River Douro.

Romaria de Nossa Senhora da Agonía (weekend nearest 20 Aug): A huge, traditional *romaria* (religious festival) in Viana do Castelo (➤ 93–94) with

Left: Germany and Portugal soccer fans (2006 World Cup). Right: Festival celebrations

RUNNING WITH THE BULLS

Especially over the summer months, you are likely to see a bullfight taking place somewhere in Portugal. The biggest difference with Spanish bullfights is that in Portugal bulls are not killed in the ring (though don't be fooled by the large declarations on posters, as they are invariably mortally wounded and dispatched out of sight after the fight).

The spectacle during a fight is certainly dramatic, with bullfighters in 18th-century costumes and scarlet cummerbunds leaping onto the bull and wrestling it to the ground, but a less controversial tradition is bull-running. This takes place in the streets at Vila Franca de Xira, north of Lisbon, during the Festa do Colete Encarnado (Festival of the Red Waistcoat) in early July and the Feira de Outubro in early October. As in Pamplona in Spain, this event involves members of the public running through the streets with bulls, and although not without its dangers, it is fun to watch.

bullfights, fireworks, folk dancing and the blessing of fishing boats.

Romaria de Nossa Senhora da Nazaré (8 Sep): Religious processions, folk dancing and bullfights take place in the fishing village of Nazaré.

Feiras Novas (third weekend in Sep): There's a market, fairground, brass bands, parades and fireworks in Ponte de Lima, a centre of Minho culture.

Festa dos Rapazes (25 Dec–6 Jan): Christmas in Portugal is a family affair, a time for eating *bacalhau* (salt cod) and *bolo rei* (fruit cake) – except in the villages around Bragança (➤ 94–95), where young men put on masks, cowbells and suits of ribbons and run through their villages in an ancient rite of passage that dates back to pre-Christian times.

Dignitaries assemble in front of a large crucifix during the Festa das Cruzes, Barcelos

FOOD traditions

The Portuguese like to eat, and not only is there an enormous variety of traditional ingredients and cooking styles, but these are being interpreted and highlighted by an increasing number of young, world-class Portuguese chefs.

Grilling fresh sardines in Portimão

Seafood Delights

With its long relationship with the sea, no prizes for guessing that there is plenty of fresh fish at many Portuguese restaurants. Depending on region and season, you can find pretty much every kind of fish you can imagine, but among the most sought after are sardines, red mullet *(salmonete)* and swordfish. If you can't decide on your favourite fish, try a *cataplana*, which is a mixed seafood dish of shellfish cooked with onions and potatoes, or a fish stew, known as *caldeirada,* a delicious blend of fish, onions, garlic, potatoes, peppers and usually copious amounts of wine.

Regional Dishes

There are also many regional dishes that give clues to the history of the individual areas. In the Trás-os-Montes, for example, you often find a chicken sausage on the menu known as an *alheira*. This dates back to the 15th century, when Jews fled to the remote mountainous region from the Spanish Inquisition. The chicken sausage was first made as a way of fooling the Inquisitors that they had renounced their Jewish ways and had started to eat pork. They are still eaten today.

The Portuguese love to eat meat, and vegetarians may find a rather limited selection on offer. Meat eaters, however, will discover a succulent array of hams, sausages, salamis (in fact 40 per cent of meat eaten in Portugal is pork). One of the best of these cured hams comes from

Alentejo's acorn-fed black pigs and is known as *presunto de porco preto bolata*. These pigs have grazed in the gentle Montados countryside and are said to offer the same benefits to your heart as olive oil.

Cheese, Wines and Olive Oils

The regional cheeses are also found in a seemingly endless array of varieties. Most cheeses are either from ewes or goats, or a combination of both. The best known is probably Queijo da Serra da Estrela (► 120), from Portugal's highest mountain range. This is a delicious mountain sheep cheese that is rich and creamy, and usually eaten straight out of the pot after six weeks of ripening.

In addition, regional wines and olive oils are also increasingly available with more and more regional single-*quinta* (from one estate) wines from quality-conscious producers, and new single-*quinta* olive oils from the Douro, Trás-os-Montes, Alentejo and Ribatejo.

"the locals can't resist a sweet start to the day, or end to a meal"

Order of Play

All meals in Portugal are likely to start with soup (and again, vegetarians beware, as even vegetable soups usually have bits of meat lurking within them). Typical soup of the north is the *caldo verde,* with cabbage, onions and potatoes, while a chilled Alentejo soup is made of bread, egg and garlic. Many dishes have spicy touches that contain flavours of cumin, cinnamon, paprika and sweet peppers brought back from former Portuguese outposts in Brazil, Goa, the Azores and further afield.

The Portuguese really come into their own with their sweet specialities. All over the country, you'll find that the locals can't resist a sweet start to the day, or end to a meal. Among the stickiest treats on offer are the *doces conventuais,* little egg-yolk sweets. Look out also for *marmelada* – not marmalade as the name suggests, but a quince paste – and jams made from the delicious Elvas (► 140–141) plums. Towns large and small can be counted on to contain at least one or two bakeries, where you should ensure you stock up on egg custard *natas.*

BACALHAU

The Portuguese passion for *bacalhau* (dried salted cod, ► 37) has its origins in the fishing fleets that sailed the waters off Newfoundland in the early 16th century. At that time, there was an abundance of cod, but it had to be preserved for the journey back to Portugal. Despite the presence of numerous fresh fish off the coast, *bacalhau* remains a Portuguese favourite and there are said to be 365 different ways of cooking it.

Best of Portugal

Portugal has so much to offer – from markets and festivals to beaches and landscape – this is just a few of its highlights.

Ten Memorable Experiences

- A blustery morning at Belém (➤ 46–49), feeling the ocean breeze as you recall the voyages of Portugal's explorers.
- An evening at one of Lisbon's *fado* clubs (➤ 20–21).
- Touring the port lodges of Vila Nova de Gaia (➤ 84–85).
- Exploring the Douro Valley by road, river or rail, or taking the scenic train line from Tua to Mirandela (➤ 176–179).
- Joining the crowds to pick up a bargain at the busy Thursday market in Barcelos (➤ 94).
- The view from the summit of Serra da Estrela (➤ 119–120).
- A boat trip from Lagos or Carvoeiro in summer to explore the cliffs, caves and cove beaches of the Algarve (➤ 159–161).
- Standing on the cliffs at Cabo de São Vicente (➤ 157–158) to watch the magnificent sight of the sun setting over the Atlantic.
- Spending the night in the medieval town of Évora, capital of the Alentejo (➤ 132–135).
- A walk in Parque Natural da Ria Formosa (➤ 162).

If You Only Visit One Market...

...make it the Thursday market at Barcelos (➤ 94), which has the atmosphere of a fair. There are also other markets at Estremoz (➤ 140) and Loulé (➤ 163).

Best Castles in the Air

Portugal has a wealth of romantic ruined castles, many in hilltop towns along the Spanish border. Among the best are Castelo de São Jorge, Lisbon (➤ 52–53) and the castles at Sintra (➤ 60–62), Guimarães (➤ 93), Bragança (➤ 94–95), Silves (➤ 164) and the walled villages of Óbidos (➤ 122) and Marvão (➤ 138–139).

Best for People-watching

The terrace of Café Nicola (➤ 175) or Pastelaria Suiça (➤ 175) in Lisbon.

Best for Kids

- Algarve beaches, boat trips and waterparks (➤ 159–161).
- Oceanário, Lisbon (➤ 58), Europe's largest aquarium.
- Portugal dos Pequenitos, Coimbra (➤ 106), a park with miniature models.

The golden sweep of sand and sandstacks at Praia da Rocha in the Algarve

Finding Your Feet

First Two Hours

There are international airports at Lisbon, Porto and Faro. All three have tourist offices, post offices, currency exchange facilities and car hire outlets. Airlines operating a frequent service to these airports include British Airways, TAP and Monarch, as well as low-cost airlines like Ryanair, easyJet and bmibaby.

Lisbon

- **Portela Airport** (www.ana.pt) is 7km (4.3 miles) north of the centre (tel: 218 413 500 for enquiries, tel: 218 413 700 for arrivals/departures).
- The **Aerobus** (inexpensive; free for passengers flying with TAP, the Portuguese national airline) departs for central Lisbon from outside the arrivals hall every 20 minutes from 7am–9pm and every 30 minutes from 9pm–11pm daily. The route takes in Avenida da Liberdade, Rossio, Praça do Comércio and Cais do Sodré (for trains to Estoril and Cascais). Tickets are also valid for one day on Lisbon's buses, trams and funiculars.
- A **taxi** to central Lisbon costs around €20. Night travel or extra luggage costs more. Fares are metered, so make sure the meter is on. Alternatively buy a pre-paid taxi voucher from the tourist office in the arrivals hall.
- By **Metro,** there is no direct connection from the airport but the nearest Metro station, Parque das Nações, is 10 minutes from the airport by taxi (www.metrolisboa.pt).

Porto

- **Francisco Sá Carneiro Airport** is 11km (6.8 miles) north of the city centre (tel: 229 432 400; www.ana.pt).
- On the **Metro** (www.metrodoporto.pt), take the Violeta Line, 6am–1am every 20 minutes (€2), which takes 20–35 minutes to the centre.
- A **taxi** to central Porto should cost around €25–30, with supplements for extra luggage or night travel.

Faro

- **Faro Airport** is 6km (3.7 miles) west of the city centre (tel: 289 800 800, www.ana.pt).
- From the airport, take **buses** No 16 and No 14 into Faro.
- **Taxi** fares to Faro and the various resorts are listed in the arrivals hall, but it is worth checking the price with the driver before you set off.

Tourist Information Offices

Most tourist office staff speak excellent English, and have maps and information in English. There are tourist offices in all main towns and cities.

- **Lisbon**: The main office (daily 9–7), **Lisboa Welcome Center**, Rua do Arsenal 15, tel: 210 312 700, www.visitlisboa.com. There are tourist offices on Praça dos Restauradores (daily 9–8) and information kiosks at Belém, Rua Augusta and Castelo de São Jorge.
- **Porto:** The main tourist office is at Rua Clube dos Fenianos 25, near the top of Avenida dos Aliados (tel: 223 393 472, www.portoturismo.pt).
- **Faro:** The tourist office is at Rua da Misericórdia 8 (near the entrance to the old town), tel: 289 803 604. There is also an office at the airport (late Jun to late Sep daily 9–7, late Sep to late Jun 9–5:30).
- **The Algarve:** There are also tourist offices at Albufeira, Alcoutim, Carvoeiro, Lagos, Loulé, Monchique, Monte Gordo, Portimão, Praia da Rocha, Sagres, Silves and Tavira.

Getting Around

Portugal's compact size makes it easy to get around. There are excellent bus and train connections between the major cities in Portugal, but to get to the more out-of-the-way places you will need a car.

Driving

- Drivers **bringing their own cars** into Portugal need to carry their driving licence, registration document, insurance certificate and display a nationality sticker on their car.
- **Car rental** is available at all airports and in major towns and resorts. To rent a car you must be aged over 21 and have a passport, driving licence and credit card. You can book in advance through the major international car rental agencies (see below). Local firms offer competitive rates, but you should check carefully the level of insurance cover and excess. Keep the car-rental documents and your driving licence with you at all times.
  Avis: tel: 218 435 550 (Lisbon Airport), www.avis.com
  Europcar: tel: 218 401 176 for reservations (Lisbon Airport), www.europcar.com
  Hertz: tel: 219 426 300 (Lisbon Airport), www.hertz.com
- Theft from rental cars is common. Never leave items on display in the car, and take all valuables with you or lock them out of sight.

Driving Essentials

- Drive on the **right**.
- **Seat belts** are compulsory for the driver and all passengers.
- The legal **alcohol** limit is 0.05 per cent.
- **Speed limits** are 120kph (74mph) on motorways, 90kph (56mph) on main roads, 50kph (31mph) in urban areas, unless otherwise indicated.
- **Driving standards** are generally poor and Portugal has one of the highest accident rates in Europe. The N125 across the Algarve is notorious for its high number of accidents. If you are involved in an accident, use the orange SOS phone on a motorway to call the police.
- A network of **motorways** and **main roads** connects Lisbon, Porto and the major cities. Motorways are prefaced with A and incur tolls. Other main roads are prefaced with IP or IC, or N (for *nacional*).
- **Check regulations before you travel** – www.theAA.com has comprehensive European driving information.

Buses and Trains

- Bus and train services connect the main towns and cities. On both, under-4s travel free, under-12s travel half fare, and over-65s receive a discount.
- **Bus** services are operated by **private companies**.
- **Train** services are operated by **Caminhos de Ferros Portugueses** (**CP**, tel: 808 208 208 or +351 707 201 280 from abroad, www.cp.pt). Tickets can be purchased in advance from stations. CP also sells a rail pass valid for 7, 14 or 21 days.
- The Alfa Pendular from Lisbon to Porto via Coimbra or to Faro will save you time, because it is a **fast train service**.
- There are five main **railway stations** in **Lisbon**. Trains depart from Sete Rios for Sintra, from Cais do Sodré for Estoril and Cascais, Óbidos and the west coast from Santa Apolónia or Oriente for Porto and Madrid and from Entrecampos for Faro and Évora.

City Transport

- **Lisbon** has an excellent network of buses, trams, Metro trains and *elevadores* (funiculars). **Single tickets** can be bought on buses or at Metro stations and validated at the machines behind the driver or at the station barriers. Less expensive options include a two-journey ticket or a one-day or three-day pass, valid on buses and trams, from the Carris ticket booth on Praça da Figueira. You can also buy a four-day or seven-day ***passe turístico,*** valid on Metro, buses and trams, on production of your passport. Metro stations sell 10-ticket *cadernetas*, which are good value for multiple journeys. Tourist offices sell the **Lisbon Card**, valid for up to three days, which gives unlimited travel on public transport and free or discounted admission to more than 80 museums, tours and places of interest.
- **Porto** has a good metro system with six different lines (named A–F), which covers most of the city, including the main part of Porto, over the bridge to Gaia and out to the airport (www.metro-porto.pt). There is also a good network of local **buses**. Single-journey tickets and one-day passes can be bought on the bus. Tourist offices sell one- or two-day passes called the **Porto Card**, which include discounts at museums and on river cruises, and free travel on buses, trams and the Metro.

Admission Charges

The cost of admission for museums and places of interest featured in the guide is indicated by the following price categories.
Inexpensive under €3 **Moderate** €3–€6 **Expensive** over €6

Accommodation

Especially outside Lisbon and the Algarve, accommodation in Portugal is very good value. Independent travellers can choose from a wide range of places and the luxury end of the market is refreshingly informal.

Booking

- Advance booking is vital in the **high season** (July and August) or if your stay coincides with events, such as local festivals or pilgrimages. In quiet periods, rates can drop to 40 per cent of the high-season price, but beware that in coastal resorts places may shut completely in the winter.
- **Tourist offices** have comprehensive lists of official accommodation or the addresses of *dormidas* or *quartos* (rooms for rent).
- Many hotels and tourist complexes in the Algarve are **block booked** throughout the summer; either reserve months ahead or choose a guesthouse, *pousada* (➤ 35) or *estalagem* (country inn) instead.

Hotels

- Hotels are invariably **clean and safe**, but you might find alternative types of accommodation (➤ opposite) more attractive and welcoming than budget hotels, especially in cities.
- An **official price list** must be displayed inside the door of every room.
- **IVA** (VAT) or sales tax must be included in the advertised room rate; breakfast tends to be included and varies from continental to a buffet.
- You may be **charged extra** for using a garage or gym.
- **Extra beds** are often supplied for a small fee.
- **Children** (usually under four years) can stay free or at a discount.

Pousadas and Accommodation with Character

- *Pousadas* (which means "a place to rest", ➤ 15–16) are privately owned hotels located throughout the country (many in the Alentejo, ➤ 127–146), aimed at tourists looking for somewhere special to stay, usually near centres of interest. They are set in **fabulous surroundings** and have elements of traditional architecture and furnishing, as well as good to excellent restaurants – open to non-residents – where you can sample Portuguese specialities and wine, often in highly atmospheric dining rooms. **Standards of comfort** are reliably high.
- With around 40, there are **four categories**: historical *pousadas*, converted castles and monasteries; historic design *pousadas*, as above but with modern boutique-style elements; nature *pousadas*, in spectacular natural settings; and charm *pousadas*, often in converted village houses. All *pousadas* are good value for money and even the most expensive, such as those at Estremoz (➤ 144) and Guimarães (➤ 97), cost less than the equivalent luxury establishments in most other countries.
- *Pousadas* are popular with honeymooners, who receive special treatment, and they also offer **discounts** to families, the under-30s and those aged 60 or over.
- The *pousadas* described in this guide are not necessarily the best, but form part of a balanced selection of accommodation for each region. For a complete listing and detailed information, including promotions and booking facilities, contact **Pousadas de Portugal**, Rua Soares de Passos 3, Alto de Santo Amaro, 1300-314 Lisbon, tel: 218 442 00, www.pousadas.pt.
- The **Solares de Portugal** and other similar schemes are on a more intimate scale. They, offer a huge choice of alternative accommodation across the whole country in the mid-budget range. Government-approved but privately owned, these tend to be farmhouses and country houses with around 12 rooms, sometimes with facilities such as swimming pools but seldom offering meals other than breakfast. A complete list is available from the following:
  Solares de Portugal, Praça da República 4990, Ponte de Lima, tel: 258 741 672, www.solaresdeportugal.pt.
  Privetur, Largo das Pereiras, 4990 Ponte de Lima, tel: 258 743 923, www.privetur.co.uk.
  CENTER (Centro de Tourismo no Espaço Rural), Praça da República 4990, Ponte de Lima; tel: 258 931 750; www.center.pt.
- Another thing to look out for is the official green tree symbol awarded to government-approved country guesthouses often advertised as a ***turismo rural***. These also offer charming accommodation in manors and farms, usually on a bed-and-breakfast basis, plus facilities such as horse-riding.
- Traditional Alentejo farmhouses, known as ***montes***, have grouped together to form **Turismo Montes Alentejanos,** Avenida da Liberdade 115, 7400-217 Ponte de Sor (tel: 242 291 226, www.montesalentejanos.com.pt).

Residencials, Pensões and *Hospedarias*

- In addition to rooms for rent, at the lower end of the budget range is the ***residencial***. These are nearly always clean and comfortable, if basic, but do not provide any meals, except possibly breakfast.
- The ***pensão*** is another good-value alternative, sometimes offering no meals at all, or sometimes breakfast and an evening meal. Often family-run, *pensões* tend to have a more local flavour than hotels and can be a charming place to stay and brush up on your Portuguese
- Alternatively, there is the ***hospedaria,*** the lowliest of all. Some rooms have their own bathroom, sometimes at a far higher rate than if you share

facilities. These are often better value than a low- to mid-budget hotel, and some of these places have wonderful character.

Youth Hostels

- ***Pousadas de Juventude*** (youth hostels) are good on the whole and some are excellent – clean, safe and friendly. Bed linen and a simple buffet breakfast are generally included in the price, and facilities often include shared kitchens, snack bars and wireless internet access.
- In **high season** you should book ahead, either through your local youth hostel association or the **Portuguese Youth Hostel Association** (Movijovem), Rua Lúcio de Azevedo 27, 1600-146 Lisbon, tel: 707 203 030 (reservations), www.pousadasjuventude.pt.
- Of all the 30 or so hostels, the one in **Leiria** has the best reputation, while the most expensive are in the big cities and the Algarve (where the favourite is at Alcoutim). The hostels in Lagos, Portimão, Coimbra and Penhas da Saúde are all acclaimed. Expect to pay around €9–€43 a night, depending on location, room type and time of year.

Camping

- ***Parques de Campismo*** (campsites) are usually well run, with facilities ranging from basic to quite luxurious, again at relatively low prices. The best ones in **prime seaside locations**, especially in the Algarve where there are several, are crowded in high season – and be warned that theft can be a problem.
- A few require an **international camping carnet**, available from national organisations. Charges hover around the €5 per person mark.
- Sites belonging to **ORBITUR** are more expensive but slightly better.
- For more details contact:
  ORBITUR, Avenida da Boavista 1681, 3°, Salas 5 a 8, 4100-132 Porto, tel: 226 061 360, www.orbitur.pt.
  Portuguese Camping Federation, Avenida Coronel Eduardo Galhardo 24 D, 1199-007 Lisbon, tel: 218 126 890, www.fcmportugal.com
  Roteiro Campista, Rua do Giestal, 5-1° Fte, 1300-274 Lisbon, tel: 213 642 370 for the invaluable booklet of the same name (www.roteiro-campista.pt).

Self-catering

- Self-catering apartments and villas are located mostly along the **south coast**, though they can be found throughout Portugal. **Facilities** range from a basic refrigerator and cooker to fully equipped kitchens, swimming pools, large gardens and a regular maid service.
- It's worth **booking privately** rather than through a tour operator to get better value for money.
- Local and national **tourist offices** should be able to supply contact names and addresses.
- Also try www.ownersdirect.co.uk or www.holidaylettings.co.uk.

Accommodation Prices

The symbols refer to the average cost of a double room per night in high season. Singles often cost more than half the double rate.

€ under €60 **€€** €60–€120 **€€€** €121–€180 **€€€€** over €180

Food and Drink

There are said to be 365 ways of preparing the national favourite, *bacalhau,* so you are sure to find it on the menu. Be adventurous and seek out other specialities and, given the subtle regional variations, the advent of several imaginative chefs, plus some remarkably low prices, you can enjoy some memorable meals without breaking the bank.

Eating Out – A Practical Guide

- Strict **dress codes** are almost non-existent, though Sunday best is still customary in the provinces. Jacket and tie is *de rigueur* in only a handful of restaurants in Lisbon and Porto.
- Often as smart as restaurants and mostly found in cities, ***cervejarias*** (beer houses) also serve high-quality Portuguese food. ***Marisquerias*** specialise in *marisco* (seafood), where *gambas* (prawns), lobster and luxury fish, served by weight, are expensive.
- **Restaurant terraces** (as opposed to café *esplanadas*) are a rarity, so the coolness of deep cellars where some dining rooms are located may prove welcome in the height of summer.
- All but the most modest places now accept **credit cards**, but check first in case you don't have enough cash on you.
- **Lunch** is over by 2, maybe 3 in the south. **Dinner** is served around 8 and you may find it hard to find a kitchen open after 10 or 11, especially in rural areas. In **Lisbon**, fashionable places serve until very late into the night, while *cervejarias* (beer houses) may stay open all afternoon, too. Some establishments may close Sunday evening; many more are closed all day Monday.
- Standard servings are **enormous**, except in chic restaurants: you can often ask for a *meia dose* (half portion) for one person.
- **Service** is rarely included and never compulsory, but a 10 per cent tip will always be welcome even in cafés and tea-rooms.
- The ***ementa turística*** (daily set menu) can be very good value (as little as €5–€6), but is normally only available at lunchtime.

Portuguese Cuisine

- **Seafood**, usually top rate and priced accordingly, is served along Portugal's long coasts, while inland, lamb, pork and game (in season) feature.
- ***Carne de porco à alentejana*** (pork simmered with clams and fresh coriander) is Portugal's answer to "surf and turf", the North American dish combining meat and seafood. The pork is marinated for four hours in white wine and spices and is then fried. The clams are added at the end. It is often served with diced potatoes or French fries.
- ***Bacalhau*** (salt cod, soaked to remove most of the salt, ➤ 27) is a favourite. There are several different recipes, such as *à Gomes de Sá* (with hard-boiled egg, boiled potatoes and black olives), *à brás* (stir-fried with eggs, onions and potatoes), *à Minhota* (with fried potatoes) and *com natas* (baked in a rich cream sauce).
- ***Churrasco*** (barbecued chicken, beef or pork), sometimes served Brazilian-style (*rodízio*), is the house speciality of many roadside grills.
- ***Leitão*** (suckling pig), cooked until crisp and succulent and infused with local herbs, is the speciality of the region between Lisbon and Coimbra, but is considered a delicacy nationwide.
- **Vegetarians** have a fairly hard time in Portugal – ask for salads or side orders, such as spinach. Although rice and potatoes are frequently on the menu, the only true concession to vegetarians will be omelettes.

Snacks and Sweets

- The Portuguese are great on **snacks** (*petiscos* are the local answer to *tapas*), and great for an informal dinner. Choose a slightly sparkling Vinho Verde white wine to go with *petiscos* like *bolinhos de bacalhau* (codfish cakes), *presunto* (cured ham), *polvo* (octopus) and *caracóis* (snails) cooked in garlic and herbs. *Lanche* (afternoon tea) is faithfully observed.
- With a good breakfast (coffee or tea, bread and jam or cheese, cold meats and eggs), you can probably survive until the evening by eating in cafés, *confeitarias* and *pastelerias* (cake shops), and *casas de chá* (tea rooms).
- **Coffee** is good and popular and a few sumptuous cafés have survived modernization in towns and cities. *Bica* (*um café* in Porto) is a strong espresso, while *galão* is a milky coffee served in a glass, perfect with a *torradas* (thick slices of toasted bread dripping with butter).
- In addition to *sandes* (sandwiches), *pregos* (bread rolls with hot slices of beef) and *bifanas* (like *pregos* but with pork), try *rissóis* (deep-fried meat or prawn patties) and *pastéis de bacalhau* (mini cod fishcakes).
- Portuguese **cakes** (*pastéis* or *bolos*) are very sweet. The main ingredient is sugar, followed by almonds, honey and egg yolks, and sometimes all four. The regional and local variations on these themes are countless. The best are the cheese-based *queijadas* from Sintra and custard-filled, cinnamon-dusted *pastéis de nata* (especially the fabulous ones at Belém, ➤ 69).
- **Dessert** fans will appreciate *arroz doce* (rice pudding with cinnamon), *pudim flan* (crème caramel) and a whole range of nut and chocolate concoctions. Baked apple *(maçã)* and quince *(marmelo)* are delicious.

Cover Charges and Starters

- In nearly every restaurant there's a *couvert* or **cover charge** – ostensibly for the bread – and in more expensive places this can be quite high.
- ***Acepipes*** – an array of olives, ham, cheese (traditionally served before rather than after meals), fish pâté and pickles. Note that even if unsolicited, they will be itemized on your bill if you so much as touch them. Politely but pointedly refuse them if you don't want to be charged.
- ***Entradas*** (starters) come in the form of vegetable soups (such as *caldo verde*, containing strips of kale cabbage) or seafood, or maybe a salad.

Drinks

- **Mineral water** is inexpensive – ask for *agua sem gas* (still) or *agua com gas* (sparkling) served *fresca* (chilled) or *natural* (room temperature).
- Apart from ***vinho do Porto*** (port, ➤ 9–11) and **Mateus Rosé**, there are other excellent **wines**, the best coming from the Dão and Douro valleys, plus full-bodied reds from Bairrada and the Alentejo. Or there's Vinho Verde – slightly sparkling young wine from the Minho (mostly whites).
- **Beer** is popular in big cities and on tap should be ordered by the *imperial* (in the south) or *fino* (in the north).
- There are some good **brandies** *(conhaque)* as well as *aguardente*, *bagaço* and *medronho*, made in the Algarve from arbutus berries. Cherry-based *ginginha* is a popular tipple, especially in Lisbon.

Restaurant Prices

The following symbols indicate the average price per person for a three-course meal excluding drinks and tips.

€ under €12 **€€** €12–€24 **€€€** €25–€36 **€€€€** over €36

Shopping

Traditional markets across Portugal can be colourful spectacles as well as great places to shop. Ceramics are often on sale along with foods, but the finest items are only sold during local fairs *(feiras)*. With its juxtaposition of extravagant boutiques and dusty groceries alongside state-of-the-art shopping malls and beguiling bookstores, Lisbon is Portugal's undisputed shopping capital, though Porto does its best. Every town and city has a busy commercial street or two where you can pick up bargains. Perhaps the best gifts are food or wine related, though sometimes you can come across interesting arts and crafts. Footwear and other leather goods are also good value.

Opening Hours

- Shops usually open daily 9–7, except Sunday, with a two-hour lunch break – *sestas* (siestas) are rare outside the rural interior.
- Modern shopping centres open 10am–midnight, seven days a week.

Clothes and Footwear

- Items such as belts, bags, wallets, shoes, jackets and purses are less expensive than in the rest of Western Europe. Leather gloves are also a bargain, still sold in old-fashioned booth-like shops.
- **Home-grown designers** are worth investigating, though few have branches outside Lisbon.

Food and Wine

- In addition to wine and port, brandy, *aguardente* (firewater) and, in the Algarve, *medronho* (➤ 169) make good gifts. Decanters and other wine-connoisseur paraphernalia can be interesting – some are designed by fashionable artists.
- The easiest foodstuffs to transport include olive oil (try and get "luxury" oil – 0.1 or 0.2 per cent acidity, packaged in smart, corked bottles), cheese (some of it at astronomical prices, so beware), *bacalhau* (➤ 27, 37), and non-perishable cakes and biscuits.
- Pine nuts, almonds and dried and candied fruit are very good value compared with prices in most other countries.

Art and Crafts

- Ceramics, basket- and wicker-ware, and copper pans tend to be the traditional items appealing to all tastes. Pottery and porcelain can be more of an acquired taste.
- The yellow-dotted brown earthenware dishes from Barcelos are universally popular with tourists – as is the *Galo* (rooster) commemorating a folk legend originating in the eponymous northern town, and now a national symbol (➤ 94).

Souvenirs

- ***Azulejos*** (traditional glazed tiles) range from mass-produced souvenirs to whole sets of antique tiles. Measure up before you come to Portugal and you can have a set tailor-made, to your own design.
- "**Scissor chairs**" are distinctive seats from Monchique in the Algarve.
- ***Cataplanas*** are metal cooking pans used to make seafood dishes.
- ***Arraiolos carpets*** are exquisite (and expensive) rugs made in the picturesque town of the same name, to ancient designs.
- ***Fado*** (➤ 20–21) – a CD of Portuguese "blues".

Entertainment

Portugal is noted for its traditional festivals – the calendar is packed with them – *fado* and, of course, football so there's usually something to suit every taste.

Information

In the Algarve, there are three monthly **English-language publications**: *Essential Algarve*, *Welcome to the Algarve* and *Algarve Guide*, all available from tourist offices and hotels. In Lisbon you can find *Follow Me* for the Greater Lisbon area, and for Sintra and Cascais *What's in Sintra* and *What's in Cascais.* Elsewhere you'll have to rely on weekly English-language newspapers *The Portugal News* and *The Resident*, Portuguese-language publications, such as the daily press, tourist office information and posters and flyers. Or check out various websites (➤ 188).

Nightlife

- Lively student populations keep the nightlife upbeat and the arts scene buoyant year-round in **Lisbon** (➤ 74), **Porto** (➤ 100) and **Coimbra** (➤ 126), where there's a a good mix of **nightclubs**, **wine bars**, **concert halls**, ***fado* venues** and **cultural centres**. Most *fado* venues (➤ 20–21) double as restaurants and have a minimum cover charge of €10–€25.
- Nightlife in the **Algarve** is **seasonal** from about Easter to September, though a few clubs, bars and pubs are open all year. **Albufeira** (➤ 170) is party central, but **Faro** (➤ 170) offers a more stylish, Portuguese scene.
- **Opening hours** vary widely. **Bars** tend to open around midday and close at midnight; lounge bars with DJs or live music may stay open until 2am or 3am. **Nightclubs** open around 10pm or 11pm and close between 4am and 6am. Most have relaxed dress codes, though more exclusive clubs may rule out denim, trainers and T-shirts. Nightclub entrance charges tend to vary between €5 and €15, though small venues are often free.

Festivals

The most important festivals are covered in the regional listings, but look for others – it's important to know if only because accommodation can be scarce. Check at local tourist offices.

Spectator Sports

- Cristiano Ronaldo is the most prominent Portuguese footballer since Eusébio and Luís Figo. Porto's Boavista and FC Porto and Lisbon's rival teams, Benfica and Sporting, have the national championship stitched up between them and fans might like to see them play at home (➤ 74).
- **Roller-hockey** is the only international sport at which Portugal regularly excels (➤ 74), while bullfighting *(touradas,* ➤ 27*)* – less cruel than in Spain but still not a sight for animal-lovers – is reappearing in some areas.

Sport and Outdoor Pursuits

- Some of Europe's best **golfing** fairways, **tennis courts, watersports** and **diving clubs** are found on the warm southern Algarve coast (➤ 170).
- The western seaboard – where wind and rollers are perennially reliable – is better for **surfing**, **windsurfing** or just a refreshing dip.
- Inland, unspoiled mountain scenery lends itself to **hiking**, **mountain-biking**, **hang-gliding** and **horse-riding** – ask at local tourist offices for outfits.
- **Boating**, **fishing** and other **watersports** can be practised at sea or on inland waterways; many places hire equipment (➤ individual chapters).

Lisbon and Around

Getting Your Bearings

The capital of Portugal since around 1255, Lisbon (Lisboa) is one of Europe's smallest and most atmospheric capitals. Tumbling down seven hills on the north bank of the Tagus (Tejo) estuary, it has a vibrant, multicultural appeal that stems from the large number of immigrants from its former African and Asian colonies. One in 10 of Portugal's population live here, creating a lively, Latin atmosphere.

Most visitors arrive in Lisbon by plane, but there's nothing like arriving on one of the ferries that breeze across the River Tagus to get a true sense of the city's layout. In front of you is Praça do Comércio, the former parade ground and symbolic entrance to the city. Ahead, beyond a triumphal arch, Rua Augusta leads through the Baixa (lower town), the downtown business and shopping district. To the west rises the party-loving Bairro Alto (upper town) and boutique-dotted Chiado; to the east, the labyrinthine Alfama, crowned by a splendid Moorish castle. Across the water, beyond Ponte 25 de Abril, a giant statue of Christ gazes down from the south bank.

The shape of Lisbon today is largely the result of the earthquake of 1755. It struck on All Saints' Day, when most people were at church, causing a tidal wave and hundreds of fires. At least 40,000 people died. The rebuilding of the Baixa on a grid plan was largely the architectural vision of the chief minister, Marquês de Pombal.

Two buildings that mostly survived the destruction were the whimsical Manueline tower and monastery at Belém (➤ 47–48), inspired by the discoveries and built on the riches that made Lisbon great – Indian spices and Brazilian gold.

In the last few years, Lisbon has seen another transformation, with new dockside leisure facilities, one of Europe's longest bridges and EU funding for glittering new facades. As Lisbon sails into the 21st century, its cityscape is a striking blend of old and new, its people all at once nostalgic and innovative.

Page 41: Torre Vasco da Gama, at Parque das Nações in Lisbon

Mosaic pavement at Parque Eduardo VII

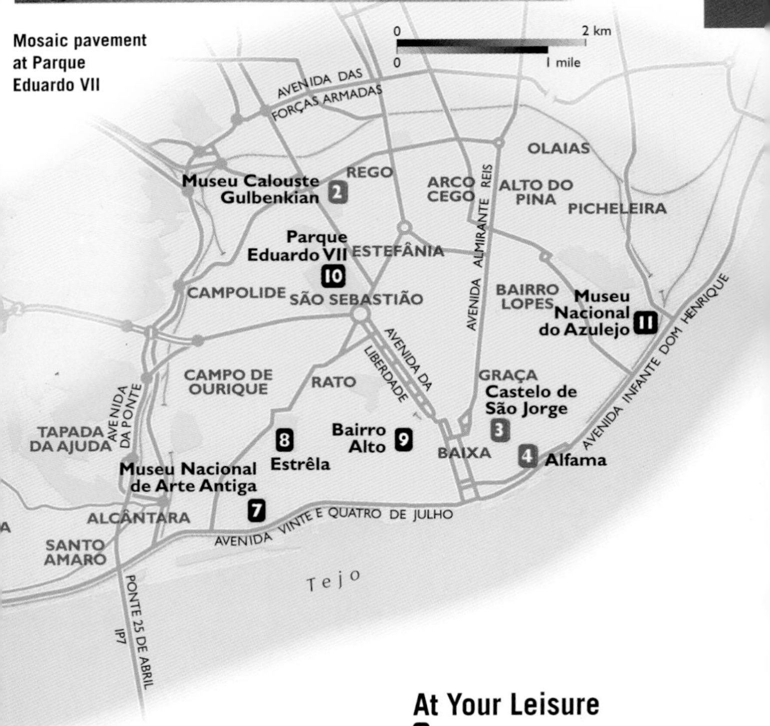

0 2 km
0 1 mile
AVENIDA DAS FORÇAS ARMADAS
OLAIAS
REGO
Museu Calouste Gulbenkian 2
ARCO CEGO
ALTO DO PINA
PICHELEIRA
AVENIDA ALMIRANTE REIS
Parque Eduardo VII 10
ESTEFÂNIA
CAMPOLIDE
SÃO SEBASTIÃO
BAIRRO LOPES
Museu Nacional do Azulejo 11
AVENIDA INFANTE DOM HENRIQUE
AVENIDA DA LIBERDADE
CAMPO DE OURIQUE
RATO
GRAÇA
Castelo de São Jorge 3
AVENIDA DA PONTE
TAPADA DA AJUDA
8 Estrêla
Bairro Alto 9
BAIXA
4 Alfama
Museu Nacional de Arte Antiga 7
ALCÂNTARA
AVENIDA VINTE E QUATRO DE JULHO
SANTO AMARO
Tejo
PONTE 25 DE ABRIL
IP7

★ Don't Miss

1 Belém ➤ 46
2 Museu Calouste Gulbenkian ➤ 50
3 Castelo de São Jorge ➤ 52
4 Alfama ➤ 54
5 Parque das Nações ➤ 58
6 Sintra ➤ 60

At Your Leisure

7 Museu Nacional de Arte Antiga ➤ 63
8 Estrêla ➤ 63
9 Bairro Alto ➤ 64
10 Parque Eduardo VII ➤ 64
11 Museu Nacional do Azulejo ➤ 65
12 Estoril and Cascais ➤ 65
13 Palácio de Mafra ➤ 66

In Four Days

If you're not quite sure where to begin your travels, this itinerary recommends a practical and enjoyable four days exploring Lisbon and the surrounding area, taking in some of the best places to see using the Getting your Bearings map on the previous page. For more information see the main entries.

Day 1

Morning

From Praça do Comércio, take tram No 15E to 1 **Belém** (➤ 46–49) to immerse yourself in Portugal's maritime past. Walk along the waterfront to the fortified Torre de Belém, then admire royal barges in the Museu de Marinha. Allow plenty of time to explore the Manueline **Mosteiro dos Jerónimos** (➤ 48), its intricate stonework celebrating the Portuguese explorer Vasco da Gama. Have a custard tart at the *azulejo*-tiled **Antiga Confeitaria de Belém** (➤ 69).

Afternoon and Evening

Return by tram as far as the Alcântara docks and explore the 7 **Museu Nacional de Arte Antiga** (➤ 63). If you want to party, head to the revitalized docks area and choose one of the sleek lounge bars or warehouse clubs (➤ 74). Otherwise return to Belém for a concert at the **Centro Cultural de Belém** (➤ 74) – the arts centre has an exciting programme of classical music, opera, jazz and dance.

Day 2

Morning

Take the Metro to São Sebastião for the wonderful 2 **Museu Calouste Gulbenkian** (➤ 50–51), then stroll through the sculpture park and have lunch at **Centro de Arte Moderna** (➤ 51).

Afternoon and Evening

Walk downhill to the centre through 10 **Parque Eduardo VII** (right, ➤ 64) and along the tree-lined Avenida da Liberdade. Take Tram 28 through the narrow streets of Castelo to the mazelike Moorish district of 4 **Alfama**. (➤ 54–57). Climb up to the

3 Castelo de São Jorge (➤ 52–53) to watch the sun set over the River Tagus. Wander back down to Alfama for a fish supper and authentic *fado* in an intimate club (➤ 20–21).

Day 3

Morning

Take the Metro to Oriente for the cutting-edge **5 Parque das Nações** (➤ 58–59). Visit the huge oceanarium (left) and ride the cable-car along the waterfront. Have lunch at one of the riverside restaurants.

Afternoon and Evening

Shop for the latest Portuguese styles in the Centro Comercial Vasco da Gama, then take the Metro to Rossio for a drink at a pavement café. Take the rickety Elevador da Glória up to the Bairro Alto – have an apéritif at the **Solar do Vinho do Porto** (➤ 72), a meal at either the jovial **Cervejaria Trinidade** (➤ 70) or the more glamorous **Pap'Açorda** (➤ 71), famous for its *açorda* (bread soup with shellfish). End at one of the lively hole-in-the-wall bars around **9 Bairro Alto** (➤ 64).

Day 4

Morning and Afternoon

Take the train from Cais do Sodré to **12 Estoril** (➤ 65–66) and stroll along the seafront to **12 Cascais** (below, ➤ 66. Explore this fishing port, then get a bus to **6 Sintra** (➤ 60–62) for lunch at **Tulhas** (➤ 72). Hike up to the fantastical Castelo dos Mouros and Palácio da Pena. Walk back through the pinewoods to Sintra or catch the bus back to the train station.

0 Belém

More than anywhere else in Portugal, it is at Belém that you feel the pull of the Atlantic and the excitement of the great Age of Discovery. For more than a century, Portuguese ships left from Belém in search of new worlds, bringing back untold riches from unknown lands. Add to that its status as Lisbon's museum district, along with the crowning glories of Manueline architecture, and there is plenty to keep you occupied here.

The best way to reach Belém is on the No 15E tram that clatters along the waterfront from central Lisbon.

On arrival, head for the imposing **Padrão dos Descobrimentos** (Monument to the Discoveries), built in 1960 to mark the 500th anniversary of Prince Henry the Navigator's (➤ 12) death. A *padrão* was a stone cairn

The Torre de Belém is Lisbon's most emblematic building

surmounted by a cross, built by Portuguese explorers to mark their presence on new territory; this modern version neatly combines the form of a caravel, a cross and a sword. The prow of a ship faces out to sea with an image of Prince Henry at the helm. Behind him are other heroes of the discoveries (➤ 12–14), including Gil Eanes, Vasco da Gama, Pedro Álvares Cabral and poet Luís de Camões, who celebrated the Age of Discovery in his epic work *Os Lusíadas* (*The Lusiads*, ➤ 87).

Take the lift to the top of the tower, which is 52m (171ft) high, for harbour views, then wander around the marble world map at its base, with dates showing Portuguese conquests in Africa, Asia and America.

Portuguese heroes are carved in stone on the Padrão dos Descobrimentos

Manueline Masterpiece

Just along the waterfront is the **Torre de Belém**, built by Dom Manuel I between 1515 and 1520 to guard the entrance to Lisbon harbour. This elegant fortress is a good example of what has come to be called the Manueline style (➤ 14), a Portuguese version of late Gothic architecture inspired by the discoveries and particularly associated with Dom Manuel.

The hallmark of the Manueline style is the extravagant use of seafaring imagery, with windows and doorways decorated with stone carvings of knotted ropes, anchors, globes, exotic fauna and flora and other maritime motifs. Two symbols that are ever present in this architecture are the armillary sphere (emblem of Dom Manuel) and the Cross of the Order of Christ.

You can go right inside the tower and up onto the terrace for closer views.

Art and Culture

The other main sights of Belém are across the railway line, around the Praça do Império gardens.

On one side is the **Centro Cultural de Belém**, built out of the same limestone as the Mosteiro dos Jerónimos (➤ 48), which has become one of Lisbon's most vibrant cultural centres, with galleries, a dynamic programme of concerts and performing arts, bookshops and cafés.

The star attraction for art buffs is the free **Museu Colecção Berardo**, harbouring the magnificent art collection of billionaire José Berardo, which includes masterpieces by Picasso, Warhol, Yves Klein and Portuguese artist Paula Rego. The works are shown in rotating exhibitions.

A Long History

However, the sight that really takes your breath away is the UNESCO World Heritage site **Mosteiro dos Jerónimos**, begun in 1502 on the site of a hermitage founded by Prince Henry the Navigator. In 1497, Vasco da Gama spent his last night here before sailing to find a sea route to India. Dom Manuel vowed he would build a church to the Virgin if he was successful. Begun by French architect Diogo de Boytac and continued by Spaniard Juan de Castillo, the monastery is full of Manueline flourishes. Don't miss the south portal, with its stonework saints and figure of Prince Henry on a pedestal. Just inside the web-vaulted church are the tombs of Vasco da Gama and Luís de Camões. Go through a separate entrance to the two-storey cloister, a Manueline masterpiece. Portugal's treaty of accession for entry to the EEC (now EU) was signed here in 1986.

Carving at the cloisters of Mosteiro dos Jerónimos, Belém

Maritime History

A 19th-century wing of the monastery houses the **Museu de Marinha**. Highlights include graffiti carved onto the African rocks by Portuguese explorer Diogo Cão in 1483, a model of Vasco da Gama's flagship, maps of the known world and a reconstruction of the state rooms from the royal yacht *Amélia*, right down to the king's private piano and roulette table.

A separate building contains the **royal barges**, including the sumptuous gilded barge built for the wedding of João VI in 1780, rowed by 78 oarsmen and last used to transport Britain's Queen Elizabeth II on the River Tagus in 1957.

Fairy-tale Coaches

The popular **Museu Nacional dos Coches** is housed in a frescoed, 18th-century building, the former royal riding arena, and features an extraordinary collection of state coaches and carriages from the 17th to 19th centuries. Highlights include Pope Clement XI's lavishly gilded Coach of the Oceans (1716), covered with red silk velvet and lined with gold brocade.

TAKING A BREAK

Treat yourself to a coffee and a custard tart at the **Antiga Confeitaria de Belém** (➤ 69).

---

196 off A1 · Tram 15E · Belém (Lisbon to Cascais line)

Padrão dos Descobrimentos

Avenida de Brasília · 213 031 950; www.padraodescobrimentos.egeac.pt
May–Sep daily 10–6:30; Oct–Apr 10–5:30 · Inexpensive

Torre de Belém

Avenida de Brasília · 213 620 034; www.mosteirojeronimos.pt
May–Sep 10–6:30; Oct–Apr Tue–Sun 10–5:30 (last entry 30 mins before closing) · Moderate; free Sun and holidays 10–2

Museu Colecção Berardo
Praça do Império ☎ 213 612 878; www.museuberardo.pt 🕘 Tue–Fri 10–7, Sat 10–10 (last entry 30 mins before closing) ✋ Free

Centro Cultural de Belém
✉ Praça do Império ☎ 213 612 400; www.ccb.pt 🕘 Mon–Fri 8–8, Sat–Sun 10–7 ✋ Free. Workshops: moderate. Concerts: prices vary; see the website for an up-to-date programme of events and ticket bookings.

Mosteiro dos Jerónimos
✉ Praça do Império ☎ 213 620 034; www.mosteirojeronimos.pt
🕘 May–Sep Tue–Sun 10–6:30; Oct–Apr Tue–Sun 10–5:30 ✋ Church: free. Cloisters: moderate; free Sun 10–2

Museu de Marinha
✉ Praça do Império ☎ 213 620 010; http://museu.marinha.pt
🕘 May–Sep Tue–Sun 10–6; Oct–Apr Tue–Sun 10–5 ✋ Moderate

Museu Nacional dos Coches
✉ Praça Afonso de Albuquerque ☎ 213 610 850; www.museudoscoches.pt 🕘 Tue–Sun 10–6 (last entry 30 mins before closing) ✋ Moderate; free Sun 10–2

The ornate facade of the Museu de Marinha in the Belém area

BELÉM: INSIDE INFO

Top tip Visit Belém on a Sunday morning when many of the museums and sights have free entrance. Avoid Mondays when almost everything is closed.

In more depth The **Museu da Electricidade** (Sun–Sat 10–6; www.fundacao.edp.pt), housed inside the thermo-electric power station at the eastern end of Belém, contains original generators and energy-themed exhibitions.

2 Museu Calouste Gulbenkian

The most significant museum in Portugal is the result of one man's passionate collecting, encompassing the entire history of both Eastern and Western art. What makes it all the more enjoyable is that although each piece is worth seeing, the small size of the collection means that it can be thoroughly explored in a visit of a couple of hours.

***The Mirror of Venus,* 1870–76, by Sir Edward Burne-Jones**

Calouste Gulbenkian (1869–1955) was an Armenian oil magnate who earned his nickname "Mr Five Per Cent" when he negotiated a five per cent stake in the newly discovered oilfields of Iraq.

He spent much of his wealth acquiring works of art, from Roman coins to old masters. During World War II, he moved to Portugal, and bequeathed his fortune and his art collection to the Portuguese. The foundation, established after his death, is now one of the largest cultural institutions in the world, which supports museums, orchestras and charitable projects.

Treasures From Around the World

The **Museu Calouste Gulbenkian** was opened in 1969 and contains the most precious objects from Gulbenkian's collection. Your tour of the museum begins with a small room devoted to ancient Egyptian art, including funerary statues, bronze sculptures and an alabaster bowl dating from 2700BC. The next room contains superb classical art from Greece and

A 14th-century mosque lamp

Rome, together with an impressive life-size relief of an Assyrian warrior from the ninth century BC.

Some of the greatest treasures are found in the **Gallery of Islamic and Oriental Art**, which features Persian rugs, Ottoman ceramics, enamelled glassware and a beautiful late 13th-century glazed ceramic *mihrab* (a prayer niche indicating the direction of Mecca) from a Persian mosque. Also in this room is a small case of illuminated gospel manuscripts from Gulbenkian's native Armenia.

This leads into the **Far East Gallery**, which has porcelain, jade, lacquered boxes and screens.

European Art

The largest part of the museum is devoted to **European art** from the 13th to the 20th centuries. It begins with early illuminated gospels and a 14th-century French triptych depicting scenes from the life of the Virgin.

Among the paintings to look out for are *Portrait of an Old Man* by Rembrandt and *Flight into Egypt* by Rubens (which features a terrified Mary clutching Jesus to her breast as the beasts of the forest surround her). From the Impressionist period there is *Self-Portrait* by Degas and *Boy Blowing Bubbles* by Manet. Other prominent European artists represented in the museum include Gainsborough, Turner, Renoir and Monet, along with some superb marble sculptures by Rodin.

The Gulbenkian Foundation is also responsible for the **Centro de Arte Moderna** (same hours as the museum), devoted to 20th-century Portuguese art. Walk through the attractive sculpture gardens and past an amphitheatre where open-air concerts are held in summer.

TAKING A BREAK

Take a **picnic** to the sculpture gardens or visit the **café** in the **Centro de Arte Moderna**, Rua Dr Nicolau de Bettencourt, (tel: 217 823 474), which has a good lunchtime cold buffet.

196 off A5 · Avenida de Berna 45 · 217 823 000; www.museu.gulbenkian.pt · Tue–Sun 10–5:45 · São Sebastião or Praça de Espanha · Moderate; free Sun · Bus 16, 726, 56, 718, 742

MUSEU CALOUSTE GULBENKIAN: INSIDE INFO

Top tips The Gulbenkian Foundation has its own **orchestra and choir** and also hosts concerts by visiting musicians. Ask for a programme at the museum reception desk or contact the box office (tel: 217 823 000).

- As well as paintings and sculpture, the European art galleries contain fine examples of **decorative arts**, including 18th-century Louis XV furniture from France and a set of gorgeous Italian tapestries depicting children playing in the woods.

Hidden gem Don't miss the **René Lalique Gallery** at the end of the European Art section, with stunning art nouveau jewellery by the French decorative artist René Lalique, who was a friend of Calouste Gulbenkian.

3 Castelo de São Jorge

Dominating the skyline above the Alfama district, the Castelo de São Jorge (St George's Castle) has a long and chequered history. Yet, despite its bloody past, this is now one of the most peaceful spots in Lisbon. The gardens make a pleasant place to escape for an hour or two, and there are fine views over the city and river from its walkways and terraces.

The castle occupies the site where Phoenician traders set up their first camp when they occupied Lisbon during the eighth century BC. It was fortified by the Romans and again by the Visigoths, and the Moorish rulers built their palace here.

The castle was taken for the Christians in 1147 by Afonso Henriques, Portugal's first king, who captured it after a 17-week siege, with the help of British and French crusaders. The victorious battle saw the death of the Portuguese knight Martim Moniz, who is honoured in the name of a Metro station and a nearby square.

After the Christian conquest, the Portuguese kings used the **Moorish palace** as their royal home until Dom Manuel I moved it to Terreiro do Paço, on the site of Praça do Comércio.

You enter the outer walls through the Arco de São Jorge, where a niche houses an image of the saint. This leads you

Climb on to ramparts for the best views

The superb views from Castelo de São Jorge

into the *bairro* of **Santa Cruz**, a village-like quarter of medieval houses around the 18th-century church of Santa Cruz do Castelo. A separate gateway leads into the castle proper, and a parade ground dominated by a **statue of Afonso Henriques**.

From the castle terrace, there are wonderful **views** and photo opportunities to be enjoyed over the River Tagus, named the *mar de palha* (sea of straw) by locals because of the way it shimmers like gold in the sun.

Walkways lead around the walls, and you can climb up onto the battlements and the roofs of the 10 towers for more superb views. In summer, peacocks strut around the gardens and artists set up their stalls beneath the ramparts.

Part of the old royal palace now contains **Olisipónia**, a multimedia exhibition. The video sequence takes you on a tour of Lisbon's history, including a simulation of the 1755 earthquake, with commentary and sound effects.

The other attraction here is the fascinating **Periscópio**, housed in the Torre de Ulisses, a device that provides live 360° images of the city and people below going about their daily business.

TAKING A BREAK

There is an attractive café and a restaurant within the castle if you want to stop for a meal, or if you want a late lunch or informal supper, try the **Wine Bar do Castelo** (➤ 69).

---

197 E4 Bus 737; tram 12, 28

Castelo

218 800 620; www.castelodesaojorge.pt Mar–Oct 9–9; Nov–Feb 9–6 (last entry 30 mins before closing) Expensive

Olisipónia

As castle, above Included in castle entry

Periscópio

Mar–Oct 9–5; Nov–Feb 10–5 Included in castle entry

CASTELO DE SÃO JORGE: INSIDE INFO

Top tips The castle can be reached by a short, steep climb from the **Miradouro de Santa Luzia**, but if you want to avoid the walk, **bus 737** goes all the way to the outer walls.

- The castle terrace is a great place to watch the **sunset**.
- A *fado* (➤ 20–21) festival is held on summer weekend evenings.

4 Alfama

The oldest quarter of Lisbon is also its most charming. Alfama sprawls across a hill between the Castelo de São Jorge and the River Tagus, a maze of cobbled lanes, alleyways, staircases and hidden courtyards whose Moorish streetplan has largely survived the damage caused by the 1755 earthquake.

View from Portas do Sol over the rooftops of Alfama

This is a district for aimless strolling through lanes, where you will be rewarded with endless surprises as you discover a flower-strewn courtyard, a public washing place or a statue of the Virgin in a niche high on a wall. Although Alfama is undergoing some changes, it is still primarily a working-class *bairro*, with a densely populated community of fishermen – who spend their spare time in local *tascas* (bars) – and their wives, who set up stalls on the street. The scent of freshly washed laundry and charcoal-sardines is ever present as the life of the community goes on in dilapidated houses with wrought-iron balconies and *azulejo* panels on the walls.

Cathedral and Teatro Romano

The name Alfama probably derives from the Arabic *al hama* (fountain) and there is evidence of Roman and Moorish settlements here. The Christians built their **sé** (cathedral) on the site of the main mosque, soon after Afonso Henriques captured the city in 1147. Constructed in Romanesque style and closely resembling a fortress, it has twin towers either side of a rose window on the main facade. The Gothic cloisters contain the excavated remains of the Roman city.

Just above the cathedral, the **Teatro Romano** is a partly excavated Roman theatre, built during the reign of Emperor Augustus and rebuilt under Nero in the first century AD. The theatre itself is found in a shed on Rua de São Mamede, and there is a small **museum** across the street displaying archaeological finds.

Miradouro de Santa Luzia

Walk (or take tram 28) uphill from the cathedral to reach **Miradouro de Santa Luzia**, a pretty garden with fine views over Alfama and the River Tagus. Notice the tiled panels on the south wall of the nearby church, one depicting Lisbon before the earthquake, the other showing Christian soldiers with helmets, swords and shields attacking the Castelo de São Jorge (➤ 52–53), which is defended by turbanned Moors.

Museu de Artes Decorativas

Around the corner is the **Museu de Artes Decorativas**, containing the applied arts collection of the Portuguese banker Ricardo do Espírito Santo Silva. The collection is particularly rich in Portuguese furniture, as well as ceramics, clocks, fans and guns, all displayed in a re-creation of a 17th-century aristocratic home. Don't miss the *Giraffe Parade*, a colourful 16th-century Flemish tapestry in the main hall. The museum also has workshops where artisans reproduce traditional skills such as bookbinding and woodcarving.

There are more views over the Alfama rooftops from the terrace at **Largo das Portas do Sol**, opposite the museum. Notice here the **statue of São Vicente**, Lisbon's patron saint, bearing the city's symbol, a boat with two ravens (the relics of the saint were said to have been brought to Lisbon by Afonso Henriques in a boat piloted by ravens).

An aristocratic drawing room in the Museu de Artes Decorativas

Two Churches

Looking east from the terrace, the skyline is dominated by two white marble churches, the vast bulk of **São Vicente de Fora** and the domed church of **Santa Engrácia**. You can hop back on the tram to visit both of them.

São Vicente de Fora means "St Vincent Beyond the Wall" as the church was originally outside the city walls. The first church was built on this site soon after the Christian conquest, though the current one dates from 1629. Go through a side entrance to visit the monastery and cloisters. There is a fine 18th-century sacristy with walls of inlaid polychrome marble and a set of *azulejo* tiles (➤ 18–19) depicting the fables of the 17th-century French satirist La Fontaine.

The superb illuminated dome of Santa Engrácia

The former monks' refectory is now the pantheon of the **House of Bragança** (➤ 137) containing the tombs of monarchs from Catherine of Bragança (Queen of England) to the assassinated Dom Carlos I and his son, Dom Manuel II, who died in exile in England in 1932.

The baroque church of **Santa Engrácia**, by contrast, has become the national pantheon, with monuments to Portuguese heroes, such as explorers Vasco da Gama (➤ 12, 13) and Luís de Camões, as well as the *fadista* Amália Rodrigues. You can take the lift up to the rooftop for fabulous views over the River Tagus and the city.

The open ground between the two churches, **Campo de Santa Clara**, is the setting for Lisbon's liveliest flea market, the Feira da Ladra (Thieves' Market), which takes place on Tuesday and Saturday from 6am to 5pm.

Fado

Alfama is the true home of the traditional music of *fado* (➤ 20–21), and there are several clubs in the back streets where you can hear it performed each night.

To find out more about this uniquely Portuguese music, visit the **Museu do Fado**, on the southern edge of Alfama, close to the river. This excellent museum describes the history and traditions of *fado* and of the Portuguese guitar, a mandolin-type instrument that was introduced by British traders in the 18th century. There are frequent live performances, and the shop sells *fado* books and CDs.

TAKING A BREAK

Cafés, *fado* bars and restaurants cluster on and around Rua de São Pedro, Rua São João da Praça and Rua dos Remédios. Try **Pois Cafe** (Rua São João da Praça 93, tel: 218 862 497) for good salads and sandwiches in arty surrounds, or **Porta d'Alfama** (Rua São João da Praça 17, tel: 218 864 536) for grilled sardines and spontaneous, free *fado* performances.

197 F3 Bus 737; tram 12, 28

Sé

197 E2 Largo da Sé 218 876 628 Museum: daily 10–5. Cloisters: 10–6. Cathedral: daily 9–7 Church: free. Cloisters: inexpensive

Narrow cobbled streets in Alfama, Lisbon's oldest quarter

Museu do Teatro Romano

197 E2 Pátio de Aljube 5, Rua Augusto Rosa 218 820 320 Tue–Sun 10–1, 2–6 Free

Museu de Artes Decorativas

197 E3 Largo das Portas do Sol 2 218 814 600; www.fress.pt Daily 10–5 Moderate

São Vicente de Fora

197 off F4 Largo de São Vicente 218 824 400 Church: Tue–Sat 9–4, Sun 9–12:30. Cloisters: Tue–Sat 10–5, Sun 19–11:30 Free

Santa Engrácia (Panteão Nacional)

197 F4 Campo de Santa Clara 218 854 820 Tue–Sun 10–5 Inexpensive; free Sun 10–2 Bus 34

Museu do Fado

197 F2 Largo do Chafariz de Dentro 1 218 823 470; www.museudofado.pt Tue–Sun 10–6 (last entry 30 mins before closing) Moderate

ALFAMA: INSIDE INFO

Top tips Come here on **weekday mornings** when the street life is at its most lively and a fish market is set up along Rua de São Pedro.

- Alfama is a poor area with a reputation for **petty crime**, so avoid flaunting anything valuable and take care when wandering at night.

Hidden gems One particularly charming spot is the **courtyard** at the top of **Escadinhas de Santo Estêvão**, between Rua dos Remédios and Santo Estêvão.

Igreja de Santo André e Santa Marinha is one of the oldest convents in Lisbon. Parts of the convent are closed to the public, but the church is open and the views over the city and river from the courtyard are stunning.

5 Parque das Nações

The former Expo'98 site has become an open-air playground where *Lisboetas* flock at weekends to enjoy its many restaurants, bars, sculpture gardens and riverside walks. With stunning modern architecture and a range of high-tech attractions, a day out at "the invented city" offers a completely different experience of Lisbon.

Hosting the World Exposition in 1998 gave Lisbon the opportunity for a major project in urban renewal. A derelict area of warehouses and oil refineries, 5km (3 miles) east of the city, was transformed into a riverside park. When Expo'98 closed, the site was renamed **Parque das Nações** and turned into a business and residential zone – in effect, a new city with cultural and sporting facilities. There are now more visitors than there were when Expo'98 was in full swing.

Most visitors arrive at the concertina-like **Estação do Oriente**, a strikingly vaulted steel-and-glass Metro station, designed by much-lauded Spanish architect Santiago Calatrava. This leads into the Vasco da Gama **shopping mall**. Walk through the mall to emerge on the waterfront.

Shops and restaurants in the Vasco da Gama mall

An Underwater World

The **Oceanário** is one of the largest oceanariums in Europe, and receives around one million visitors per year. It is based around a huge tank with windows at two levels so you can watch the sharks near the surface and flatfish on the seabed.

Gathered around this are four separate tanks devoted to the ecosystems of the North Atlantic, South Atlantic, Pacific and Indian oceans. More than 15,000 marine animals and birds are on show, including puffins, penguins, sea otters and spider crabs, together with some superb examples of coral reefs.

From here you can walk or take the **cable-car** along the banks of the River Tagus, passing the Garcia de Orta botanical gardens. The ride ends close to the sail-shaped **Torre Vasco da Gama**, a skeletal concrete-and-steel structure that is Lisbon's tallest building, rising 145m (476ft) above the river.

The ultra-modern and extraordinary Wall of Water Fountain

The tower was being converted into a luxury hotel at the time of writing.

The extraordinary 18km (11-mile) bridge, **Ponte Vasco da Gama**, spans the River Tagus; it passes over water for 10km (6 miles) of its length and almost seems to be floating.

TAKING A BREAK

There are more than 40 restaurants, serving everything from fast food to Brazilian, Cuban, Chinese, Italian, Spanish and Portuguese cuisine. There's also a wide choice of ice-cream parlours, pizza houses, *tapas* bars and cafés along the waterfront.

---

200 B2 218 919 333; www.parquedasnacoes.pt Oriente

Oceanário

218 917 002; www.oceanario.pt Jun–Sep daily 10–8; Nov–Mar daily 10–7 (last entry one hour before closing) Expensive

Teleférico (cable-car)

218 956 143; www.parquedasnacoes Jul–Sep Mon–Fri 11–8, Sat–Sun 10–8; Oct–Jun Mon–Fri 11–7, Sat–Sun 10–8 Moderate

The waterfront area is a pleasant place to relax

PARQUE DAS NAÇÕES: INSIDE INFO

Top tips If you have small children with you, you can get around the various attractions on a **miniature road train** that makes regular circuits of the park.

- The **Cartão do Parque** gives free entry to the Oceanário and on the cable-car, as well as discounts on audio tours and bike rental, and is good value if you intend doing them all.

In more depth Take a botanical stroll through Portugal's former colonies at the riverside **Jardim Garcia de Orta** (daylight hours, free). Flame-like birds of paradise flowers, pepper trees and frangipani all flourish here. If the weather is unfavourable, head to the **Pavilhão do Conhecimento** (Tue–Fri 10–6, Sat–Sun 11–7, moderate), an interactive science museum (www.pavconhecimento.pt).

6 Sintra

If you only have time for one excursion, you should make it Sintra. Once the summer residence of the kings of Portugal, this UNESCO World Heritage site is pure fairy-tale stuff with its whitewashed *quintas* set on green hillsides among palaces, pinewoods and granite crags.

Palácio Nacional de Sintra

The centre of the town is dominated by the fairy-tale **Palácio Nacional**, with its two enormous conical chimneys. This royal palace was begun by João I in the late 14th century and completed by Manuel I (1469–1521) in the Manueline style.

Look out for the Renaissance-inspired **Sala dos Cisnes** (Swan Room) and **Sala das Pegas** (Magpie Room), named after the136 magpies in the ceiling frescoes.

The **Sala dos Brasões** (Arms Room) has *azulejo* (➤ 18–19) walls depicting hunting scenes and a coffered gilded ceiling with the coats of arms of 72 noble families.

Also in the palace is the **bedchamber of Afonso VI**, the deranged king held prisoner here by his brother Pedro II, who added insult to injury by marrying his queen.

The Castle

Sintra's other main sights speckle the hills above it. The **Castelo dos Mouros** (Moors' Castle) was built in the ninth century and captured by Afonso Henriques in 1147. You

The Palácio Nacional's conical chimneys are hard to miss

The fantasy facade of Palacio da Pena

can walk around the snaking ramparts, with views stretching beyond Lisbon and out to sea, to reach the royal tower, where there is a fine view of the Palácio da Pena, on a granite peak.

Palácio Nacional da Pena

The climb to the the **Palácio Nacional da Pena** winds through the woodlands of Parque da Pena, dotted with lakes and follies. With its minarets, towers and golden domes, the palace is famous throughout Portugal. It was built in the 1840s by Prince Ferdinand of Saxe-Coburg-Gotha, husband of Dona Maria II and honorary king of Portugal, on the site of a monastery established by Manuel I to give thanks for the sighting of Vasco da Gama's fleet returning from India.

This was the last royal palace built in Portugal and Baron Eschwege, the German architect, let his imagination run wild. Gargoyles gaze down from doorways and life-size statues hold up chandeliers. Meissen porcelain dominates the queen's antechamber and the Arabic Room features playful *trompe-l'œil* walls. Everything is preserved as it was when Dom Manuel II went into exile in 1910. From the belvedere you can look out to Cruz Alta, the highest point of the Serra de Sintra, marked by a stone cross and a statue of Baron Eschwege.

Toys, Romantic Follies and Modern Art

There are three museums worth visiting in the town centre. The **Museu do Brinquedo** (Toy Museum), in the old fire station, contains a collection of João Arbués Moreira, gathered over 50 years, including Egyptian marbles, Roman bronze figures, tin soldiers and vintage Barbie dolls.

Explore whimsical follies, underground chambers, grottoes and fountains in the lush grounds of 19th-century **Quinta da Regaleira**, the vision of Italian set designer Luigi Manini.

The outstanding **Museu de Arte Moderna**, in the old casino, features rotating exhibits from the Berardo Collection (➤ 47) of 20th-century art, including works by Dalí, Miró, Picasso and Warhol. Don't leave without trying *queijadas*,

(➤ 38) sweet cheese and cinnamon pastries, at **Fábrica das Queijadas da Sapa** near the Palácio Nacional at Volta do Duche.

The rugged battlements of the Castelo dos Mouros are worth the climb

200 A2 Praça da República 23, tel: 210 991 882; www.cm-sintra.pt From Estação do Rossio to Sintra

Palácio Nacional de Sintra
Largo Rainha Dona Amélia 219 106 840; www.ippar.pt Jun to mid-Oct Thu–Tue 9:30–7; mid-Oct to May Thu–Tue 9:30–5:30 Expensive; free Sun 10–2

Castelo dos Mouros
219 237 300; www.parquesdesintra.pt Apr–Sept, daily 9:30–8; Oct–Mar daily 9:30–6; (last entry one hour before closing) Moderate Bus 434

Palácio Nacional da Pena
Estrada da Pena 219 105 340; www.parquesdesintra.pt Oct–Mar Apr to mid-Sep daily 9:45–7; mid-Sep to Mar daily 10–6 (last entry 30 mins before closing) Expensive Bus 434

Museu do Brinquedo
Rua Visconde de Monserrate 219 242 171; www.museu-do-brinquedo.pt Tue–Sun 10–6 Moderate

Quinta da Regaleira
Rua Barbosa du Bocage 219 106 656 Nov–Jan daily 10–5:30; Feb, Mar and Oct 10–6:30; Apr–Sep 10–8 (last entry 30 mins to one hour before closing) Moderate

Museu de Arte Moderna
Avenida Heliodoro Salgado 219 248 170; www.cm-sintra.pt or www.berardocllection.com Tue–Sun 10–6 (last entry 5:30) Free

SINTRA: INSIDE INFO

Top tips The main sights are connected by a **circular bus route** (No 434) that links the station, old town, Castelo dos Mouros and Palácio Nacional da Pena. A single ticket is valid all day. If you are coming from Estoril or Cascais, buy a Day Rover ticket *(bilhete turístico diário)*, which includes travel within Sintra.

- The **Sintra Music Festival**, which takes place in June and July, is one of Portugal's top classical music festivals. Details from Sintra tourist information office.
- A tram runs direct between Praia das Maçãs beach and the Museu de Arte Moderna in Sintra every weekend in summer

In more depth Another of Portugal's elaborate royal palaces, **Palácio de Queluz** (tel: 214 343 860, www.pnqueluz.imc-ip.pt, Wed–Mon 9–5, last entry 30 minutes before closing, expensive), lies close to the Sintra train line and can be visited on the way back to Lisbon.

At Your Leisure

7 Museu Nacional de Arte Antiga

It may not have the treasures of the Calouste Gulbenkian (➤ 50–51), but the National Museum of Ancient Art does have the most complete collection of Portuguese art, together with the cultures that influenced it. Among the items to look for are Indo-Portuguese furniture, Sino-Portuguese ceramics, a carved-ivory salt cellar from Africa, and 16th-century lacquer screens showing the arrival of Portuguese explorers in Japan. Many of the religious paintings, such as Nuno Gonçalves' 15th-century *St Vincent Altarpiece*, were confiscated from churches following the dissolution of the monasteries in 1834. The museum also contains a complete baroque chapel from the Carmelite convent that once stood on this site, with gilded woodwork and outstanding *azulejo* tiles (➤ 18–19).

196 off A1 ✉ Rua das Janelas Verdes, Lapa ☎ 213 912 800; www.mnarteantiga-ipmuseus.pt ⏲ Wed–Sun 10–6, Tue 2–6 Moderate; free Sun 10–2 Bus 713, 714, 732; tram 15, 18, 25

Baroque gilded silverwork

LISBON FOR KIDS

- **Parque das Nações** (➤ 58–59): for aquatic encounters at the Oceanário and science experiments at the Pavilhão do Conhecimento Virtual, with hands-on exhibits. There's a mini road train to take you round.
- **Planetário Calouste Gulbenkian:** next to the Museu de Marinha (➤ 48,49), this planetarium has children's shows at weekends.
- **Museu da Carris:** take tram No 15 to the tram museum (Mon–Sat 10–4:30, www.carris.pt, inexpensive).
- **Jardim Zoológico:** take the Metro to Jardim Zoológico to visit Lisbon's zoo (Oct–Feb daily 10–6 (last entry 5), Mar–Sep 10–8, tel: 217 232 900, www.zoo.pt, expensive).

8 Estrêla

Estrêla, a well-to-do neighbourhood some 2km (1.2 miles) west of Bairro Alto, is dominated by its late 18th-century baroque **Basílica**, whose graceful white dome is visible across the city. Opposite, the **Jardim da Estrêla** is one of Lisbon's prettiest public gardens, with a bandstand, play area and duck pond. Walk through the gardens to reach St George's Anglican church (service Sun 11:30) and the **Cemitério Inglês**, where British novelist Henry Fielding is buried.

196 off A3 Tram 25, 28

Basílica da Estrêla

✉ Praça da Estrêla ☎ 213 960 915 ⏲ Mon–Sat 8:30–12, 1–7, Sun 10–11:45, 3–6:45 Free

Cemitério Inglês

✉ Rua de São Jorge à Estrêla ☎ 213 906 248 ⏲ Mon–Sat 9–5, Sun 9–1 Free

9 Bairro Alto

The grid of 16th-century lanes that makes up the Bairro Alto (upper town) is best known as Lisbon's nightlife quarter, where the plaintive strains of *fado* compete with African and Latin vibes.

Traditionally a working-class area, Bairro Alto has been given a new lease of life, with cocktail bars and a glut of live music venues, bars, pubs and discos.It is also a great spot for late-night shopping, where the shops sell everything from alternative fashion to vintage accessories, cutting-edge art to designer garb.

Near here is the Jesuit **Igreja de São Roque**, whose plain facade belies the richness of its interior, especially its lavish side chapels. The Capela de São João Baptista, fourth on the left, is a riot of marble, alabaster, lapis lazuli, amethyst, mosaic, silver and gold, built in Rome and taken to Lisbon on the orders of Dom João V.

Just down the hill, on the edge of the chic shopping district of Chiado, the **Museu Arqueológico do Carmo** occupies the old Carmelite convent, destroyed in the earthquake of 1755 and now a Gothic shell. Among the items on display are Egyptian and Peruvian mummies, Roman mosaics and a stone bust of Afonso Henriques dating from the 12th century.

196 A3 Tram 28, Elevador da Glória

FOUR BEST VIEWPOINTS

- **Castelo de São Jorge** (➤ 52–53): standing at the top of Alfama, there are fine views from the castle ramparts.
- **Miradouro de Santa Luzia**, Alfama (➤ 55): views over the River Tagus and Alfama.
- **Miradouro de São Pedro de Alcântara**, Bairro Alto (➤ above, 174): views from the top of the Elevador da Glória over the Baixa and River Tagus.
- **Ponte 25 de Abril**: stretching across the River Tagus, the views from the bridge are breathtaking.

The atmospheric streets of the Barrio Alto area at night

Igreja de São Roque

196 A4 Largo Trindade Coelho 213 235 380 Church: daily 8:30–5. Museum: Tue–Sun 10–5 Church: free. Museum: inexpensive

Museu Arqueológico do Carmo

196 B3 Largo do Carmo 213 478 629; www.museusportugal.org/AAP/html/historia.htm May–Sep Mon–Sat 10–7; Oct–Apr 10–6 Inexpensive

10 Parque Eduardo VII

This large, formal park was laid out at the end of the 19th century and named after the English king, Edward VII. The best reason for coming here is the magnificent view from the terrace at the top of the park, where a stone monument commemorates the 1974 revolution. From here you look down over sweeping lawns and along the broad Avenida da Liberdade all the way to the River Tagus. Near here is a garden dedicated to the *fado* singer Amália Rodrigues. On one side of the park is a pavilion, named after the 1984 Olympic marathon champion Carlos Lopes; on the other side lie the *estufas* (greenhouses), with delightful lakeside walks and hothouses full of tropical plants.

196 off A5 Marquês de Pombal, Parque, São Sebastião Daily 9–sunset

Walkways intersect lengths of grass with manicured hedges at Parque Eduardo VII

11 Museu Nacional do Azulejo

It's worth making the short trek out of the centre of Lisbon to visit the National Tile Museum, housed in the former convent of Madre de Deus. The museum traces the development of *azulejo* tiles (➤ 18–19) from the 15th century onwards, in the setting of a lovely baroque church with Manueline cloisters and tiled walls. The highlight is an 18th-century panel of more than 1,300 tiles, which gives a panoramic view of pre-earthquake Lisbon. The 20th-century galleries show how *azulejos* have moved out of monasteries and into shopping malls, Metro stations and the realms of abstract art.

197 off F2 Rua Madre de Deus 4
218 100 340; http://mnazulejo.imc-ip.pt
Wed–Sun 10–6, Tue 2–6 Moderate (free Sun 10–2) Bus 718, 742, 794

12 Estoril and Cascais

These twin resorts, linked by an attractive seafront promenade, lie at the heart of the Lisbon coast. Estoril is more cosmopolitan and chic, with a casino, golf course, racetrack and a mock castle on the beach.

The busy resort at Praia do Tamariz, Estoril, is popular with tourists and locals

A corridor in the spectacular Palácio-Convento de Mafra

During World War II, when Portugal remained neutral, Estoril was a refuge for diplomats, spies and exiled royalty – King Juan Carlos of Spain spent his childhood here.

Although a growing resort, Cascais retains its fishing village charm, with daily fish auctions beside the beach, Praia da Ribeira.

Beyond Cascais, a coastal corniche leads past Boca do Inferno (Hell's Mouth), where waves crash against the cliffs, to the dunes at Praia do Guincho, a popular windsurfing beach, and Cabo da Roca, mainland Europe's westernmost point.

This area makes a good base for a short stay near Lisbon, combining a beach holiday with a city break. Trains to Lisbon follow a scenic line along the coast, via the resorts of São Pedro do Estoril and Carcavelos.

200 A2 From Cais do Sodré

13 Palácio-Convento de Mafra

The pink marble Palácio-Convento de Mafra, 40km (25 miles) northwest of Lisbon, was built by Dom João V in 1717 to give thanks to God for the birth of a royal heir. Like El Escorial in Madrid, it served both as a royal palace and a monastery.

Financed by profits from Brazilian gold, the palace employed 50,000 workers in its construction; originally intended to hold 13 monks, it ended up accommodating 300 monks and the entire royal family. You can visit the basilica and the palace, including the monks' cells, the pharmacy, and the baroque library, on guided tours. There are also tours of the royal hunting ground, now a wildlife park.

200 A3 261 817 550; www.cm-mafra.pt/turismo/palacio.asp Wed–Mon 10–5:30 (last entry 4:30) Moderate Mafrense bus links palace to Lisbon, Ericeira and Sintra

LISBON RIDES

It is fun (and has the advantage of being much cheaper) to join the locals on public transport.

- **Ferries**: Commuter ferries cross the Tagus to Barreiro and Cacilhas. The boats for Barreiro depart from Terreiro do Paço, with superb views of the city.
- **Trams**: A ride on one of Lisbon's bright yellow, wood-panelled vintage trams is an experience in itself. The most enjoyable route is No 28, which rattles up and down the steep streets of Alfama on its way from Graça to Estrela.
- **Elevadores**: These ancient lifts and funiculars are part of Lisbon's public transport system. Take Elevador da Glória from Praça dos Restauradores to Bairro Alto, or Elevador de Santa Justa for views over Baixa.

Where to... Stay

Prices
Expect to pay for a double room per night in high season:
€ under €60 **€€** €60–€120 **€€€** €121–€180 **€€€€** over €180

LISBON

Albergaria Senhora do Monte €€–€€€

The gorgeous pink and white décor and marble bathrooms in this modern hotel complement the romantic location, high up in the quiet *bairro* of Graça. The panoramic restaurant-bar (open to non-guests for drinks) is a wonderful place to linger over breakfast. More expensive rooms with south-facing terraces also have air conditioning – ask for one when booking. It's a short tram ride into downtown Lisbon.

197 E5 Calçada do Monte 39 218 866 002; www.albergariasenhoradomonte.com Martim Moniz Tram 12, 28

Hotel Bairro Alto €€–€€€

Chic, luxurious and in a great neighbourhood, this restored 18th-century townhouse makes for a memorable stay in Lisbon. Every detail has been thought about here – generous beds in sleekly designed bedrooms, 24-hour concierge, a good café-bar, a small gym and spa. The sixth-floor terrace offers views over the rooftops of Bairro Alto and down to the River Tagus. Everything suggests understated luxury, but it can all get rather expensive. If you want to experience the hotel without quite the same price tag, the loft rooms are smaller, with sloping roofs, but are well designed and offer excellent value.

196 A2 8 Praça Luís de Camões 213 408 288; www.bairroaltohotel.com Baixa-Chiado

Britania Hotel €€€–€€€€

Tucked down a quiet street near the boutique-lined Avenida da Liberdade boulevard, this art deco boutique hotel gets rave reviews. Polished marble, geometric cork floors and chrome lighting whisk you back to the 1940s. However, the plush rooms come with modern creature comforts such as Molton Brown cosmetics, free WiFi internet, DVD players and bathrobes. Head down to the shipshape bar to watch the world go by over a coffee and the daily papers or a cocktail.

196 off A5 Rua Rodrigues Sampaio 17 213 155 016; www.heritage.pt Avenida

Casa do Bairro €€

Housed in a beautifully converted 19th-century town house in Lisbon's hilltop Santa Catarina district, this B&B is just five minutes' walk from Bairro Alto. Wood floors and bold colours contrast strikingly with original features like stucco and *azulejos* in rooms with cable TV and WiFi internet. Enjoy home-made Portuguese cakes at breakfast, which, when the weather is fine, is served on the patio shaded by lemon and fig trees. There is a minimum two-night stay.

196 off A3 Beco do Caldeira 1, Rua Fernandes Tomás 914 176 969; http://casadobairro.pt Bus 794 to Conde Barão

Hotel Heritage Av Liberdade €€€–€€€€

This hotel is the most recent addition to a small chain of renovated historic buildings that have been turned into luxury boutique hotels in key areas of Lisbon. Renovated by Portuguese architect Miguel Câncio Martins, this 18th-century townhouse was the winner of the Historic Rehabilitation Prize 2008 of the Portuguese Real State Oscars. The hotel feels chic and intimate, with good-sized bedrooms, large marble bathrooms and a heated lap pool in the basement. No restaurant, but there's a cosy, well-decorated bar downstairs, where breakfast is served and bar snacks in the evenings. Even better, it's an easy walk into the centre of town. Babysitting services are available, and there's WiFi in all rooms.

196 A5 Avenida da Liberdade 28 213 218 200; www.heritage.pt/heritage_av_liberdade.html Restauradores

Jerónimos 8 €€–€€€

Situated opposite the magnificent Jerónimos monastery (➤ 48, 49) in Belém, this contemporary and cleverly designed hotel is perfectly placed for exploring the many monuments, museums and waterfront of Belém. Discreet from the outside, the public areas of the hotel are sleek and modern, with low-level sofas in bright colours and large artworks hanging on the walls. Outside, there are several terraces on higher floors for enjoying a drink on warm days. The bedrooms are reasonably sized, uncluttered and comfortable – ask for one with a view of the monastery. A lively and popular bar serves a range of drinks and cocktails (including a house wine made in the vineyards of a sister hotel), together with a range of simple but well-cooked bar food.

196 off A1 Rua dos Jerónimos 8 213 600 900; www.jeronimos8.com Tram 15; Elevador da Glória

Hotel Olisseppo Oriente €€

This is one of the newer hotels in this area, on a street with plenty of smart places to stay. The comfortable, if functional, rooms have kitchenettes if you want to self-cater. You also have the Parque das Nações (➤ 58–59), on the doorstep, with its shopping, eating and entertainment opportunities and all rooms have staggering views of its futuristic buildings, the "Sea of Straw" (River Tagus) and the Ponte Vasco da Gama (➤ 59).

200 B2 Avenida Dom João II, Parque das Naçoes 218 929 100; www.olissippohotels.com Oriente

Pensão Londres €–€€

This simple, reliable *pensão* is superbly located for exploring the sights in the Principe Real district, and many of the rooms command fabulous views across the rooftops to the Ponte 25 de Abril or Castelo São Jorge (➤ 52–53). The 40 rooms, ranging from well-appointed singles, doubles, triples and suites, all have their own bathrooms. The largest doubles have attractive period furniture. A full breakfast is served in a charming dining room, which also has a fine view.

196 off A4 Rua Pedro V 53/1- 213 462 203; www.pensaolondres.com.pt Bus 91; Elevador da Glória

Sé Guesthouse €€

The well-appointed Sé Guesthouse is a relaxing place to stay and is in fact two guesthouses in the same building – one with five bedrooms and the other with four. In a good location, just behind the *sé* (cathedral, ➤ 54–55), and on the edge of Alfama, Lisbon's old town, this nine-room *pensão* is on the first floor of a beautiful town house. Tastefully furnished with African artefacts and antique furniture, the rooms are large and comfortable but some don't have their own bathrooms, so book early if you want an en-suite room. Breakfast is copious. The owners speak English.

197 E2 Rua de São João da Praça 97/1 218 864 400 Bus 737; tram 28

Zuzabed & Breakfast €€

It's well worth the stiff climb up the Calçada do Duque to reach this homely B&B, where Luís Zuzarte is your affable and knowledgeable host. He has put his artistic stamp on the individually decorated

rooms, done out in bright colours and all opening out onto balconies. Head up to the terrace for dreamy views over Lisbon to the castle. Free WiFi and home-made cakes at breakfast sweeten the deal.
196 B3 Calçada do Duque 29 934 445 500 Rossio Elevador da Glória

SINTRA

Cinco B&B €€
High on a hill and surrounded by gardens, this is one of Sintra's most charming retreats. You'll receive the warmest of welcomes from Carole and Stuart the minute you arrive at their attractive family stone cottage. The spacious, tastefully decorated one-bedroom apartment is completely private and also features a well-equipped kitchenette, bright living room with DVD player and a terrace with tremendous views across the valley to the Atlantic. Guests are also welcome to use the family's swimming pool. Rates apply to one to two people in the apartment, with an additional charge per extra adult or child per night.
200 A2 Largo da Caracota 5 914 502 255; www.stayatcinco.com From Estação do Rossio

Lawrence's Hotel €€€€
This beautiful house near to central Sintra, Lawrence's claims to be the oldest hotel in Iberia and is highly recommended. The exquisitely decorated 11 rooms and five suites have the latest facilities, including air conditioning and satellite TV; some have jacuzzis in the huge bathrooms, and open fireplaces. At the top-class restaurant you can sample some of the best cooking in Sintra – even if you're not a hotel guest. A refined cellar backs up the Portuguese-influenced cuisine. Golfing packages are also offered, with discount rates at the best local golf course links.
200 A2 Rua Consiglieri Pedroso 38–40 219 105 500; www.lawrenceshotel.com From Estação do Rossio

Where to...
Eat and Drink

Prices
Expect to pay per person for a three-course meal, excluding drinks and tips:
€ under €12 **€€** €12–€24 **€€€** €25–€36 **€€€€** over €36

LISBON

100 Maneiras €€€€
This is the place for imaginative food made from market-fresh ingredients. Service is attentive and the setting arty yet unpretentious. There's one tasting menu, but come with an open mind and an empty stomach and you won't be disappointed. Dishes such as marinated sardines with toasted basil and passion fruit, tender loin of lamb in a pistachio crust and palate-cleansing ginger sorbet strike a perfect balance. Book ahead.
196 A4 Rua do Teixeira 35 210 990 475 Bus 202, 758, 790; Elevador da Glória

Antiga Confeitaria de Belém €
Although you can order a range of delicious sandwiches and cakes, most people come here for the *pastéis de nata* (➤ 38). You can find these crisp tartlets filled with egg-custard in *pastelarias* across the country, but those made here are unanimously regarded as superior – and they are noticeably less sweet.
196 off A1 Rua de Belém 84–88 213 637 423; www.pasteisdebelem.pt Jun–Sep daily 8am–midnight; Oct–May, 8am–11pm Bus 714, 729, 751; tram 15

A Bica do Sapato €€€€

Leading light Manuel Reis – who owns Lux (➤ 74), the nearby nightclub – has an eye for location and impeccable taste in décor. Right on the waterfront at up-and-coming Santa Apolónia, this three-in-one temple to good food is currently the place to eat and be seen, whether in the stylish café-bar, the sushi section or the restaurant. In the latter you can sample clever concoctions such as soft-shell crab tempura, salmon *temaki* and spicy *hosomaki*. The restaurant is one of the few places in Lisbon with a dedicated vegetarian menu.

197 E2 Avenida Infante Dom Henrique, Armazém B 218 810 320; www.bicadosapato.com Restaurant: Tue–Sat 12:30–2:30, 8–11:30. Sushi Bar: Mon–Sat 9:30pm–1:30am. Café: Mon 5pm–1am, Tue–Sat 12–3:30, 7:30–1am Santa Apolónia Bus 9, 28, 35, 81, 82, 90

A Brasileira €–€€

Few old-style cafés have survived in Lisbon, but this one, thankfully, has – the timeless atmosphere is enhanced by a handless clock at the far end of the mirrored salon. It's a meeting place for students, intellectuals and other regulars drawn by the excellent coffee and *pastéis* (➤ 38), and also a shrine to Fernando Pessoa who frequented it – witness the bronze statue on the small *esplanada*, next to which many tourists have their picture taken, often having never heard of the great 20th-century poet. It is a bit touristy, and not the cheapest place, but a real institution.

196 B3 Rua Garrett 120 213 469 541 Daily 8–2 Baixa-Chiado

Café Martinho da Arcada €€

Superbly located at the foot of the Alfama district, under the arcades and on one of the city's main squares, this is one of Lisbon's oldest cafés, with more than 200 years of service, and a dining experience that should not to be missed. The wine list is excellent and the very friendly waiters are more than happy to offer suggestions for dishes that have been sourced that morning from fishing boats or local markets.

196 C1 Praça do Comérçio 3 218 879 259 Mon–Sat 7am–11pm Tram 15, 28

Casa da Comida €€€€

Tucked away in a side street just above the Rato, this is one of Lisbon's finest restaurants, with prices to match. Inside it has the sophisticated décor of a noble mansion and a beautiful patio. The superb cuisine gives a French angle to traditional Portuguese dishes, using local crab and clams, pheasant and partridge. Desserts are fabulous too and there's an excellent wine cellar. This is the perfect place for an celebration or expensive treat.

196 off A4 Travessa das Amoreiras 213 860 889; www.casacomida.pt Mon 8pm–11pm, Tue–Fri 1pm–3pm and 8pm–11pm, Sat 8pm–11pm; closed Sun Rato Bus 706, 713, 727

Casa do Alentejo €–€€

Behind a run-of-the-mill facade and up a gloomy staircase, there's a fantastic, if slightly decadent, patrician mansion, with Moorish patios and beautiful skylights, decorated with carved wood, gleaming *azulejos* and huge palms. The reliably good and well-priced food served in two dining rooms, one more subdued, the other lined with bright tiles, gives you a taste of the Alentejo, with classic dishes such as *carne de porco à alentejana* (pork with coriander and clams). Exhibitions and other events are also held in this house dedicated to "a people, a region and a culture".

196 B5 Rua das Portas de Santo Antão 58 213 405 140; www.casadoalentejo.pt Daily 12–3, 7–11 Restauradores

Cerverjaria Trindade €–€€

This boisterous but cheerful beerhouse (*cerverjaria*, ➤ 37) also serves seafood, and is popular with artists and locals. Once a convent,

the Trindade has beautiful vaulted ceilings and a splendid display of *azulejos*, which make it an atmospheric place to eat. Draught Portuguese beer served ice-cold is the perfect accompaniment to the simple delicious, seafood dishes.
196 B3 Rua Nova da Trinidade 20 213 423 506; www.cervejariatrindade.pt Daily 10–midnight Rossio Bus 202, 758, 790

Chafariz do Vinho €–€€

Located in a very attractive traditional building that also houses an interesting water museum (with exhibitions on the history of aqueducts), you'll find a good choice of wines here, all chosen by award-winning Portuguese wine writer João Paulo Martins. Good food too, with *tapas* and other food and wine tasting plates.
196 off A5 Chafariz da Mãe d'Água, Rua da Mãe d'Água à Praça da Alegria 213 422 079; http://chafarizdovinho.com Tue–Sun 6–2am Avenida Bus 202, 758, 773

Comida de Santo €€–€€€

Of Lisbon's many Brazilian restaurants, this one has the most reliably good food, all served with a smile amid tropical surroundings. It can get very busy, especially on Sundays when almost everywhere else is closed, so book. Cocktails are excellent and the delicious Bahia-dominated cuisine includes generous portions of dishes such as thick *vatapás* (spicy shrimp purée) and succulent chicken *muquecas* (cooked in coconut milk) and *feijoada* (pork and black bean stew) with trimmings of toasted manioc and orange slices. Fresh mango and papaya round off your meal.
196 off A4 Calçada Engenheiro Miguel Pais 39 213 963 339 Jun–Sep Tue–Sun 12:30–3:30, 7:30–1am; Oct–May daily 12:30–3:30, 7:30–1am Rato Bus 202, 758, 773

Cultura do Cha €

A neighbourhood institution, this lovely teashop has a calming atmosphere, friendly staff and plenty of character. Choose from a range of herbal and black teas, plus coffees, healthy smoothies and juices, hot chocolates and good snacks. There is plenty to look at inside because the walls are covered with works by local artists.
196 A3 38 Rua das Salgadeiras, Bairro Alto 213 430 272; www.culturadocha.com Mon–Sat noon–10pm Baixa-Chiado

Pap'Açorda €€€

This Bairro Alto haunt of the rich, famous and glamorous never seems to go out of fashion. Although service can receive mixed reviews and customer reaction may vary, the lavish décor of crystal chandeliers, plentiful plants, lively atmosphere and expertly prepared food explain the restaurant's popularity. The emphasis is on mussels, clams and other seafood. The house speciality is the Lisbon delicacy, *açorda*, a concoction of bread, oil, egg and coriander that tastes far better than it sounds or looks. The *açorda real*, with lobster and prawns, is truly "regal". To round off a delicious meal, the chocolate mousse is famous for being the best in town.
196 A3 Rua da Atalaia 57–59 213 464 811 Tue–Sat 12:30–2, 8–11 Rossio Bus 92

Pavilhão Chinês €

Located on the edge of the Bairro Alto, the Chinese Pavilion is a classy tea room and cocktail bar combined, popular with tourists and locals alike (though there are more locals from around 11pm). It must be among the world's most eccentric bars. The walls, cabinets and ceilings of its three red lacquer salons are crammed with ornaments, including fans and oriental porcelain, statues and dolls, lead soldiers and iron helmets, all of which have been collected by Lisbon celebrity Luís Pinto Coelho, who is also responsible for the aptly named Paródia (Rua do Patrocínio 26) in Campo de Ourique. Both are unusual places for an aperitif.

196 off A4 Rua Dom Pedro V 89 213 424 729 Mon–Sat 6–2am, Sun 9–2am Bus 92

Primeiro de Maio €€

With friendly service and a loyal clientele of journalists, intellectuals and bohemian types, this favourite restaurant dishes up very tasty Portuguese specials. This is one of the best places to try starters such as *pastéis de bacalhau* (bite-sized cod cakes), *peixinhos da horta* (green bean fritters) or *favas com enchidos* (broad beans and sausage). As an *adega* (wine cellar), one of the few traditional ones left in the Bairro Alto, it also has decent house wine and bottled vintages.

196 A3 Rua da Atalaia 8 213 426 840 Mon–Fri 12–3, 7–10:30, Sat 7–10:30 Bus 92; tram 28

Solar do Vinho do Porto €–€€

A cosy but modern place, furnished with comfortable sofas and a dimly lit bar, Solar do Vinho do Porto is the perfect place to taste your way through a bewildering list of more than 300 ports, with the help of the expert staff. It's the ideal way to find out which ones are to your taste – to buy elsewhere afterwards – and which ones are within your budget range. Vintage ports, however, can only be sampled by the bottle, so come with other port fans so you can share the bill. Incidentally, there's another *solar* in port's home city of Porto, housed in the Museu Romântico, Rua de Entrequintas (➤ 81).

196 A4 Rua de São Pedro de Alcântara 45 213 475 707; www.ivp.pt Mon–Fri 11am–midnight, Sat 2pm–midnight Bus 202, 758, 790; Elevador da Glória

Tágide €€€€

For reliable, classic Portuguese cuisine with a pronounced French influence, Tágide remains at the pinnacle of gastronomic Lisbon and well worth the pricey bill. If you want a window seat – book well ahead and specify this requirement – you are also treated to incredible views of the city and river that would distract you from the food were it not so delicious. Not surprisingly the wine cellar is one of the most refined in the city, and you can choose a suitable wine to accompany different regional dishes. The baked *bacalhau* (➤ 29, 37) is the omnipresent house special and the cheese board is first class. Recommended for a fine, albeit expensive, dining experience.

196 B2 Largo da Academia Nacional de Belas Artes 18 213 404 01 Tue–Sat 12:30–3, 8–midnight Tram 28

Wine Bar do Castelo €€–€€€

If you are not in the mood for a formal dinner, this inviting little wine bar near the castle is great for a light supper. Exposed brick and warm wood set the scene for some of Portugal's best wines (around €4 per glass) – ask the friendly manager Nuno for his recommendations. Wines from crisp Alentejo whites to full-bodied Douro reds pair well with *tapas* such as olives, cheese, cured ham, chutney and crusty bread.

197 E3 Rua Bartolomeu de Gusmão 11–13 218 879 093 Daily 2–10 Bus 737; tram 28

SINTRA

Tulhas €€

A charming restaurant located right in the centre of Sintra (➤ 60–62), Tulhas is in a beautiful, rustic former barn. The food is varied, with both fish and meat dishes, and you should certainly try the house special, *lombos de vitela com vinho de Madeira* (medallions of veal in Madeira sauce). An *ementa turística* (set menu of the day) makes this an ideal place for a quiet and relaxing authentic lunch during a day's sightseeing in this beautiful hilltop town.

200 A2 Rua Gil Vicente 4–6 219 232 378 Thu–Tue 12–3:30, 7–10 From Estação do Rossio

Where to... Shop

MARKETS AND SHOPPING MALLS

Feira da Ladra (Campo de Santa Clara, São Vicente, Tues and Sat 6am–5pm) is Lisbon's flea market. **Mercado da Ribeira** (Cais do Sodré, Avenida 24 de Julho, closed Sunday) is the most interesting traditional market.

Visit the modern mall of **Armazéns do Chiado** (Rua do Carmo) for independent shops and international chain stores.

The landmark towers of **Amoreiras** (Avenida Engenheiro Duarte Pacheco), **Centro Comercial Colombo** (Avenida Lusíada, Benfica) and **Centro Comercial Vasco da Gama** (Avenida Dom João II, out at the Parque das Nações) are great places to go to window shop.

CLOTHES AND FOOTWEAR

In the hip Bairro Alto, **Eldorado** (Rua do Norte 23), **Fátima Lopes** (Rua da Atalaia 36) and **Manuel Alves & José Manuel Gonçalves** (Rua das Flores 105/1D) are three fashion boutiques, the first specializing in retro clothing.

In Chiado, **Ana Salazar** (Rua do Carmo 87) is still a leading name of local couture, while **Atelier Gardénia** (Rua Nova do Almada 96 and Rua Garrett 54) sells great clothes by Luís Buchinho, Nuño Gama and others. **José António Tenente** (Travessa do Carmo 8) is the place for suits. Tiny **Luvaria Ulisses** (Rua do Carmo 87A) sells exquisite hand-made kid gloves.

In the Baixa and around the Rossio, for vintage fashion, head for **A Outra Face da Lua** (Rua da Assunção 22) for items ranging from 1960s platform shoes to glittery ballgowns.

ANTIQUES AND CRAFTS

Religious statues are worth a look at **Galeria da Arcada** (Rua Dom Pedro V 49). **António Trindade** (Rua do Alecrim 79) has antiques.

You can find delicate lead crystal at **Atlantis Cristal** (Centro Colombo and branches). Another excellent Portuguese design shop is **Alma Lusa** (363 Rua de Sao Bento) with branches in Lisbon and at Lisbon Airport.

For *azulejos*, visit **Ratton** (Rua Academia das Ciências 2C, São Bento) for modern designs; **Sant'Ana** (Rua do Alecrim 95, Chiado) for reproductions; **Solar** (Rua Dom Pedro V 68) for antiques; and **Viúva Lamego** (Calçada do Sacramento 29, Chiado) for bespoke tiles. **Casa dos Tapetes Arraiolos** (Rua da Imprensa Nacional 116) sells hand-made carpets from **Arraiolos** (➤ 146).

FOOD AND DRINK

Buy *bacalhau* (➤ 29, 37) at **Manteigaria Silva** (Rua Dom Antão de Almada 1C-D) and sausages, cheese, cured hams and candied fruit at **Manuel Tavares** (Rua da Betesga 1A-B). For freshly roasted coffee and delicious chocolate, stop by the delightful, old-world **A Carioca** (Rua da Misericórdia 9). It is rumoured that the best bread is sold at the **Garrafeira Nacional** (Rua dos Douradores 149–157) and **Pasteleria San Roque** in Bairro Alto (57 Rua Dom Pedro V). The shop also won Wine Merchant of the Year and has a wine museum. Wine connoisseurs should not miss **Coisas do Arco do Vinho** (Centro Cultural de Belém) for speciality corkscrews and fine vintages. At the **Antiga Confeitaria de Belém** (Rua de Belém 84–88, ➤ 69), you can buy boxes of fresh *pastéis* (➤ 38).

Where to... Be Entertained

INFORMATION

Get tickets at the **Agência Alvalade** (Alvalade Shopping, Praça de Alvalade 6, tel: 217 955 859), at the **ABEP booth** (Praça dos Restauradores, tel: 213 475 823/4) or FNAC stores in shopping malls.

ARTS AND CULTURE

You can hear chamber, choral and orchestral music at **Fundação Calouste Gulbenkian** (➤ 51). The **CCB** (**Centro Cultural de Belém**, ➤ 47) stages exhibitions, theatre and dance events.

Movie fans should check out the programme at the **Cinemateca** (Rua Barata Salgueiro 39, box office tel: 213 596 266, www.cinemateca.pt) and the **Monumental** (Praça Duque de Saldanha, tel: 213 142 223), Lisbon's best art-house cinema.

See the superb Companhia Nacional de Bailado (National Ballet) at **Teatro Camões** (tel: 218 923 477, www.cnb.pt).

FOOTBALL

Watch a match at either **Sporting** (Estádio de Alvalade, Edificio Visconde de Alvalade, Rua Professor Fernando da Fonseca, tel: 217 516 000) or **Benfica** (Estádio da Luz, Avenida General Norton de Matos, tel: 217 219 500).

Roller hockey is played at **Paço d'Arcos** (Pavilhão Gimnodesportivo, Avenida Bonneville Franco, tel: 214 432 238) at weekends.

MUSIC

Clube de Fado (Rua São João da Praça 94, tel: 218 852 704, www.clubede-fado.com) is one of Lisbon's top *fado* venues, while **Ateneu Café** (Rua das Portas de Santo Antão, 110, tel: 917 231 484) is a lively restaurant/bar with live jazz sessions. It's carnival every night (except Sundays) at **Brazilian Bruxa Bar** (Rua São Mamede 35). The **Teatro Nacional de São Carlos** (Rua Serpa Pinto 9) has excellent acoustics.

FAMILY FUN

The best **beaches** are at Caparica, across the River Tagus or between Carcavelos and Guincho on the city side of the Tagus.

Puppets, marionettes, shows and guided visits amuse the little ones at the **Museu da Marioneta** (Convento das Bernardas, Rua da Esperança 146, tel: 213 942 810, www.museudamarioneta.pt).

NIGHTLIFE

For a noisy night, visit the **Bairro Alto** (➤ 64). For a more relaxed evening, head for **Baixa**. **Alfama** is the place for authentic *fado* (➤ 20–21). If you want Lisbon's pulsating club scene (go late), check out **Avenida 24 de Julho** and the **Alcântara docks** for the **Blues Cafe** (Rua Cintura do Porto, Armazém 3, www.bluescafe.pt), **Kapital** (Avenida 24 de Julho 68) or **Kremlin** (Escadin has da Praia 5) or, more centrally, **Lux** (Avenida Infante Dom Henrique, Armazém A, Santa Apolónia, www.luxlisbon.com), or its sister club **Frágil** (Rua da Atalaia 126, www.fragil.com.pt).

For gay venues, visit the **Principe Real district**. Try **Frágil** (➤ above), **Harry's** (Rua São Pedro de Alcântara 57, Bairro Alto) or **Trumps** (Rua da Imprensa Nacional 104B, www.trumps.pt). Lesbian bars include **Memorial** (Rua Gustavo Matos Sequeira 42A) and **Tejo Bar** (Beco do Vigário 1a).

Northern Portugal

Getting Your Bearings

The north is the cradle of Portugal and Guimarães, the European Capital of Culture 2012, was its first kingdom. Portugal's first king, Afonso Henriques, was born here in 1109 and later extended the city south during the Reconquest from the Moors. It was the north, too, that produced Portugal's last and longest ruling dynasty, the dukes of the House of Bragança, who came to power in 1640 and ruled until the foundation of the republic in 1910.

Porto, the biggest city of the north, grew rich when merchants travelled to Brazil, returning with gold and diamonds, which financed the city's extravagant churches and palaces. Later, it profited from the port wine trade, which still dominates Vila Nova de Gaia and the valleys of the Upper Douro.

The north is divided into two contrasting regions. The Minho, which occupies the historic boundaries of Portucale between the Douro and Minho rivers, is a land of lush, green countryside fed by the highest rainfall in Portugal. Much of it is given over to smallholdings, though there are also manor houses, many of which take in guests. This densely populated region hosts some of Portugal's biggest country markets and fairs. It also contains two important historical towns – Portugal's first capital, Guimarães, European Capital of Culture 2012, which has a medieval centre that is a UNESCO World Heritage site, and its religious centre, Braga.

Trás-os-Montes is a wild and rugged region of mountains and remote villages with a harsh climate. Few crops survive except the hardiest vines, and the region grows some of the grapes for Mateus Rosé, as well as for port wine production.

Above: The aristocratic manor house of Casa de Mateus

Page 75: Looking up from the Gaia area of Porto

★ Don't Miss

1. Porto ➤ 80
2. Vila Nova de Gaia ➤ 84
3. Casa de Mateus ➤ 86
4. Braga and Bom Jesus ➤ 88
5. Parque Nacional da Peneda-Gerês ➤ 91

At Your Leisure

6. Guimarães ➤ 93
7. Viana do Castelo ➤ 93
8. Chaves ➤ 94
9. Bragança ➤ 94
10. Miranda do Douro ➤ 95

Decorated interior of Braga Cathedral

In Three Days

If you're not quite sure where to begin your travels, this itinerary recommends a practical and enjoyable three days out in northern Portugal, taking in some of the best places to see using the Getting your Bearings map on the previous page. For more information see the main entries.

Day 1

Morning

Start exploring the old town of **1 Porto** (➤ 80–83) by climbing Torre dos Clérigos for views over the city's red rooftops and spires to the River Douro. Then visit the Bolhão market and have a coffee at **Café Majestic** (➤ 98) before walking uphill to the cathedral. Go down to the Ribeira district (above) to admire the neoclassical Bolsa (Stock Exchange) and lavishly gilded São Francisco church before lunch in one of the riverside cafés.

Afternoon and Evening

Walk across Ponte Dom Luís I to **2 Vila Nova de Gaia** (➤ 84–85). Spend the afternoon touring the wine lodges and tasting port. In summer, you can take a boat cruise on the River Douro. Return to the north bank for dinner on Cais da Ribeira at one of the restaurants overlooking the quayside.

Day 2

Morning

Leave Porto on the IP4/A4 to Amarante and Vila Real, to visit the **3 Casa de Mateus** (➤ 86–87). After a stroll around the manicured formal gardens, take the N2 south to vine-strewn **Peso da Régua** for lunch by the river.

Afternoon and Evening

From here, you can do a shortened version of the Port Country tour (➤ 84), travelling through the steeply terraced vineyards between Peso da Régua and Pinhão on a beautiful stretch of the Douro Valley. Returning to Vila Real, take the IP4 to Amarante and head north on the N101 to 6 **Guimarães** (➤ 93). Follow the signs to the castle (castle statue, right), then wander down to the old town for a drink at one of the cafés on Largo da Oliveira. For a treat, stay at **Pousada de Santa Marinha** (➤ 16), in a 12th-century convent. One of the finest of all the *pousadas* (➤ 35), this one has fountains and *azulejo*-tiled cloisters (➤ 18–19).

Day 3

Morning

Start early to visit the magnificent 11th-century 4 **Braga** (➤ 88) and the hilltop sanctuary at 4 **Bom Jesus** (➤ 89–90). From here, drive north on the IP1/A3 to the picture-perfect town of Ponte da Lima for a walk along the River Lima and a drink in a café by the Roman bridge. Follow the N203 along the Lima Valley to enter the granite wilderness of the 5 **Parque Nacional da Peneda-Gerês** (below, ➤ 91–92).

Afternoon and Evening

Allow plenty of time to explore the mountainous national park. Tour the villages of Soajo and Lindoso before entering Spain on the way to Caldas do Gerês (➤ 92). Take the N103 to 8 **Chaves** (➤ 94). If you have time, visit 9 **Bragança** (➤ 94–95).Take the motorway back to Porto for dinner.

1 Porto

Portugal's second city enjoys a magnificent position, tumbling down the steep slopes on the north bank of the River Douro. A workaday, rough-and-ready port city, frayed at the edges but wonderfully charismatic, Porto makes a good introduction to the many delights of northern Portugal.

Porto (the English name, Oporto, derives from *o porto*, "the port") has been occupied for at least 3,000 years. The Romans built a harbour here at *Portus*, an important river-crossing on the route from Lisbon to Braga. The settlement on the south bank (now Vila Nova de Gaia) was called *Cale*. These gave their names to the county of "Portucale", part of the dowry of Teresa of Castile when she married Henry of Burgundy in 1095. When their son, Afonso Henriques, ousted the Moors from the rest of the country, he named his kingdom Portugal.

Relations between Portugal and England had been cordial for 150 years when, in 1387, Porto celebrated the marriage of João I (► 112) and Philippa of Lancaster, creating a military alliance between Portugal and England that is still valid today. Their son was Henry the Navigator (1394–1460, ► 12), one of the greatest Portuguese explorers – most famous for his conquests in Africa – and a pioneer of the Age of Discovery.

Above: The Ponte Dom Luís I bridge crosses the River Douro from Ribeira to Porto

The Modern City

The heart of Porto is **Avenida dos Aliados**, whose central promenade, with flowerbeds and a mosaic pavement, leads to the town hall. From the foot of the avenue, on Praça da Liberdade, you can see the baroque church of **Clérigos** to the west. Designed by the Italian architect Nicolau Nasoni, this was the first oval church in Portugal. You can climb its 75m (246ft) tower, one of the tallest in the country, for views over the city and Vila Nova da Gaia (► 84–85).

Left: View of the Ribeira area of Porto

East of Avenida dos Aliados, **Baixa** is the main shopping district, centred around the covered Bolhão market. Vegetables are sold upstairs, while downstairs stalls offer maize bread, fresh fish, live chickens, pigs' ears and tripe. Across the road are several tempting *confeitarias* and shops featuring Porto's other speciality, *bacalhau* (► 29), slabs of salt cod.

Rua de Santa Catarina is lined with leather and jewellery shops and the old-world Café Majestic (► 98), and leads to Praça da Batalha.

The sé (cathedral) is visible, built on a rocky outcrop above the Douro. Begun as a Romanesque fortress church in the 12th century, it was remodelled in Gothic style. The 14th-century cloisters are decorated with *azulejos* (➤ 18–19) showing the life of the Virgin. A grand staircase leads to the chapter house and an upper gallery that has fine views.

A warren of narrow alleyways, steep staircases and candy-coloured houses, the area between the *sé* and the waterfront became a UNESCO World Heritage Site in 1996. Walk down through the **Bairro da Sé**, the oldest quarter, similar to Alfama (➤ 54–57) in Lisbon. The daily life of the district mingles

ART VERSUS PORT

The **Museu Nacional Soares dos Reis** (Rua Dom Manuel II, tel: 223 393 770, http://mnsr.imc-ip.pt, Tue 2–6, Wed–Sun 10–6, moderate, free Sun 10–2) is Portugal's oldest national museum, dedicated to Portuguese art, including the work of the 19th-century sculptor António Soares dos Reis. The **Museu Romântico** (Quinta da Macieirinha Palace, Rua de Entrequintas 220, tel: 226 057 033, Tue–Sat 10–12:30, 2–5:30, Sun 2–5:30, inexpensive, free Sat–Sun), is a re-creation of a 19th-century aristocratic home. The same building houses the Solar do Vinho do Porto (➤ 72).

ART, MUSIC AND BEACHES
Take the bus to Serralves to the **Museu de Arte Contemporânea** (Rua Dom João de Castro 210, tel: 808 200 543, www.serralves.pt, Apr–Sep, Tue–Fri 10–5, Sat–Sun 10–8, Oct–Mar, Tue–Fri 10–5, Sat–Sun 10–7, moderate, free Sun 10–1), situated in the gardens of the art deco Casa de Serralves, designed by Álvaro Siza Vieira. Enjoy the rose garden, arboretum, tea-house, lake and sculpture park. Continue on the bus to **Foz** where the main Avenida da Boavista, which runs from the centre to the waterfront promenade at Foz do Douro, has recently been given a cutting-edge makeover with eye-catching architecture. The highlight, however, is the new, strikingly angular **Casa da Música** (610 Avenida da Boavista, tel: 220 120 220, www.casadamusica.com).

Statue of Henry the Navigator on Praça do Infante

with ancient churches and *azulejo*-tiled walls as housewives gather at the public washhouse and shop in the local market.

A statue of Henry the Navigator (➤ 12, 80) stands on **Praça do Infante**, near the former customs house where it is thought he was born. Also on the square stands the **Palácio da Bolsa**, the Stock Exchange built in 1834 over the ruins of the São Francisco convent. Its highlight is the Arabian Room, modelled on the Alhambra in the Spanish city of Granada.

Behind the building, the **Igreja de São Francisco** is richly ornamented with gilded baroque carvings. Before the church was ransacked by Napoleon's troops, there were more than 400kg (880lbs) of gold covering the chestnut-wood walls. The church authorities were so shocked at this blatant display of extravagance that they ordered the church

A traditional grocers shopfront in Porto

to be deconsecrated. Notice the **Tree of Jesse**, in carved and gilded wood, adorning the north wall. The visit takes in the **catacombs**, where there is an ossuary of human bones.

Ribeira, the fishermen's district with its narrow streets and painted houses rising above riverside arcades, is Porto's most atmospheric quarter. The area comes alive at night, with busy restaurants and bars in the shadow of **Ponte Dom Luís I**, the bridge that links Porto to Vila Nova de Gaia (➤ 84–85).

TAKING A BREAK

Café Majestic (➤ 98) is a belle époque beauty with oak-framed mirrors and leather banquettes, serving delicious breakfasts, pastries and cakes.

---

198 A3 Rua Clube dos Fenianos 25 (top of Avenida dos Aliados); tel: 223 393 472; www.portoturismo.pt

Torre dos Clérigos

Rua de São Felipe Néry 222 001 729 Apr–Oct daily 9:30–1, 2:30–7; Aug 10–7; Nov–Mar 10–12, 2–5 Inexpensive

Sé

Terreiro da Sé 222 059 028 Church: Apr–Oct daily 9–12:30, 2:30–7; Nov–Mar daily 9–12:30, 2:30–6. Cloisters: Apr–Oct, Mon–Sat 9–12:15, 2:30–6:30, Sun 2:30–6:30; Nov–Mar, Mon–Sat 9–12:15, 2:30–5:30, Sun 2:30–5:30 Church: free. Cloisters: inexpensive

The ornate baroque altar in Porto's cathedral

Palácio da Bolsa

Rua Ferreira Borges 223 399 000; www.palaciodabolsa.pt Apr–Oct daily 9–6:30; Nov–Mar daily 9–12:30, 2–5:30 Moderate

Igreja de São Francisco

Rua do Infante Dom Henrique 222 062 100 Daily 9–6/7/8 Moderate

PORTO: INSIDE INFO

Top tips The best way to get around Porto is **on foot**, but you will need a good pair of shoes for all the steep hills and cobbled streets.

- Take one of the **river cruises** that depart regularly in summer from the quayside at Cais da Ribeira or the waterfront at Vila Nova de Gaia. Just turn up and buy a ticket. For trips of one hour, try **Doura Acima** (tel: 222 006 418, www.douroacima.pt) or **Rota do Douro** (tel: 223 759 042). For longer cruises hop aboard the **Douro Azul** (tel: 223 402 500, www.douroazul.com).
- For the **best views of Porto**, cross the upper level of the Dom Luís I bridge to reach the terrace of Nossa Senhora da Serra do Pilar on the south bank.
- Visit the new **Port Wine Museum**, housed in an 18th-century building on Rua de Monchique, (tel: 222 076 300).

2 Vila Nova de Gaia

The names of famous port shippers, Sandeman, Ferreira and Taylor, spelled out in neon letters on the hillside, draw you irresistibly across the water to Vila Nova de Gaia, the home of the port wine trade. Here, barrels of port mature in cool cellars and lodges, many of which can be visited.

Although the grapes for port are grown in the Douro Valley, the ageing process takes place at the river mouth, in Vila Nova de Gaia, which was chosen in the 18th century by British traders for its north-facing position, cool ocean breeze and high levels of humidity.

These days, however, the port houses are, increasingly, moving their warehouse facilities out of town and converting their lodges (a corruption of the Portuguese word *loja*, meaning "warehouse") into restaurants, hotels and open houses with guided tours.

The city council also has plans for increasing tourism, including a cable car, new pedestrian bridge to Ribeira, a port wine cultural centre and a museum dedicated to *barcos rabelos*, the traditional flat-bottomed boats that are used to transport the port wine downriver from the Duoro Valley. Currently, you can still see the *barcos rabelos* moored outside many port houses (➤ 177–178), or sailed once a year during the annual regatta on 24 June (➤ 100). The cable car has opened (see below), the other projects are still in the pipeline.

Opened in April 2011, the **Teleférico de Gaia** has given

View of the famous port lodges

THE DOURO BY TRAIN
Take a train journey through the Douro Valley, from Porto to Pocinho by the Spanish border. It runs for 100km (62 miles) by the River Douro, through seemingly endless stretches of beautiful scenery. There's a steam train on Saturdays from Regua to Tua (www.cp.pt).

The tasting terrace at Taylor's

the neighbourhood a huge boost. The 562m (1844ft) cable car links the Cais de Gaia to the Jardim do Morro on the Avenida da República, affording wonderful views of the city.

The best way to approach Vila Nova de Gaia is to walk from Porto (➤ 80–83) across **Ponte Dom Luís I**. The new tram also goes across the bridge from Porto to Vila Nova de Gaia.

To visit the **port lodges**, get a list and map from the tourist office. Most people start with top producer **Sandeman** (Largo Miguel Bombarda 3, tel: 223 740 500, www.sandeman.eu, moderate), founded by Briton George Sandeman in 1790.

It is interesting to compare Sandeman with a smaller firm. such as **Ferreira** (Avenida Ramos Pinto 70, tel: 223 746 107, inexpensive), which was founded in 1751 and is still Portuguese owned. The tasting room is decorated with *azulejos* and there is an archive of historical exhibits.

Other lodges include **Cálem** (tel: 223 746 660, www.calem.pt), which has a good visitor centre; **Ramos Pinto** (Avenida Ramos Pinto 400, tel: 223 775 011, www.ramospinto.pt); and **Real Companhia Velha** (Rua Azevedo Magalhães 314, tel: 223 775 100, www.realcompanhiavelha.pt), founded by Dom José I in 1756 to challenge Britain's monopoly on port.

TAKING A BREAK

There are several restaurants and cafés by the waterfront, or book at **Barão de Fladgate** (➤ 98), housed in the Taylor's Lodge (see panel below), for superb seafood and port wine.

198 A3 **Avenida Diogo Leite, tel: 223 703 735**

VILA NOVA DE GAIA: INSIDE INFO

Top tip Let your tastebuds explore the many **different styles** of port: the aperitif, dry white, amber-coloured tawny, rich ruby and vintage (➤ 10–11).

Hidden gem It's worth making the steep climb to **Taylor's** (Rua do Choupelo 250, tel: 223 742 800), owned by the Fladgate partnership, which also owns Croft, Fonseca and Delaforce. Founded in 1692, and the last surviving family-owned British port house, it is housed in an old-style lodge and offers a very friendly welcome, although this is due to be converted into an 84-room luxury hotel. The free tour is helpful, the tastings are generous and there are wonderful views from the terrace over the Douro and Ponte Dom Luís I.

3 Casa de Mateus

The building that graces the label of every bottle of Mateus Rosé is as perfect a Portuguese manor house as you can find. With fine furniture, paintings, formal gardens and family chapel, a visit to the Casa de Mateus offers a rare glimpse into the lives of the Portuguese aristocracy.

It was built in 1745 by the third *Morgado* de Mateus. His descendants, the counts of Vila Real, still live in a wing of the house. The architect is unknown, but it is attributed to Nicolau Nasoni, the Italian who designed the Clérigos tower in Porto (➤ 80) and was a major influence on the development of Portuguese baroque.

The facade of the house is immediately impressive, a contrast of whitewash and granite reflected in a pool that was added when the gardens were extensively remodelled in the 1930s. The forecourt is dominated by an immense double stairway, whose balustrades lead the eye up towards the pediment, flanked by classical statues and crowned by a family escutcheon.

The house can only be visited on 30-minute guided tours, and the guides tend to rush you through. You begin in the entrance hall, with its carved chestnut ceiling, 18th-century

The landscaped gardens and elegant facade of the Casa de Mateus

CASA DE MATEUS: INSIDE INFO

Top tips **Classical music concerts** are held in the grounds on summer weekends.

- If you're looking for **Mateus Rosé**, don't look here – it is produced by the Sogrape company (www.sogrape.pt) from vineyards in the Beiras and has no connection with the Mateus estate, other than the label on the bottle. They do have their own wine on the estate also, called Alvarelhão, which you can buy in the shop.

In more depth The nearby town of **Vila Real** (Royal Town), dramatically perched above a gorge at the confluence of the Corgo and Cabril rivers, is the capital of the Upper Douro. The best sights are the Gothic cathedral and the house on the main street where the explorer Diogo Cão, who "discovered" the mouth of the Congo in 1482, was born.

sedan chairs and family coat of arms on the wall. This leads into the **Four Seasons Room**, which takes its name from the strange paintings of seasonal vegetables in human form. On the table in the centre stands a 16th-century Hispano-Arab plate, the oldest item on display.

The neighbouring **Blue Room** features Chinese porcelain in a 17th-century Chinese cabinet, while the **Dining Room** has a Brazilian jacaranda wood dresser containing stunning Portuguese china and silver.

The highlight of the **Four Corners Room**, where ladies gathered after dinner while the men smoked and drank port, is a fine, hand-carved Indo-Portuguese ivory and wood travelling desk.

The family **museum** has several rare treasures, including the original copperplates by Jean Fragonard for a limited edition of *Os Lusíadas* (*The Lusiads*) by Portuguese poet Luís de Camões, produced in 1817 and sent by the Morgado de Mateus to 250 libraries and noble families in Europe to promote Portuguese history and culture. Some of the letters of thanks are displayed, along with religious vestments and chalices, relics of saints and martyrs, a 17th-century ivory crucifix and a statue of the Virgin carved from a single piece of ivory.

Be sure to walk around the **gardens**, with their dark avenue of cedar trees, neatly clipped box hedges and peaceful views over the surrounding countryside.

TAKING A BREAK

There is a small **café** in the gardens for snacks and refreshments, which is open in summer.

198 C4 · 4km (2.5 miles) east of Vila Real · 259 323 121; www.casademateus.com · Mar–May, Oct daily 9–1, 2–6; Jun–Sep 9–7:30; Nov–Feb 10–1, 2–5 · House: expensive. Gardens: moderate · Bus 1

4 Braga and Bom Jesus

Braga likes to describe itself as the Portuguese Rome. The largest city in the Minho has a long history as a religious capital that has left it with churches, Renaissance mansions and Portugal's most spectacularly sited sanctuary, Bom Jesus.

Braga

A saying has it that "while Coimbra studies and Lisbon plays, Porto works and Braga prays". The Roman bishop St Martin of Braga converted the local Swabian tribe to Christianity in the sixth century AD and established the custom, still used in Portugal, of naming the days of the week in numerical order rather than after pagan gods (Monday, *segunda-feira*, is "second day", Tuesday, *terça-feira*, "third day", etc). In the 12th century, following the Christian conquest, Braga became, and remains, the seat of the Portuguese archbishops.

Start your visit at **Praça da República**, an arcaded square at the end of a long public garden with fountains and playgrounds. Stallholders sell Minho artefacts, such as clogs and wooden toys, and there are old-fashioned cafés under the arches close to the 14th-century town keep. From here, walk down Rua do Souto, a pedestrianized shopping street, passing the former bishop's palace on your way to the sé (cathedral).

The exquisitely ornate **cathedral** was begun in 1070 on the site of a mosque and is Portugal's oldest cathedral. Originally

Leisurely outdoor dining at the Café Vianna, Praça de República

built in Romanesque style, the subsequent Gothic, Renaissance and baroque additions give it an eclectic feel. The main Romanesque doorway survives at the western end, though it is covered by a Gothic porch that was added in the late 15th century. Among the artists who worked on the cathedral are Manueline master João de Castilho, one of the architects of the Mosteiro dos Jerónimos in Lisbon (➤ 48), and the French sculptor Nicolas Chanterene, whose statue of **Nossa Senhora da Leite** (Our Lady of the Milk) is sheltered beneath a Gothic canopy at the cathedral's eastern end.

The cloister gives access to the **Museu de Arte Sacra**, whose junk-shop atmosphere is both fascinating and frustrating. There are amazing treasures here – gold, silver, ivory, diamonds, emeralds, pearls and jade – but it's all arranged haphazardly without labelling, and the guides do not allow you much time to linger. Among the items on display is a simple cross, used by Pedro Álvares Cabral in 1500 to celebrate the first ever Mass in Brazil.

The hilltop sanctuary of the Church of Bom Jesus

The tour of the museum also includes the **Capela dos Reis**, where Henry of Burgundy and Teresa of Castile (➤ 80), parents of Portugal's first king, are buried in 16th-century tombs.

A more expensive ticket also gives you entry to the **Coro Alto** (upper choir), which has gilded baroque organs and carved choir stalls.

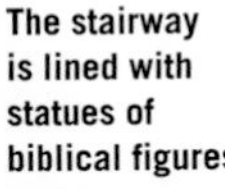

The stairway is lined with statues of biblical figures

Bom Jesus

At weekends, pilgrims and tourists flock to one of Portugal's most important religious sites, Bom Jesus do Monte, a hilltop sanctuary 5km (3 miles) east of Braga. Although primarily a place for prayer and quiet contemplation, it is also a popular picnic spot, with gardens, woodland and a lake.

The spectacular centrepiece is the **baroque stairway** with more than 1,000 steps, which was begun by the archbishop of Braga in 1722 but not finished until the 19th century. True pilgrims ascend on their knees, especially during *Semana Santa* (Holy Week, the week before Easter), but most people walk or take the old-fashioned funicular (daily 8–8, every 30 minutes). It's best to make the climb on foot to appreciate the architecture.

Via Sacra (Holy Way) begins with a winding path lined with chapels depicting the Stations of the Cross. Each chapel, dripping with wax from pilgrims' candles, is filled with life-size terracotta figures evoking scenes from Christ's Passion. As you near the summit, you reach a magnificent ornamental double stairway. Fountains depict the five senses, with water gushing out of ears, eyes, nose and mouth, while further up, the **Staircase of the Three Virtues** features the allegorical figures of Faith, Hope and Charity.

The monumental stairway to Bom Jesus

TAKING A BREAK

Visit the old-world **Café Vianna** (➤ 99) on Praça da República for coffee or a light snack, but if you want a more substantial, traditional Portuguese meal try Arcoense (➤ 98).

---

198 B4 **off Praça da República; tel: 253 262 550**

Sé/Museu de Arte Sacra
Rua Dom Paio Mendes **253 263 317; www.geira.pt/MSeBraga/**
Jun–Sep Tue–Sun 9–12:30, 2–6:30; Oct–May Tue–Sun 9–12:30, 2–5:30 **Church: inexpensive. Church museum and choir: moderate**

BRAGA AND BOM JESUS: INSIDE INFO

Top tips Leave your car in the **underground car park** beneath Praça da República, from where everything of interest can be reached in a short walk.
- There are **regular buses** from Braga to the foot of Bom Jesus do Monte, or you can drive your car right up to the summit.

In more depth The **Palácio dos Biscainhos** (near the Arco da Porta Nova gateway, Tue–Sun 10–12:30, 2–5:30, inexpensive, free Sun 10–12) is a 17th-century mansion with stucco ceilings and *azulejo* tiles (➤ 18–19), which has been turned into a decorative arts museum featuring Portuguese furniture, silverware and ornamental gardens.

5 Parque Nacional da Peneda-Gerês

Portugal's only national park, covering an area of 700sq km (270sq miles), is a wild and dramatic place of windswept peaks, granite crags, deep river valleys and pretty rural villages. These are the sort of villages where the shepherds still migrate to higher ground each spring in search of pasture for their flock. The park consists of two main *serras* (mountain ranges), Serra da Peneda and Serra do Gerês, which are divided by the River Lima.

With few clear entry points and villages scattered around, most of the time it doesn't seem as if you are in a national park at all. Despite the presence of wildlife, such as golden eagles, wild horses and wolves, and rare varieties of Gerês lilies and ferns, it is a way of life as much as anything that is preserved here.

You can visit the park by car on a day trip from Braga or the Minho coast. The easiest approach is along the Lima Valley from Ponte da Barca. This brings you to **Soajo** and **Lindoso**, both of which have some village houses for rent (Aldeias de Portugal, tel: 258 931 750, www.aldeiasdeportugal.pt).

Rio Cávado, with the hills stretching far into the distance

WALKING IN THE PARK
Pick up a walking map from the information centres in Braga, Ponte da Barca or Caldas do Gerês to tackle some of the *trilhos* (walking trails) in the park. Two of the best are the Trilho da Peneda, around the village of the same name, and the Trilho Castrejo from the village of Castro Laboreiro, known for its special breed of mountain dogs.

Both villages are known for their ***espigueiros***, communal stone granaries topped with a cross and raised above the ground as a precaution against pests. At Lindoso, a group of 60 *espigueiros* are huddled beneath the castle, resembling tombstones in a cemetery. The castle here, right next to the Spanish border, has been attacked many times. Nowadays it is a peaceful spot, with long-horned Minho cattle grazing beneath its walls.

A minor road runs north between the two villages, with views over the Lima Valley on the way to **Peneda**. This small village contains a remarkable sanctuary, **Nossa Senhora da Peneda**, modelled on Bom Jesus (➤ 89–90) and reached by a similarly long staircase. The chapel, which from below seems almost to be built into the cliff, is the focus for a huge pilgrimage each September.

The most direct route between the two sections of the park means crossing the Spanish border at Lindoso and re-entering Portugal at Portela do Homem. The road dips down through a delightful wooded glade to the spa resort of **Caldas do Gerês**, where wild herbs, wildflower honey and chunky woollen sweaters are for sale and the main street is lined with spa hotels. Just outside town, a ***miradouro*** (viewpoint) offers fabulous panoramas over the reservoir of Caniçada.

Long-horned Minho cattle

TAKING A BREAK

There are **cafés and bars** in the villages of Soajo, Lindoso and Caldas do Gerês. Apart from that, a good option would be to stock up on **picnic** provisions in any of the nearby towns.

---

198 B5

Park Office
Avenida António Macedo, Braga ☎ 253 203 480; www.icn.pt Mon–Fri 9–12:30, 2–5:30

PARQUE NACIONAL DA PENEDA-GERÊS: INSIDE INFO

Top tips Allow **plenty of time** for driving within the park – the roads are steep and narrow, and the distances are greater than they look on the map.

- Arrive in **Soajo** on a Sunday morning and you will find market stalls set up on the main street selling sausages, leather boots and farming tools.
- This is Portugal's wettest area so don't forget to take **waterproofs**.

At Your Leisure

6 Guimarães

Becoming European Capital of Culture in 2012 has put Guimarães firmly on the tourist map and sparked wide-scale regeneration. As well as the medeival sites of its lovely, car-free medieval old town centre (a UNESCO World Heritage Site), visitors will now also see exciting new developments such as the Platform for Arts and Creativity in the former old market and the Design Institute reviving the fortunes of a converted factory.

The first capital of Portugal and the birthplace of its first king, Afonso Henriques (1109–85, ➤ 80), Guimarães has a special place in the heart of the Portuguese nation. Most of the sights are situated in the old town beneath the castle. Climb over the ramparts of the 10th-century fortress, and visit the Romanesque chapel of São Miguel do Castelo, where Afonso Henriques was baptized, and where the warriors who helped him to conquer Portugal are buried.

Nearby, is the **Paço dos Duques de Bragança**, built by the first Duke of Bragança in the 15th century and restored under the Salazar dictatorship as a presidential palace. It has Flemish tapestries, Persian carpets, Portuguese furniture and a gallery of paintings by local artist José de Guimarães.

A short walk along the cobbled Rua de Santa Maria reveals an area that has remained unchanged for centuries. Leading from the castle to the old town, there are restored medieval houses lining the street, ending in a pair of delightful squares, the Praça de Santiago and Largo da Oliveira, where a morning market is held on Saturdays.

Praça de Santiago is surrounded by wooden-balconied houses, while Largo da Oliveira has a Gothic shrine outside Nossa Senhora da Oliveira (Our Lady of the Olive Tree), whose cloisters house a museum of sacred art. The remains of the old city walls are also worth exploring.

The commanding position of the Santa Luzia overlooking Viana do Castelo

198 B4 · Largo Cónego José Maria Gomes; tel: 253 518 394

Paço dos Duques de Bragança

Rua Conde Dom Henrique · 253 412 273; www.cm-guimaraes.pt · Jul–Aug daily 9:30–6:30; Sep–Jun Tue–Sun 9:30–12, 2–5 · Moderate; free Sun 9:30–12:30

7 Viana do Castelo

The capital of the Costa Verde enjoys a perfect setting on the north bank of the Lima estuary, overlooked by the pinewoods of Monte de Santa Luzia. Once a small fishing port, Viana supplied many of the seafarers who sailed during the Age of Discovery and returned to the town to build Manueline and Renaissance mansions. The main square, Praça da República, is the focus of daily life, with its 16th-century fountain and Renaissance palace.

BARCELOS

The largest weekly market in Portugal takes place on Thursday mornings on a vast open square in the centre of Barcelos. Look out for the local Barcelos pottery and brightly coloured *galos de Barcelos* "Barcelos cocks", which recall the legend of an innocent Galician pilgrim, miraculously saved from the gallows when a roast cockerel, on a plate at the time, began to crow. He invoked the help of St James, saying that if he were innocent the cockerel being prepared for the judge's dinner would sit up and crow.

In summer it is a busy resort. You can walk or take the funicular through the pinewoods to reach a basilica and the ruins of a Celto-Iberian settlement, or take the ferry across the river to Praia do Cabedelo, the town's splendid beach.

198 A4 Rua do Hospital Velho; tel: 258 822 620

8 Chaves

A drive from Braga on the N103 threads through the Gerês and Barroso mountains to Chaves, which sits prettily on the banks of the Tâmega River 10km (6 miles) south of the Spanish border, and is famous for its smoked hams and red wine.

Founded by the Romans as the spa town of *Aquae Fluviae*, Chaves ("keys") was awarded by Dom João I to Nuno Álvares Pereira as a reward for his victory against the Spanish at the battle of Aljubarrota (➤ 113).

A statue of the first Duke of Bragança, who lived in the castle, stands on Praça de Camões, the main square of the old town. Also here are the Misericórdia church, with a gilded altarpiece, painted ceiling and *azulejo*-tiled walls, and the **Museu da Região Flaviense**, devoted to archaeology and local crafts.

199 D4 Terreiro de Cavaleria; tel: 276 340 661

Inscriptions on a column on the Roman bridge across the Tamega, Chaves

Museu da Região Flaviense/Museu Militar
Praça de Camões 276 340 500 Daily 9–12:30, 2–5:30 Inexpensive

9 Bragança

The remote capital of Trás-os-Montes is closely identified with Portugal's last ruling dynasty, descendants of an illegitimate son of João I who became the first Duke of Bragança – though later dukes preferred to live in their palace at Vila Viçosa (➤ 136–137).

The city is built around a 12th-century citadel, a walled village and

The Romanesque five-sided Domus Municipalis in Bragança

museum where ancient monuments sit side by side with whitewashed houses and cobbled streets. The **castle** contains a small **military museum**, and there are great views from the tower. Near here is a medieval pillory, an ancient stone pig on its pedestal, and the five-sided Domus Municipalis, Portugal's only surviving example of Romanesque civic architecture, where public meetings were held and the *homens bons* (good men) would gather to settle disputes.

Just beneath the citadel, on the way to the cathedral, the Igreja de São Vicente is where Dom Pedro is believed to have secretly married Inês de Castro (➤ 110).

Bragança is a good base for excursions into the Montesinho natural park (➤ 24).

199 E5 · Avenida Cidade de Zamora; tel: 273 381 273

Castelo and Museu Militar
273 322 378 · Tue–Thu, Sat–Sun 9–12, 2–5, Fri 9–12 · Inexpensive; free Sun 9–12

10 Miranda do Douro

Set on a cliff overlooking a deep gorge in the River Douro, Miranda is a medieval border town whose inhabitants speak their own particular dialect, *mirandês*. The 16th-century sé (cathedral) includes the Menino Jesus da Cartolinha, a statue of the child Jesus in 17th-century costume and a top hat, who is said to have appeared to rally the Portuguese forces during a Spanish siege in 1711.

The excellent **Museu da Terra de Miranda** features a reconstruction of a farmhouse kitchen and folk costumes such as those worn by the *pauliteiros* (stick dancers) at festivals.

199 F4 · Largo do Menino Jesus da Cartolinha; tel: 273 431 132

Museu da Terra de Miranda
Largo Dom João III · 273 431 164 · Tue 2–5:30, Wed–Sun 9–12:30, 2–5:30 (6 in summer) · Inexpensive; free Sun

WHAT TO DO WITH THE KIDS

- Douro boat trips at Porto (➤ 83).
- The climb to Bom Jesus either on foot or by funicular railway (➤ 89–90).
- Parque da Cidade, by Castelo do Queijo, has duck ponds and play areas.
- Shopping for clay cockerels at Barcelos market.
- The spectacular beaches of the Costa Verde around Viana do Castelo (➤ 93–94).

Where to... Stay

Prices
Expect to pay for a double room per night in high season:
€ under €60 **€€** €60–€120 **€€€** €121–€180 **€€€€** over €180

PORTO

4 Rooms AL €€–€€€
Tucked away in the historic area of old Foz, this superb B&B, with helpful owners, is a two-minute walk from the River Douro and a 15-minute bus ride from the town centre. Clean lines, bold art and glass walls define the minimalist-chic rooms featuring white marble bathrooms with rain showers. The overall look is sleek and contemporary. You'll wake up to an excellent breakfast of fresh fruit, juice and home-made sweets.
198 A3 Padre Luis Cabral 1015 929 190 406; www.4rooms.org

Hotel da Bolsa €€
Well located close to the Stock Exchange building and 50m (55 yards) from the Port Wine Institute, this three-star hotel (with car park next door) is built on the site of the São Francisco monastery. Its 19th-century facade conceals a modern interior and, although the rooms are a little dated, this is a pleasant base from which to explore the city.
198 A3 Rue Ferreira Borges 101 222 026 768; www.hoteldabolsa.com

Pestana Porto Hotel €€–€€€
Located on the riverfront in Ribeira with views to Vila Nova de Gaia (➤ 84–85) and the Dom Luís I Bridge, this luxury boutique hotel interconnects six former town houses (all UNESCO World Heritage sites) from the 16th, 17th and 18th centuries, which have been restored and converted to the highest standards. The rooms are well appointed and comfortable. There is an excellent restaurant and bar, with the emphasis on regional food and wine. Ask for a room with river views.
198 A3 Praça da Ribeira, No 1 223 402 300; www.pestana.com

VILA REAL

Casa da Quinta de São Martinho €€
You will need to book ahead to stay at this tiny, popular guesthouse. It is a 200m (218 yards) hop across the main road from the Casa de Mateus (➤ 86–87), a short way east of Vila Real. A lovely swimming pool in the quiet grounds is the only luxury at this home-from-home country house. The two rooms inside the house and two self-contained flats are well decorated and the resident family is very welcoming. They also have a well-stocked cellar of port.
198 C4 Mateus 933 202 326/933 437 291; www.quintasaomartinho.com

BRAGA

Albergaria Bracara Augusta €–€€
This is a cheerful, well-decorated and perfectly located guesthouse in the pedestrianized centre of town – what more could you ask for? Some of the rooms have views over the attractive cathedral (➤ 88–89), all are cosily decorated in warm colours with thick carpets. The well-regarded Centurium restaurant is elegant, with stone walls and columns, and crisp white tablecloths. There is also a terrace for eating outside when the weather is warm – make use of this, if possible, for afternoon tea in the garden.
198 B4 Avenida Central 134 253 206 260; www.bracaraaugusta.com

Dona Sofia €€

A five-minute stroll from the main square, this welcoming guesthouse is an excellent deal and the affable English-speaking staff will help you make the most of Braga. The rooms are spotless and modern, decorated in earthy hues with flat-screen TVs, minibars and free WiFi. Relax in the living room, complete with grand piano, or with drinks at the bar. Room rates include a generous breakfast buffet, with cold cuts, fresh fruit and cereals.

198 B4 ✉ Largo São João do Souto 131 ☎ 253 263 160; www.hoteldonasofia.com

GUIMARÃES

Pousada Santa Marinha da Costa €€€

A highly atmospheric place to stay, this is one of the most impressive *pousadas* in Portugal. A 12th-century former monastery, it is set on a hill overlooking the city of Guimarães, and has all kinds of balconies and terraces from which you can admire the magnificent views. The 49 bedrooms are large and stately, many with four-poster beds and ornate bathrooms. You can relax in the large gardens with fountains and a stream, a lovely outdoor swimming pool and underground caves. The restaurant is also excellent.

198 B4 ✉ Largo Domingos Leite Castro ☎ 253 511 249; www.pousadas.pt

VIANA DO CASTELO

Estalagem Casa Melo Alvim €€–€€€

Next to Viana do Castelo's railway station, this delightful Manueline *solar* (➤ 16–17), built in 1509 by the Conde da Carreira, was successfully extended in the 17th and 19th centuries. During the 1990s, it was turned into a first-class inn, fully respecting the appearance of the imposing stone building. Furnishings and décor, including superb carpets and bedsteads, are a subtle blend of traditional styles with a modern preference for sobriety and sleek lines. Each of the 20 bedrooms is different. Alto Minho cuisine is on offer at the exemplary Conde do Camarido restaurant.

198 A4 ✉ Avenida Conde da Carreira 28 ☎ 258 808 200; www.meloalvimhouse.com

BARCELOS

Quinta do Convento da Franqueira €€

Perched on a hill overlooking Barcelos and surrounded by manicured gardens and pine and eucalyptus woods, this converted 16th-century Franciscan monastery (with spring-fed swimming pool) is a charming retreat. The hosts, Piers and Kate, will make you feel welcome in their elegant home. Centred on a fountain-dotted inner courtyard, the spacious rooms are furnished with antiques, paintings and Portuguese fabrics, and have tea-making facilities. For romance, choose the Blue Room, complete with hand-painted four-poster bed. Breakfasts are delicious. Be sure to pop down to the winery for Piers' tangy Vinho Verde. The guesthouse is open from April to October.

198 A4 ✉ Carvalhal ☎ 253 831 606; www.quintadafranqueira.com

TRÁS-OS-MONTE

Quinta Entre Rios €€

Welcoming farmhouse accommodation about 3km (1.5 miles) outside of the town of Mirandela, with comfortable rooms and a lovely large drawing room for guests to use. The 18th-century building has good sized bedrooms, attractively furnished although aiming at functionality rather than luxury. There are plenty of opportunities to relax here – a snooker room, cards, chess, a large terrace for reading, and a pool. Enjoy home-cooked breakfasts of local cheeses and sausages.

199 D4 ✉ Chelas, Mirandela ☎ 278 263 160; www.quintaentrerios.pt.vu

Where to... Eat and Drink

Prices
Expect to pay per person for a three-course meal, excluding drinks and tips:
€ under €12 **€€** €12–€24 **€€€** €25–€36 **€€€€** over €36

PORTO

Café Majestic €

An intellectuals' haunt dating from the 1920s, this is arguably Portugal's most beautiful café. Miraculously, it has survived intact, complete with stucco cherubs and mouldings, chandeliers, leather upholstery, marble-top tables, huge art deco mirrors and a grand piano. Ideal for coffee or tea and *pastéis*. Snacks and simple meals at lunchtime, served by liveried waiters.
198 A3 Rua de Santa Catarina 112 222 003 887; www.cafemajestic.com Daily 9:30am–midnight

Casa da Música Restaurant €€–€€€

This fusion restaurant is on the 7th floor of the imposing Casa da Música, and is one of the best – and most fashionable – places to eat in Porto. Bold light panels hang above the restaurant and the chessboard-like terrace affords sweeping views over Porto. Chef Artur Gomes puts his creative stamp on fresh, seasonal dishes – think peppered tuna fish tataki with papaya and lemon sauce. The fixed-price lunch and dinner menus (€–€€) represent excellent value. The wine list is extensive also, with a good selection of reds from the local Douro Valley, and further afield in Portugal.
198 A3 Avenue da Boavista 220 107 160; www.casadamusica.com/restaurante Mon–Wed 12:30–3, 7:30–11; Thu–Sat 12:30–3, 7:30–midnight

O Comercial €€–€€€

High ceilings, chandeliers and rich fabrics set the scene at this refined restaurant in the 19th–century Palácio da Bolsa (Stock Exchange Palace). The service is polished and the food is prepared with top-quality ingredients. Try the tender veal in Douro sauce or steamed turbot. The three-course set lunch is very reasonable (€€).
198 A3 Palácio da Bolsa, Rua Ferreira Borges 223 322 019; www.ocomercial.com Mon–Fri 12:30–3, 8–11; Sat 8–midnight

VILA NOVA DE GAIA

Barão de Fladgate €€€

Set in the hilltop Taylor's wine lodge, this restaurant has peerless views over Porto's rooftops and the River Douro. The classic Portuguese cuisine places the emphasis on seafood – the fresh tuna tartar from the Azores and the *bacalhau* (salted cod, ➤ 29, 37) in a bread and olive crust are particularly good. Finish off with a glass of the excellent house port.
198 A3 Rua do Choupelo 250 223 742 800; www.tresseculos.pt Mon–Sat 12:30–3, 7:30–10:30; Sun 12:30–3

BRAGA

Arcoense €€

A seriously good local restaurant, serving up food that draws on Portuguese ingredients, such as wood-fired lamb or Barrosa beef from Trás-os-Montes, plenty of local cheeses and a large range of sweet custard-based desserts. The location is excellent, right next to the pretty River Este. Book ahead.
198 B4 Rua Engenheiro José Justino Amorim 96 253 278 952 Mon–Sat 12–3, 7:30–10:30

Café Vianna €

Like its equally atmospheric neighbour, the Astória, this low–key and great value art nouveau coffee-house is a great place for people-watching, either inside or on the *esplanada* (terrace) on warm days. The coffee, cakes and *pregos* (bread rolls filled with a sliver of sizzling steak) are excellent. Some of the delicious local pastries to sample are *rabanadas* (cinnamon-flavoured French toast) and *charutos de chila* (pumpkin-filled pastry rolls).

198 B4 Praça da República 253 262 336 Daily 9am–2am

GUIMARÃES

Solar do Arco €€

Situated near a stone arch along Guimarães' prettiest street, this is not the usual tourist trap, despite the multilingual menu (try the good-value *ementa turística* – tourist menu, ➤ 37). The menu is varied but with a Portuguese emphasis. Roast *bacalhau* and *tamboril* (monkfish) are specials, but veal and pork dishes are also excellent.

198 B4 Rua de Santa Maria 48–50 253 513 072; www.solardoarco.com Mon–Thu 12–10:30, Fri–Sat 12–11, Sun 12–10.30

VIANA DO CASTELO

Os Três Potes €€

With its traditional granite walls and dark-wood furniture, this place may seem a little sombre. Nonetheless, it offers a good variety of Minho specialities. Try the wood-oven-roasted kid *(cabrito)* or the chargrilled octopus *(polvo na brasa)*. There are folkloric shows on Saturday evenings.

198 A4 Beco dos Fornos 7/9 258 829 928 Daily 12–3:30, 7–10:30

BRAGANÇA

Geadas €€

Good regional produce in attractive surroundings, with warm exposed stone walls, and a long wall of windows that open onto the pretty view. This is just the kind of local restaurant that you hope to stumble across, and has consistently high standards of food and service. Expect plenty of freshly caught fish and local meats on the menu, and all served up in generous portions.

199 E5 32 Rua do Loreto 273 324 413; www.geadas.net Restaurant: Tue–Sun 12–2, 7–11. Pub: Tue–Sat 12–11

TRÁS-OS-MONTES

Bagoeira €€

A cavernous place to dine on the Campo da Feira (marketplace), this inn has been catering to merchants and visitors since the 19th century. *Minho* dishes and gargantuan roasts are served in traditional style, with jugs of Vinho Verde. *Bacalhau à Bagoeira* is the house variation on *à minhota*, with onions and potatoes. It has a few ensuite rooms, too (€).

198 A4 Avenida Sidónio Pais 495, Barcelos 253 811 236 Daily 12–2:30, 7–10:30

Where to... Shop

PORTO

A triangle between the Estação São Bento, the University and the City Hall is the main shopping area, with stationers, grocers and clothes and shoe shops along **Rua de Santa Catarina**. **Via Catarina** is a shopping mall with nearly 100 shops in which to browse.

For a more authentic experience, head for the covered **Bolhão Market**, on Rua Sá da Bandeira, by Bolhão station. It is held all week and is a noisy, colourful sight where you can haggle over everything from vegetables to lampshades.

For crafts, go to the **Centro Regional de Artes Tradicionais** (Rua da Reboleira 33–37, tel: 223 320 201) and **Artesanato Clérigos**

(Rua da Assunção 33–34, tel: 222 000 257) for ceramics, candles and embroidered tablecloths.

For fine wines and ports, visit **Garrafeira do Carmo** (Rua do Carmo 17, tel: 222 003 285, www.garrafeiracarmo.com) or the charmingly old-world **Casa Oriental** (Campo Mártires da Pátria 111/112, tel: 222 002 530), which also shows off an amazing display of *bacalhau*. If you are stuck for time visiting the various lodges at **Vila Nova de Gaia** (➤ 84–85), go to **Sandeman's** (➤ 85) or **Taylor's** (➤ 85).

BARCELOS

Every Thursday, the lively **Campo da Feira** takes over. Pottery, wicker baskets, fresh fruit and flowers, clucking chickens, coffee, crusty bread – you'll find it all here.

The "Barcelos cock" (➤ 94) and distinctive Barcelos pottery – a rich brown with cream dots – originated here. Items are signed RR or JR.

Where to... Be Entertained

FESTIVALS

São João (St John's Day), 24 June, is celebrated everywhere. In Porto, it is a huge street festival with music, dancing, feasting, and hitting people on the head with squeaky hammers! It ends with a regatta of traditional *barcos rabelos* (➤ 84) and fireworks. The Pálacio da Bolsa holds concerts all year as part of its **Festival de Música**. **Noites Ritual Rock** takes place at the Palácio de Cristal in August.

At Freixo de Espada à Cinta, the **Romaria de Sete Paços**, a famous Good Friday procession, starts at the Igreja Matriz. Viana do Castelo has its famous ***romaria*** (pilgrimage), a three-day carnival held around 20 August.

SPORT AND OUTDOOR PURSUITS

Hire **surf** gear at Viana do Castelo; the **Surf Club de Viana** (Rua Manuel Fiúza Júnior 133, tel: 917 762 807, www.surfingviana.com) offers lessons while **Amigos do Mar** (Parque Empresarial da Praia Norte, tel: 258 827 427, www.amigosdomar.pt) offers diving, sailing and canoeing.

Hiking is popular in the national parks such as Peneda-Gerês (➤ 91–92); enjoy watersports on the Caniçada reservoir; hire boats and gear at **AML** (Lugar de Paredes, Rua 6, Rio Caldo, tel: 253 391 779, www.aguamontanha.com).

For one- or two-day cruises on the Douro, contact **Douro Acima** (tel: 222 006 418) or **Douro Azul** (tel: 223 402 500).

MUSIC AND NIGHTLIFE

For classical music, there's Porto's **Auditório Nacional Carlos Alberto** (Rua das Oliveiras 43, tel: 223 395 050) or **Casa da Música** at the Rotunda da Boavista (Avenida da Boavista 604-610, tel: 220 120 220, www.casadamusica.com). *Fado* (➤ 20–21) is performed at **Mal Cozinhado** (Rua do Outeirinho 13, tel: 222 081 319). **Hot Five Jazz Club** (Largo Actor Dias 51; 934 328 583, www.hotfive.eu) is a great little venue for live jazz and blues.

Sip fine wines and ports at **Vinologia** (Rua de São João 46, tel: 936 057 340, www.lamaisondesporto.com) or head to Ribeira for bars, pubs, lounge bars and open-air cafés. Check out **Plano B** (Rua Cândido dos Reis 30, tel: 222 012 500, www.planobporto.com), for theatre, dance, live music and DJ nights.

In Braga, the clubs are around Praça da República – try **Sardinha Biba** (Lugar dos Galos, Carandá).

Central Portugal

Getting Your Bearings

Central Portugal stretches almost from Lisbon to Porto and from the Spanish border to the Atlantic coast – yet apart from the charming university city of Coimbra and the fascinating pilgrimage town of Fátima it receives few visitors and is little known outside the country.

The heart of central Portugal is the Beira (border) region, a group of three provinces between the Douro and the Tagus rivers. This was the historic homeland of the *Lusitani* tribe, Celto-Iberians who resisted the Roman invasion of Portugal, whose leader Viriatus, killed in 139BC, remains a national hero. Coimbra, which takes its name from the Roman settlement at Conímbriga, was the capital of Portugal for more than 100 years. These days it is the capital of Beira Litoral, a seaside province of sandy beaches, pine forests and dunes, which is popular with Portuguese holidaymakers in summer.

Further inland, Beira Alta is a region of solid towns and granite villages, where Dão wines and Serra cheese are made, the latter by the sheep farmers of the highlands of Serra da Estrela, while remote Beira Baixa is the setting for Monsanto, one of Portugal's most spectacular hilltop villages.

The twin provinces of Estremadura and Ribatejo are dotted with castles and monuments recalling the time when the Christian armies marched south through this region, reconquering land from the Moors. This is where you will find the holy trinity of great Portuguese churches, at Alcobaça, Batalha and Tomar, as well as the moving modern shrine at Fátima, attracting pilgrims from across the Catholic world.

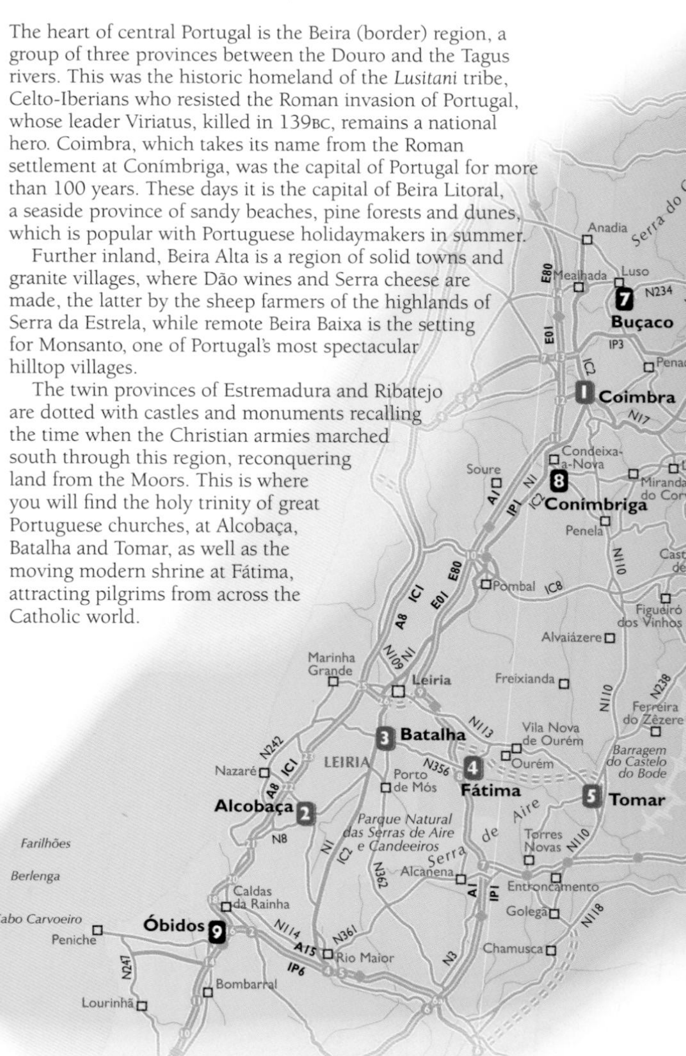

Church of São Miguel in the castle ruins, Monsanto

Page 101: The basilica of Our Lady of Fátima

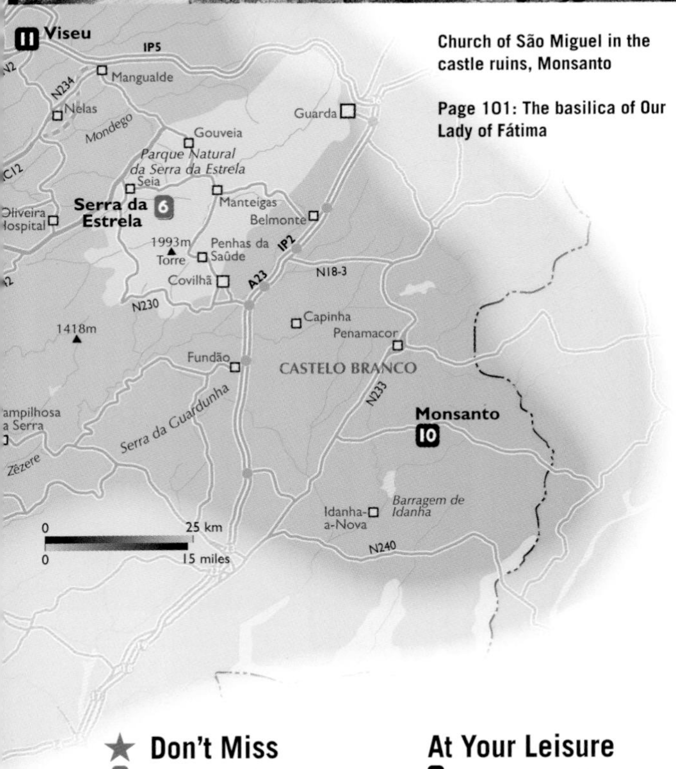

★ Don't Miss

1. Coimbra ➤ 106
2. Mosteiro de Alcobaça ➤ 110
3. Mosteiro da Batalha ➤ 112
4. Fátima ➤ 114
5. Tomar ➤ 116
6. Serra da Estrela ➤ 119

At Your Leisure

7. Buçaco ➤ 121
8. Conímbriga ➤ 121
9. Óbidos ➤ 122
10. Monsanto ➤ 122
11. Viseu ➤ 122

In Four Days

If you're not quite sure where to begin your travels, this itinerary recommends a practical and enjoyable four days out in central Portugal, taking in some of the best places to see using the Getting your Bearings map on the previous page. For more information see the main entries.

Day 1

Morning

Start by exploring **1 Coimbra** (➤ 106–109) on foot. Climb the hill to visit one of the oldest university's in the world to see its library, chapel and graduation halls, then drop down through the old town, passing the old cathedral on the way to the church of Santa Cruz. Have lunch in the neighbouring **Café Santa Cruz** (➤ 124).

Afternoon and Evening

Cross the river and drive south on the N1 to see the Roman remains at **8 Conímbriga** (below, ➤ 121–22). Continue as far as Leiria, then pick up the A8/IC1 motorway to pretty **9 Óbidos** (➤ 122). Book ahead to stay in the castle, a *pousada* (➤ 124); walk around the hilltop ramparts.

Day 2

Morning

Admire the views and whitewashed houses in Óbidos, then go back along the A8/IC1 north to **2 Alcobaça** (➤ 110–111) to visit the monastery and wine museum before lunch.

Afternoon and Evening

Take the short drive to visit the **3 Mosteiro da Batalha** (➤ 112–113). Then head east on the N356 to the sanctuary at **4 Fátima** (➤ 114–115). Stay at the *pousada* (➤ 123) in the walled town of Ourém. Climb the hill to the castle for views across the plain.

Day 3

Morning

Drive to riverside 5 **Tomar** (➤ 116–118) to visit the UNESCO Templar church-fortress, then visit the town centre to see Portugal's oldest synagogue before enjoying lunch by the river. Bring a hearty appetite to try *leitão* (roast suckling pig, ➤ 37), a speciality of central Portugal.

Afternoon and Evening

Allow three hours for the drive to rugged 6 **Serra da Estrela** (➤ 119–120), Portugal's highest mountain range. From here, go east on the IP6, then north on the IP2, towards Manteigas to stay at Pousada de São Lourenço (tel: 275 980 050), in a stone-built house above Manteigas with views over the Zêzere Valley (above) or, slightly north to Solar de Alarcão (tel: 271 214 392) in Guarda outside the national park. An alternative route leads south of Manteigas to the boulder-strewn village of 10 **Monsanto** (➤ 122) along the N239, N345 and N232, taking in rugged hill country, meadows and postcard-perfect hill villages.

Day 4

Spend a full day exploring the mountains. Visit the Manteigas tourist office for walking maps, then take a picnic to **Poço do Inferno waterfall** (➤ 119). If you don't want to walk, drive the circuit from **Penhas da Saúde** (➤ 119) to **Torre** (➤ 120) for spectacular views of the high sierra.

Coimbra

Portugal's oldest university sits on the crown of a hill overlooking the River Mondego. With historic buildings and churches, parks and gardens, and a lively student feel, Coimbra is one of the most enjoyable Portuguese cities in which to spend some of your time.

The first king of Portugal, Afonso Henriques (1109–85, ➤ 80), moved the capital here from Guimarães (➤ 93), but it was his successor, Dom Dinis, who founded the university that is today synonymous with Coimbra. Established in 1290 by papal decree to teach medicine, arts and law, the university moved back and forth between Lisbon and Coimbra before settling in João III's royal palace at Coimbra in 1537. Despite clinging to traditions, the students here are known for their liberal outlook. During the 20th century, Coimbra was a focus for radical opposition to the Salazar régime.

Visiting the University

The university is in the upper town, on the summit of Alcáçova hill. Despite the steep gradients, Coimbra is best explored on foot and it is easiest to start by climbing to the top of the hill and working your way back down.

From the river, head for the **Pátio das Escolas**. This handsome quadrangle, with buildings on three sides and a

ACROSS THE RIVER

Walk across Ponte de Santa Clara for the best view of the old town and university. On the south bank, the Gothic convent of **Santa Clara-a-Velha**, once home to Inês de Castro (➤ 110, 111), has been sinking for centuries but is being recovered and stands behind a new riverside park. The convent ruins reopened to the public in April 2009 with a new visitor centre and tours (Rua das Parreiras, tel: 239 801 161, Jun–Sep Tue–Sun 10–7, Oct–May Tue–Sun 10–5:30). Near here is **Portugal dos Pequenitos** (Rossio de Santa Clara, tel: 239 801 170, www.portugaldospequenitos.pt, Mar–May, 16–30 Sep 10–7, Jun–15 Sep 9–8; Oct–Feb 10–5, moderate–expensive). Aimed mainly at children, the park has a play area and miniature models of houses, monuments and historic buildings. Behind the park, the peaceful gardens of **Quinta das Lágrimas** (Villa of Tears) mark the spot where Inês de Castro was murdered. The palace at the centre of the gardens is now a luxury hotel (➤ 123).

Cross the water for the best views of Coimbra

The venerable Coimbra University

terrace overlooking the Mondego, is at the heart of the old university. A statue of João III stands at the centre and in one corner is a baroque bell-tower.

You can visit most of the buildings, but you need a ticket to enter the frescoed **Biblioteca Joanina** (library), which has a collection of more than 30,000 books dating back to the 12th century, and the ruby-red **Sala dos Capelos** (ceremonial hall). The ticket office for both is in the main university building, at the left end of the colonnaded walkway on the north side of Pátio das Escolas. The baroque library, named after its benefactor, João V, is the main attraction, decorated in gilded wood and lacquered in green, red and gold. The Sala dos Capelos, where investitures and degree ceremonies take place, occupies the grand hall of the Manueline (➤ 14) palace, with a panelled ceiling and portraits of Portuguese monarchs.

A corridor, offering fine views over the Coimbra rooftops, leads to the private examination hall, with a painted ceiling, tiled walls and portraits of former rectors.

The courtyard at the Museu Nacional Machado de Castro

On the east side of the square, the **Porta Férrea** (Iron Gate), built in 1634, contains carved figures representing the original faculties and statues of Dom Dinis and João III. This leads to the modern university buildings, including the faculties of medicine, science and technology. Most of these date from the 1960s, when the dictator António Salazar, a former economics professor at Coimbra, destroyed Manueline and Renaissance buildings in the name of modernization.

Two Cathedrals

From the statue of Dom Dinis, steps lead down to **Praça da República**, with its student cafés. Behind the 21-arch São Sebastião Aqueduct, which was completed by Italian architect Filippo Terzi in the late 16th century, is the vast **Jardim Botânico** (tel: 239 855 233, Mon–Fri 9–12, 2–5, Sat, Sun only if booked in advance, gardens free, greenhouses inexpensive). It is Portugal's largest botanical garden and the formal gardens were laid out in the late 18th century.

Go back up the steps and turn right to explore the rest of the upper town. The **Sé Nova** (New Cathedral) was built in 1598 and includes the choir stalls and font from the old cathedral. Just down the hill, the **Museu Nacional Machado de Castro** is housed in the 16th-century bishops' palace. It includes medieval paintings, sculpture and the *cryptoporticus*, a series of underground galleries and part of the old Roman forum. The museum is currently being expanded – ring for information.

Further downhill, the **Sé Velha** (Old Cathedral) is a Romanesque church-fortress on the site of the first cathedral in Portugal. Of interest here are the 13th-century cloisters and the Hispano-Arab tiles covering the walls.

Mosteiro de Santa Cruz

From here you can walk down to **Arco de Almedina**, the 12th-century gateway to the city. Go through the arch and turn right along a busy pedestrian street to the **Mosteiro de Santa Cruz**. Many of the leading artists of the Coimbra school, such as Jean de Rouen, worked on pieces for the monastery in the 16th century. The Renaissance porch is by Diogo de Castilho and Nicolas Chanterène, who also designed the pulpit and was responsible for the tombs of Portugal's first kings, Afonso Henriques and his son, Sancho I, behind the high altar. Buy a ticket to visit the **Sala do Capítulo** (chapter house) by Diogo de Boytac, with its Manueline ceiling, and the **Claustro do Silêncio** (Cloister of Silence), one of the purest examples of Manueline art.

Turn left on coming out of the church to return to the river at Largo da Portagem.

TAKING A BREAK

Try the **trendy student cafés** around Praça da República. **Trovador** (➤ 125), by the Sé Velha, is good for lunch.

Sé Velha dates back to the reign of King Afonso Henriques

198 B1 Largo Dom Dinis; tel: 239 832 591

Universidade Velha (Biblioteca Joanina and Sala dos Capelos)
Paço das Escolas 239 482 001; http://bibliotecajoanina.uc.pt/en Apr–Oct 8:30–7 (tickets), 9–7:30 (visits); Nov–Mar 9:30–5 (tickets), 10–5:30 (visits) Moderate

Museu Nacional Machado de Castro
Largo Dr José Rodrigues 239 482 001; http://mnmachadodecastro.imc-ip.pt Apr–Sep Wed–Sun 10–6; Oct–Mar Wed–Sun 10–12:30, 2–6

Sé Velha
Largo da Sé Velha 239 825 273 Mon–Thu, Sat 10–1, 2–6, Fri 10–1, Sun only for services Church: free. Cloisters: inexpensive

Mosteiro de Santa Cruz
Praça 8 de Maio 239 822 941 Daily 10–12, 2–6 Church: free. Cloisters: inexpensive

COIMBRA: INSIDE INFO

Top tips Parking in central Coimbra is difficult – it is generally easier to park across the river and walk across Ponte de Santa Clara.

- To avoid the climb to the university, take **tram No 1** from Largo da Portagem.
- In summer, there are river trips from a jetty in the park beside the Santa Clara bridge on the north bank.
- Look out for the chance to hear the **Coimbra version of *fado*** (➤ 20–21), sung by men rather than women, with musicians and singers dressed in long black capes. It is less melancholy than its Lisbon counterpart. You are mostly likely to hear this in bars and restaurants and in the streets during student festivities. Or try to catch it at Trovador (➤ 125).

Hidden gem Following signs from Praça Dom Dinis, walk upstairs and ring the bell to be let into the **Museu Académico** (tel: 239 827 396, Mon–Fri 10–12:30, 2–5, inexpensive), with costumes, photos and artefacts describing university traditions such as *bedels* (beadles), *repúblicas* (communally run student houses) and the Queima das Fitas (Burning of the Ribbons) in May.

2 Mosteiro de Alcobaça

The largest church in Portugal is a supreme example of Gothic architecture and would be worth a visit to Alcobaça for the building alone. What makes it even more special is that the church has become a shrine to one of the most tragic love stories in Portuguese history.

The **Mosteiro de Alcobaça** (sometimes referred to as Mosteiro Santa Maria) was founded by Afonso Henriques (➤ 80) in 1153 to give thanks for victory over the Moors at Santarém. The baroque facade dates from the 18th century, but once you are inside everything is pure Gothic.

Clean Lines and Soaring Columns

Unlike many Portuguese churches, the central nave is simplicity itself. The only exception to the almost complete absence of decoration is the richly sculpted sacristy portal behind the high altar, designed by João de Castilho in 16th-century higly floral Manueline style (➤ 47).

The tomb of Dom Pedro I and Inês de Castro

DOM PEDRO I AND INÊS DE CASTRO

Visitors crowd the transept to see the tombs of Dom Pedro I and his lover, Inês de Castro. Inês was lady-in-waiting to Pedro's wife, Constanza of Castile, but Pedro's father, Afonso IV, had her banished from court to end the affair. After Constanza died, Inês lived with Pedro at Coimbra, where she was murdered in 1355 on the orders of Afonso IV who feared Spanish influence over the Portuguese throne. Two years later, when Pedro assumed the throne, he wrought revenge on the killers by having their hearts torn out and eating them. He also revealed that he and Inês had been secretly married at Bragança; her corpse was exhumed and he ordered the court to pay homage to their dead queen by kissing her decomposed hand.

The baroque facade of the monastery at Alcobaça

Tombs and Cloisters

The limestone **tombs of Dom Pedro I and Inês de Castro**, carved with scenes from the Bible (► 110, box), face each other across the aisle. The reclining figure of Inês is held by six angels, while her assassins are thrown into Hell at her feet. On Pedro's orders, the lovers were buried foot to foot, so that they could see one another when they rose on Judgement Day. The tombs are inscribed with *Até ao fim do mundo* ("Until the end of the world").

The entrance to the cloisters is through the **Sala dos Reis**, with statues of Portuguese kings and tiled walls telling the story of the monastery. The **Claustro de Silêncio**, added in the 14th century, is considered one of the finest Gothic cloisters in Portugal, with its orange trees and a Renaissance *lavabo* for the monks to wash their hands before entering the refectory.

Along here are the rather grand 18th-century **kitchens**, once famed for their extravagant banquets, with huge conical chimneys, and a stream that flowed straight from the River Alcôa, providing a plentiful supply of fish. Next to the kitchens is the rib-vaulted **refectory**. Note the pulpit on the western flank where the monks once read holy scriptures. A staircase from the cloister leads to the 13th-century dormitory.

TAKING A BREAK

Café Dom Pedro (Praça 25 de Abril, tel: 965 359 180) across the square from the monastery, has a good range of snacks. There is also a smaller café in the gardens behind the cloister.

200 B4 ☎ 262 505 120; www.mosteiroalcobaca.pt ⌚ Apr–Sep daily 9–7; Oct–Mar 9–5 (last entry 30 mins before closing) 💶 Moderate; free Sun 9–2

MOSTEIRO DE ALCOBAÇA: INSIDE INFO

Top tip Climb the hill to the ruined castle above the town for the **best views** of the monastery.

In more depth The **Museu Nacional de Vinho** (Rua de Leiria, Olival Fechado, tel: 262 582 222, Mon–Fri 9–12:30, 2–5:30, plus May–Sep Sat–Sun 10–12:30, 2–6, inexpensive) explains the history of wine making for which the region is famous and has a fascinating collection of old wine bottles, wine-making equipment and decorative posters.

3 Mosteiro da Batalha

As you round a corner on the busy N1, a great church comes into view, with pinnacles, turrets and flying buttresses in honey-coloured limestone. This is the Mosteiro da Batalha, a masterpiece of Gothic architecture that has become a symbol of Portuguese history and of independence from Spain.

Abbey of the Battle

The **Mosteiro de Santa Maria da Vitória**, commonly known as the Mosteiro da Batalha (Abbey of the Battle), was built to celebrate the Portuguese victory over the Spanish at the Battle of Aljubarrota in 1385. Three years after King João I's victory work on the abbey began.

Admire the worn exterior of the abbey and the **statue of Nuno Álvares Pereira** (► box opposite) on horseback on the square in front of the church. The main portal, beneath a Gothic window, features carved statues of Christ and the apostles, with angels, saints and João I's coat of arms. The long, tall nave is beautifully simple, with Gothic pillars and vaulting and stained glass.

THE BATTLE OF ALJUBARROTA

King Fernando I of Portugal died in 1383 without leaving a male heir. King Juan I of Castile claimed the throne from his marriage to King Fernando's daugher, Beatriz, but was opposed by Fernando's illegitimate half-brother, João I. Heavily outnumbered by Spanish troops, João promised to build a magnificent church to the Virgin if he was successful, and with the help of his faithful lieutenant Nuno Álvares Pereira, and 500 English archers supplied by King Richard II, his supporters won the day. João's victory ushered in a new era for Portugal, with 200 years of independence under the rule of the House of Avis.

The Founder's Chapel

Immediately to the right as you enter is the **Capela do Fundador** (Founder's Chapel), where João I and his wife, Philippa of Lancaster

The church is full of space and light

(➤ 80), are buried beneath an octagonal lantern, their tombs carved with effigies of the couple lying hand in hand. Also buried here are their four younger sons, including Henry the Navigator (➤ 12, 80).

The original **Claustro Real** (Royal Cloister) was embellished with rich Manueline tracery by Diogo de Boytac, architect of the monastery at Belém (➤ 48). All the main symbols of Manueline art are here, including armillary spheres, crosses of Christ, twisted branches and exotic foliage.

On one side of the cloister, the **Sala do Capítulo** (chapter house) contains Portugal's two Unknown Soldiers, one from World War I and the other from Portugal's wars in Africa. A museum dedicated to them is in the former refectory.

A second cloister leads to the **Capelas Imperfeitas** (Unfinished Chapels), begun by Dom Duarte, João I's eldest son, as a royal mausoleum, containing the tombs of Duarte and his queen, Éleonor of Aragón. The chapels, also accessible from behind the main abbey, are perhaps the highlight of the entire complex, with an Indian-inspired Manueline portal and a magnificent roofless octagonal rotunda.

TAKING A BREAK

Behind the abbey, the **Circunstancia Bar** (15 Estrada de Fatima, tel: 244 768 777, www.circunstancia.com.pt) is a good place for a glass of wine and a light snack.

200 B4 · 244 765 497 · Apr–Sep 9–6:30; Oct–Mar 9–5:30 (last entry 30 mins before closing) · Moderate; free Sun 9–2

BATALHA: INSIDE INFO

Top tips The abbey is best seen on a **day trip** from Nazaré or Fátima, although there are express buses from Lisbon.

- During the weekends of **13 May and 13 October**, Batalha is packed with people visiting from Fátima (➤ 114–115).

In more depth Visit the **battlefield of Aljubarrota**, 4km (2.5 miles) south of Batalha in the village of São Jorge. There is a small chapel, a military museum, a shop and café (tel: 244 480 060, www.fundacao-aljubarrota.pt, May–Sep Tue–Sun 10–7, Oct–Apr Tue–Sun 10–5:30, expensive).

4 Fátima

The so-called "altar of Portugal", Fátima is Portugal's greatest Roman Catholic shrine. The story of what happened to three shepherd children in 1917 has moved millions, and made the town one of the biggest centres of pilgrimage in the Roman Catholic world.

The Vision

It was on 13 May 1917 that the Virgin Mary appeared in an oak tree to 10-year-old Lúcia dos Santos and her cousins Jacinta and Francisco as they were tending their family's sheep in the village of Cova da Iria, near Fátima. The children spoke of a lady "brighter than the sun" who called them to return at the same time each month for six months. Although their story was greeted with much scepticism, the children returned and the visions continued.

On the final occasion, 13 October, a crowd of 70,000 people witnessed the sun dancing in the sky like a ball of fire and countless miracles occurred – the blind could see, the sick were cured and the lame walked.

On the same day, the Virgin revealed to Lúcia the "three secrets of Fátima", which are said to have foretold World War II, Russian communism and the assassination of a pope.

The Children

Jacinta and Francisco died of pneumonia in 1920, but Lúcia entered a Carmelite convent in Coimbra in 1928, where she died in 2005, age 97. Jacinta and Francisco, who are buried inside the basilica, were beatified in 1989 by Pope John Paul II, the first step on the path to sainthood.

The Basilica of Our Lady of Fátima towers over its steps and the tarmac esplanade

Pilgrims light candles for Our Lady of Fátima

The Basilica

A vast, neoclassical basilica was completed in 1953, and accommodates the millions of pilgrims who flock here from Portugal and all over the world. The esplanade in front of the basilica can hold a million people and is twice the size of St Peter's Square in Rome. In a corner of the square stands the **Capela das Aparicões** (Chapel of the Apparitions), on the site of the original visions, where pilgrims pray, offer gifts and light candles to a statue of the Virgin. The sea of candles and dripping wax is a captivating sight. Inside the basilica are 15 altars symbolizing the 15 mysteries of the Rosary.

Pilgrimages to Fátima take place all year, and particularly on 13 May and 13 October, with many of the pilgrims making their way to the basilica on their knees.

TAKING A BREAK

The *pousada* at Ourém (► 123), built on a hilltop 10km (6 miles) northeast of Fátima, makes a good overnight stop.

---

200 C4 Avenida Dom José Alves Correia da Silva; tel: 249 531 139

Shrine of Our Lady of the Rosary of Fátima
Apartado 31 249 539 600; www.santuario-fatima.pt

FÁTIMA: INSIDE INFO

Top tips From Easter to October, there are **candlelit processions** in front of the basilica at 9:30 each night. The largest procession is on 12th of the month.
■ You should be silent around the basilica and the Chapel of the Apparitions.

In more depth You can visit the village of **Aljustrel**, outside Fátima, to see the **Casa Museu de Aljustrel** where the three children grew up (further on in Valinhos, a statue marks the spot of the fourth vision), and the ethnographic museum next door (tel: 249 532 828, May–Oct Tue–Sun 9–1, 2:30–6:30, Nov–Apr Tue–Sun 9–1, 2:30–6, house free, museum inexpensive).

5 Tomar

The third in the trio of medieval churches, the Convento de Cristo, stands in the grounds of a castle on a wooded slope overlooking Tomar. Once a powerful military and religious capital, Tomar is now a peaceful town on the banks of the River Nabão and makes a pleasant base to stay for exploring the surrounding area.

The Templar's 12th-century Convento de Cristo

The Monastery

The Knights Templar castle dominates the town. Within its walls stands the **Convento de Cristo**, one of Portugal's UNESCO World Heritage Sites. It was begun in 1160 but has Gothic and Manueline (➤ 14) additions.

The tour of the monastery begins in a pair of cloisters, **Claustro da Lavagem** and **Claustro do Cemitério**, both added by Henry the Navigator (1394–1460, ➤ 12, 80), whose ruined palace can be seen through the arches.

Next you come to the **Charola** (Rotunda), the spiritual heart of the complex, a 12th-century round church that was modelled on the Holy Sepulchre of Jerusalem, with an octagonal chapel where the knights are reputed to have held services on horseback. The columns are richly painted with 16th-century frescoes. The Charola now forms the eastern end of a Manueline church, built under the reign of Manuel I.

From here you move into the **Claustro Principal** (Great Cloister), added in 1557 in neoclassical and Renaissance style. Climb onto the roof for the best views of the **great western window** by Diogo de Arruda and the **south portal** by João de Castilho, two of the most sumptuous examples of Manueline art

A restored spiral staircase in the monastery

THE KNIGHTS AND TOMAR

Tomar was founded in 1157 by Gualdim Pais, the first Grand Master of the Knights Templar of Portugal, a military force with powerful religious overtones. The town was created on land donated by Afonso Henriques (➤ 80) in return for the knights' help in the reconquest of Portugal from the Moors. Tomar subsequently became the knights' base. In 1314, the order was deemed too powerful and was suppressed by Pope Clement V, but it was reconstituted in Portugal by Dom Dinis under the name the Knights of Christ. Henry the Navigator became "governor" in the 15th century and tapped the order's wealth to fund his explorations, while the Knights of Christ were given spiritual control over all Portuguese conquests.

in Portugal. The window in particular contains all the familiar symbols of the Manueline era, including anchors, cables, twisted ropes, an armillary sphere and the Cross of the Knights of Christ. From here you can wander along corridors of monks' cells and step onto the rooftop terrace before finishing with the walkway around the castle walls.

The Town

The old town, to the west of the river, is centred around the elegant **Praça da República**, where a statue of Gualdim Pais stands in front of the town hall. On one side of the square, the church of **São João Baptista** has an elegant Manueline portal and a pulpit carved with the Templar cross and the royal coat of arms.

Just south is the oldest surviving **synagogue** in Portugal, lovingly maintained by one of two remaining Jewish families in Tomar. Built around 1430, and abandoned after the expulsion of the Jews in 1497, it has been used as a prison, chapel, hayloft and cellar, but is now a museum containing 13th- and 14th-century Jewish tombstones as well as sacred items donated by members of Jewish communities across the world.

Tomar's other museum, **Museu dos Fósforos** (Matchbox Museum) is housed in a wing of a 17th-century convent. An eccentric display features more than 40,000 matchboxes, the largest collection in Europe, beginning with Queen Elizabeth II's coronation in 1953 and continuing with Portuguese politicians, Spanish bullfighters and Japanese topless models.

Praça da República, with the statue of Gualdim Pais

A warren of narrow streets leads down to the River Nabão, where the shady Parque do Mouchão, on an island in the middle of the river, has open-air cafés and a waterwheel, said to date from Roman times. The park is a cool, calm place planted with willow trees and enclosed by the river.

A Manueline carving in Tomar

TAKING A BREAK

Chico Elias (tel: 249 311 067, daily 12–3, 7–10) is a traditional restaurant in a large old tavern. **O Tabuleiro** (➤ 125), close to the main square, is another fine choice for hearty Portuguese cuisine.

200 C4 Avenida Dr Cândido Madureira; tel: 249 329 000; www.rttemplarios.pt

Convento de Cristo
15-minute walk above the town 249 313 481 Jun–Sep daily 9–6; Oct–May 9-5 Moderate

Sinagoga
Rua Dr Joaquim Jacinto 73 249 322 427 Thu–Tue 10–1, 2–6 Free

Museu dos Fósforos
Varzea Grande 249 329 829 Tue–Sun 11–5 Free

TOMAR: INSIDE INFO

Top tip Come here on Friday when the riverbanks are taken over by a **large market**, with fresh food and flowers on the east bank, and clothes, shoes and household goods on the west bank.

- Try a ***Fatias de Tomar*** (a slice of Tomar), a sweet treat made with a mixture of egg yolks, sugar and water, purchased in many shops and restaurants around the town.

Hidden gems Cross the Ponte Velha (Old Bridge) to the chapel of **Santa Iria** (Tue–Sun 10–6, free), Tomar's patron saint, a young nun who was murdered. The church, built in the 16th century, features a stone-carved calvary, a coffered painted ceiling and rich 17th-century *azulejos* (➤ 18–19).

A short drive away from Tomar is **Constância**, one of the most attractive villages in the area. The Festival of the Tabuleiros takes place here once every four years. The next one will be held in June and July 2015.

6 Serra da Estrela

Rocky hillsides are carved up by glacial valleys in the Serra da Estrela, Portugal's highest mountain range. In summer you can walk across carpets of scented grasses and wild flowers, and in winter the peaks are covered in snow. Much of the area has been designated a natural park.

The Serra da Estrela forms a 100km by 30km (62 miles by 19 miles) range, with a summit of 1,993m (6,537ft), and is Portugal's largest protected wildlife area. This is a land of shepherds, long-horned sheep, cheese-making and wool. The mainstays of the economy are farming and forestry, though outdoor tourism is becoming ever more important. In winter, there is skiing and hunting; in summer. there is trout fishing in the rivers and walking in the hills.

Getting into the Mountains

There is good access to the mountains from Covilha, a busy textile town with views over the mountains, where you can buy gloves, jackets and woollen goodies. From here, the N339 climbs through **Penhas da Saúde**, Portugal's only ski resort, on its way to the high sierra. In winter, you can try dog sledging and sleigh rides as well as skiing. This is a good starting point for a circular tour, allowing at least half a day. Soon after Penhas da Saúde, turn right on the N338 for a beautiful drive along the Zêzere Valley, a deep glacial gorge.

All along the valley, there are distant views of **Manteigas**, the small town at the centre of the park. Here you can pick up information on walking and hiking in the mountains, including the half-day circular walk from Manteigas to the **Poço do Inferno** (Hell's Well) waterfall.

The glacial scenery of the Zêzere Valley

Magnificent views of the High Sierra near Torre

From Manteigas, you can follow the twisting N232 towards Gouveia. You pass a *pousada* and the source of the River Mondego, which empties into the sea near Coimbra. The scenery is stunning, with rock formations of wind-sculpted granite such as the Cabeça do Velho (Old Man's Head).

A minor road leads to **Sabugueiro**, Portugal's highest village, where cheese, ham, sausages and woollen blankets are on sale. Turn left on the N339 for the slow climb to **Torre**. The highest mountain in Portugal (1,993m/6,537ft) takes its name from the stone tower built here in the 19th century so that the peak would top 2,000m (6,560ft). On winter weekends, families flock here to go sledging. On the way down to Penhas da Saúde, look out for the statue of **Nossa Senhora da Boa Estrela**, carved into a niche in the rock.

Two towns that make good bases for visiting the park are **Guarda**, the highest town in Portugal (1,056m/3,464ft), with a 14th-century Gothic cathedral, and **Belmonte**, birthplace of Pedro Álvares Cabral (➤ 13), who "discovered" Brazil. Belmonte was once home to a large population of *marranos* (Jews who fled here after their expulsion from Portugal in 1497) and it still has a large Jewish community.

TAKING A BREAK

There are **cafés** in all the main villages offering sandwiches made with the local cheese, *queijo da serra* (see below).

198 C1/D1

Park Tourist Information Office
Rua 1 de Maio, Manteigas 275 980 060; www.icn.pt

SERRA DA ESTRELA: INSIDE INFO

Top tips Try ***queijo da serra*** (➤ 29), a strong cheese made from sheep's milk and curdled with thistle flowers. The runny, ripe cheese, usually scooped out with a spoon, is at its best in winter.

- The mountains need to be **treated with respect.** The weather can change quickly – it can be sunny in Manteigas while Torre is obscured in mist, or you might drive through the mist to emerge in sunshine above the clouds. Be prepared for anything, even in summer, and allow plenty of time.

At Your Leisure

Gardens at Palace Hotel do Bussaco

7 Buçaco

Buçaco is a place where you can still believe in fairies. Once a monastic retreat from which women were banned by papal decree, the walled Mata Nacional (National Forest) is a landscape of sylvan glades and cedar-scented woods dotted with fountains, hermitages and shady walks, even its own vineyard. At the centre is the bizarre neo-Manueline Buçaco Palace, designed as a royal hunting lodge and now one of Portugal's top hotels (➤ 124). The **Carmelite convent** next door has cork-lined cells and mosaic walls. Walk through the Buçaco forest up to Cruz Alta (High Cross), which offers impressive views over the ocean, and a museum, which tells of the Battle of Buçaco in 1812, in which the Duke of Wellington fought the French.

198 B1

Mosteiro dos Carmelitas

231 939 226 Jun–Sep Tue–Sun 9–12:30, 2–5:30; Oct–May Tue–Sat 9–12:30, 2–5:30
Inexpensive

8 Conímbriga

The best-preserved Roman remains in Portugal are situated 15km (9 miles) south of Coimbra. Some of the houses have detailed mosaics, with images of birds, fish, horses and dragons. Note the **Casa das Fontes**, a second-century villa with ornamental gardens and pools. The excavations here have uncovered evidence of a forum, aqueduct, shops, taverns and

BEST FOR KIDS

- **Portugal dos Pequenitos**, Coimbra (➤ 106), a theme park of Portugal in miniature.
- Visit a **sheep farm** in the hills of Serra da Estrela.
- **Forest walks** in Buçaco (➤ 119–120), which has a special place in the hearts of the Portuguese.
- The beaches of the **Costa da Prata**, the coastline running along Central Portugal.

public baths. A museum contains archaeological finds, some of which date from a Celto-Iberian settlement before the arrival of the Romans in the first century BC.

200 C5 Condeixa-a-Velha 239 941 177; www.conimbriga.pt Daily 10–7 Moderate; free Sun 9–2

9 Óbidos

This walled town of whitewashed houses and mazelike Moorish lanes was traditionally given as a wedding gift by the Portuguese kings to their queens, a custom begun by Dom Dinis for Isabel of Aragón in 1282 that continued for 600 years. Porta de Vila, the town's gateway, is lined with 18th-century *azulejos* (➤ 18–19) and leads to Rua Direita, the main street, with its souvenir shops and *ginja* (cherry brandy) bars. Halfway up the street, the church of Santa Maria has *azulejo* walls and there is a striking Manueline pillory in the church square. The castle, at the top of town, was converted into a royal palace in the 16th century and is now one of Portugal's finest *pousadas*, the Pousada do Castelo (➤ 124). From here, climb onto the ramparts to make a circuit of the walls, which should take around 45 minutes. The castle is atmospherically illuminated by night.

200 B4

10 Monsanto

Inhabited in pre-Roman times, Monsanto is one of Portugal's oldest settlements. It is perched on the side of Monte Santo (Sacred Mountain), its houses built into the mountainside between huge granite boulders. This village has the odd claim to fame of having been once voted "Most Portuguese village in Portugal". Climb to the ruined 12th-century castle, for magnificent views stretching as far as the Serra da Estrela (➤ 119–120). On 3 May, during the Festa das Cruzes, the younger village women throw flowers from the ramparts in memory of a famous siege when the starving inhabitants threw their last calf from the castle walls in a successful attempt to fool their attackers into thinking that they were able to last out for a long time. There are a few signs of tourist development – a small *estalagem* (➤ 34) a couple of restaurants and craft shops – but mostly life goes on as it always has in this remote, quintessential hilltop village.

201 F5

The roofless Church São Miguel in the ruins of the castle in Monsanto

11 Viseu

The capital of the Beira Alta and the Dão wine region, Viseu is an attractive town. At the heart of the old town is Largo da Sé, with two churches facing one another across the square. The larger and more imposing facade is that of the baroque church of Misericórdia; the Sé (cathedral) has Renaissance cloisters and a Manueline ceiling.

The main attraction is the **Museu de Grão Vasco**, named after Vasco Fernandes (1475–1542), a leading figure in the 16th-century Viseu school of painting. It includes his painting, *St Peter Enthroned*.

198 C2 Avenida Calouste Gulbenkian; tel: 232 420 950; www.cm-viseu.pt

Museu de Grão Vasco

Paço dos Três Escalões 232 422 049; www.ipmuseus.pt Tue 2–5:30, Wed–Sun 10–6 Moderate; free Sun 9:30–12:30

Where to... Stay

Prices
Expect to pay for a double room per night in high season:
€ under €60 **€€** €60–€120 **€€€** €121–€180 **€€€€** over €180

COIMBRA AND ENVIRONS

Casa nas Serras €€

Attractively renovated, this B&B in the foothills of the Serra da Estrela (➤ 119–120) has enchanting views. Enjoy them from the poolside terrace. The young Belgian owners are very welcoming; rooms, some of which have terraces and kitchenettes, are decorated in a light and contemporary style. Breakfast is good. This is a quiet, relaxing base if you want to hike or cycle in the surrounding region. It's located in Vila Nova de Poiares, 25km (15 miles) east of Coimbra.

198 C1 Santa Maria, Arrifana, Vila Nova de Poiares, Coimbra 914 288 447; http://casanasserras.com

Casa Pombal €

By the university and commanding views across the rooftops to the river, this guesthouse is a delightful place to stay. You feel as though you are staying at one of the famous *repúblicas* or student houses. A steep staircase leads to a number of antiquated but comfortable rooms, some with bathrooms. A hearty breakfast is served in the dining room, where delicious meals can be prepared to order.

198 B1 Rua das Flores 18 239 835 175; www.casapombal.com

Quinta das Lágrimas €€€–€€€€

Famous for receiving the Duke of Wellington in 1808, this luxurious hotel is set in wooded parkland, with a pool, spa, tennis courts and a golf academy with a nine-hole pitch-and-putt and driving range. Inside the main house, the décor is elegant and the bedrooms huge; rooms in the modern spa wing are minimalist-chic. There is a restaurant, and a cellar offering more than 200 vintages.

198 B1 Rua António Augusto Gonçalves, Santa Clara 239 802 380; www.quintadaslagrimas.pt

OURÉM

Pousada Conde de Ourém €€–€€€

This charming, renovated *pousada*, (➤ 15–16, 35) converted from medieval houses, is a good base from which to visit Fátima and Tomar. Climb to the castle for distant views of Fátima. Rooms are spacious and comfortable, and a pool is open in summer. The *pousada*'s restaurant offers local specialities, such as *Conde de Ourém* (fried rabbit with cabbage).

200 C4 Largo João Manso 249 540 930; www.pousadas.pt

TOMAR

Estalagem de Santa Iria €–€€

As Tomar's *pousada* is a long way out of town, this is the best choice, especially if charm and tranquillity are your criteria. Even the early 20th-century writer Somerset Maugham has signed the visitors' book. This unpretentious inn, with 14 bright, spacious rooms, is idyllically located on a wooded island in the middle of the town. The dining room serves delicious, well-cooked dishes.

200 C4 Parque do Mouchão 249 313 326; www.estalagemsantairia.com

BUÇACO

Hotel Palace do Bussaco €€€€

The Buçaco Forest (➤ 121), where Napoleon suffered a major defeat in the Peninsular Wars, benefits from a microclimate and has been under papal protection since the 1800s. The hotel was built as a royal hunting lodge just before the monarchy was abolished in 1910, but it's still fit for a sovereign. The mock-Manueline palace houses 34 luxurious rooms, a fabulous dining room and some impressive *azulejos*. There are also tennis courts. The cellar is one of Portugal's best.

198 B1 ✉ Mata do Buçaco, Luso ☎ 231 937 970; www.almeidahotels.com

ÓBIDOS

Casa das Senhoras Rainhas €€€

The whitewashed walls make this hotel feel like a haven of peace and relaxation. The building itself has been perfectly renovated and preserved, but inside there is a luxurious space with good sized, well-appointed bedrooms, a large terrace for outside eating and a cosy drawing room with fireplace. It is right next to the old city walls, so it is perfectly located for exploring.

200 B4 ✉ 6 Rua Padre Nunes Tavares ☎ 262 955 360; www.senhorasrainhas-obidos.com

Pousada do Castelo €€€–€€€€

The magnificent site – commanding fantastic views – alone justifies splashing out to stay here. It's one of the most prestigious *pousadas* in Portugal, if only because there are only nine rooms, a couple of them in the eyrie tower. Exuberant tapestries enhance the romantic atmosphere in the impeccably restored medieval interior. Rooms are comfortable and well appointed. Traditional meals are served in the charming refectory – or you could drop by for afternoon tea.

200 B4 ✉ Paço Real ☎ 262 955 080; www.pousadas.pt

Where to... Eat and Drink

Prices

Expect to pay per person for a three-course meal, excluding drinks and tips:

€ under €12 **€€** €12–€24 **€€€** €25–€3 **€€€€** over €36

COIMBRA AND ENVIRONS

Arcadas Restaurante €€€

At this Michelin-starred restaurant, award-winning chef Albano Lourenço has made this a must destination for foodies in Portugal. Seasonal, local ingredients are the key here, and the elegant restaurant looks out over the gardens of this attractive hotel, Quinta das Lágrimas. There are two tasting menus, where the chef will suggest various fresh ingredients, and can match each one with local wines. There are over 300 Portuguese and international wines on offer. Wild rabbit, duck and free-range chicken feature on the slightly unusual menu, while *ensopado de enguias* (eel stew) draws customers from a wide radius. This goldmine of a restaurant (30km/19 miles west of Coimbra), with its rustic décor and charming *patio*, is renowned for its locally grown or caught produce and expert Bairrada cooking. It gets packed on market day (every other Wednesday). Advance bookings are recommended.

198 B1 ✉ Rua António Augusto Gonçalves ☎ 239 802 380; www.quintadaslagrimas.pt ⌚ Jul–Sep daily 7pm–10pm, Oct–Jun 12–2, 7–10

Café Santa Cruz €

University students keep this wonderfully atmospheric café-bar buzzing, especially in the evening. It is housed in the former sacristy of the 16th-century Igreja Santa Cruz. Coffee, wine, beer and snacks are served in a fabulous vaulted room – stone walls and leather benches. The superb *esplanada* (terrace) is packed out in summer.

198 B1 Praça 8 de Maio 239 833 617; www.cafesantacruz.com Mon–Sat 7am–11:30pm (1:30 in summer)

Fangas Mercearia Bar €–€€

This is just the place for an informal dinner. Occupying an old grocery, with bistro-style tables and *fado* (➤ 20–21) playing, it's an atmospheric spot to snack on *tapas*, such as tangy salami, cured ham, cheese, and tuna in tomato sauce, which you can pair with top-notch regional wines.

198 B1 Rua Fernandes Tomás 45–49 934 093 636 Tue–Thu 1–1, Fri–Sat 1pm–2am

Trovador €€–€€€

Not only is the food good, but this is one of the few places in Coimbra where you can be sure to hear the local version of *fado* (➤ 20–21) sung by men instead of women, and more important for the lyrics than the tune. All kinds of regional specialities are available, including *chanfana* (goat in a wine sauce). The wine list is top notch, including local Bairradas, but there are also vintages from all over Portugal. The delightful décor, with wood panelling and crisp white linen, plus charming service and great food, make this restaurant the best in the old town.

198 B1 Largo da Sé Velha 17 239 825 475 Mon–Sat 12–3, 7:30–10. Closed 15–31 Dec

ALCOBAÇA

Restaurante Antonio Padeiro €€–€€€

Going strong since 1938, this inviting restaurant is just steps from the monastery. Sit on the terrace or in the contemporary cellar restaurant for well-prepared regional cuisine. The generous *couvert* (appetiser plate, ➤ 38) of cured meats, cheese and garlicky dips is followed by specialities such as *cabrito no forno*, (oven-baked goat) and *frango na púcara*, a hearty chicken stew flavoured with garlic, pepper and Port wine. Round out with *trouxos de ovos*, a rich, sticky convent dessert made from eggs and sugar.

200 B4 Rua Dom Maur Cocheril 27 262 582 295 Daily 12–3:30, 7–10:30

O Cantinho €€–€€€

This is a favoured local, with friendly owners and a good range of hearty meals that are based on traditional, regional ingredients. Try the chicken casserole, a speciality of the house. There are some lighter snacks and *tapas*-style meals available, too.

200 B4 Rua Engenheiro Bernardo Vila Nova 262 583 471 9–12

TOMAR

O Tabuleiro €

For simple Portuguese fare and a warm welcome, head to this unassuming family-run place close to the main square. It's a laid-back spot for grilled fish and other regional dishes, such as bean casserole with pork and roast lamb. If you aren't feeling very hungry, opt for a "*meia dose*," or small portion.

200 C4 Rua Serpa Pinto 140-148 249 312 771 Jul–Sep Mon–Sat 12–11, Oct–Jun Mon–Sat 12–2, 7–11

FÁTIMA

Tia Alice €€

This restaurant is a real find with its simple interior and well-cooked traditional food, including *morcela com arroz* – a type of black pudding of pork mixed with red wine, rice, herbs and spices.

200 C4 152 Rua do Adro 249 531 737 Tue–Sat 12–2:30, 7:30–10:30, Sun 12–2:30

Where to... Shop

MARKETS

Viseu holds a market at **Largo Castanheiro dos Amores** every Tuesday. A cheese market is held in **Celorico da Beira** every other Friday. In the **Serra da Estrela**, Gouveia's Thursday markets are worth seeing, as is the **Montemor-o-Velho**, 30km (18.5 miles) west of Coimbra, every other Wednesday. The daily market in **Coimbra** is in a hangar behind the City Hall.

CRAFTS

Óbidos has ceramic and craft shops along Rua Direita – try the **Centro de Artesanato**. In **Alcobaça**, quality earthenware is sold at **Raul da Bernarda** (Ponte Dom Elias). In **Coimbra**, you can pick up earthenware goods along **Rua Quebra Costas**. **Ruas Ferreira Borges** and **Visconde da Luz** are Coimbra's main shopping streets, lined with boutiques, grocers, bookshops and tobacconists. Just outside, at Condeixa-a-Nova, factories sell hand-painted ceramics.

FOOD AND DRINK

In **Coimbra, A Camponesa** (Rua da Louça) has an excellent range of wines and spirits or try **Dom Vinho** on Rua Armando Sousa. Buy bottles of Dão wine in Viseu's grocers.

Buy *Queijos da serra* (mountain cheeses, ➤ 29) at **Guarda's** covered market on Rua Dom Nuno Álvares Pereira on Saturday mornings. Try **Pastelaria Horta** (Rua Formosa, **Viseu**) for pies and cakes.

Where to... Be Entertained

SPORT AND OUTDOOR PURSUITS

Surfing is first class at **Buarcos**, near Figueira da Foz. In **Aveiro**, rent bikes from **Agência de Viagens Culturália** (Rua Trinidade Coehlo 16, tel: 234 423 142, www.culturalia.pt) or use **BUGA**, Aveiro's free bike service. **Hiking** in the **Serra da Estrela** (➤ 119–120) is great, and trails well marked.

There are several **spas** in this region – **Termas de Monfortinho** (www.monfortur.pt) enjoys a stunning location and you can play tennis and hire mountain bikes.

FESTIVALS

Coimbra's Queima das Fitas (Ribbon Burning) occurs in May. Don't miss **Aveiro's Festa da Ria**, in the second half of August, when the distinctive *moliceiro* boats are decorated. "Holy Bathing" can be witnessed at **Figueira da Foz**, along with other partying, on and around **St John's Day** (24 June).

MUSIC AND NIGHTLIFE

Nightlife is focused on **Coimbra** and **Figueira da Foz**, where there's also a **film festival** in September. A good nightclub is **Bergantim** (Rua Dr Lopes Guimarães 28, Figueira da Foz). In Coimbra, **A Capella** (Rua Corpo de Deus, www.acapella.com.pt), housed in a converted 14th-century chapel, is the best place for local *fado* (➤ 20–21). **Boémia** (Rua do Cabido 4–8) is a beautiful venue for jazz. **Via Latina** (Rua Almeida Garrett 1) is a lively disco.

The Alentejo

Getting Your Bearings

The Alentejo ("Beyond the Tagus") is a sun-baked plain that stretches across southern Portugal, occupying land between the River Tagus and the Algarve. This is both the largest and the most sparsely inhabited region of Portugal, where just 12 per cent of the population are scattered across a third of the country in isolated hamlets and small market towns. It is a proud region whose people share a strong sense of identity, expressed through their music, rural traditions and hearty country cooking.

Looking down on the walled hilltop village of Monsaraz

The landscape of the Alentejo is almost entirely man-made and agricultural. The Romans established vast feudal estates (*latifúndios*) to grow olives, vines and wheat, many of which survived right up to the 1974 revolution. Even today, when many of these estates have become co-operatives, the whitewashed *monte* (farmhouse) surrounded by vineyards is still a familiar sight. Wine and wheat are still important products, but the region is best known for its cork oaks, which provide more than half of the world's cork, used in everything from aircraft insulation to bottle stops.

Alongside the wide open spaces and strong elemental colours of the landscape, the region has also made some important gourmet contributions to Portugal. The most famous of these is the Alentejo black pig.

Upper Alentejo in particular has several interesting sights, from the Renaissance city of Évora to the marble towns of Estremoz and Vila Viçosa, and the hilltop villages of Monsaraz and Marvão. The Moorish history of the region is more evident in Lower Alentejo, in towns like Mértola and Serpa, with their low, whitewashed, blue-trimmed houses.

Page 127: Whitewashed houses and cobbled streets in Marvão

★ Don't Miss
1 Évora ➤ 132
2 Vila Viçosa ➤ 136
3 Marvão ➤ 138

At Your Leisure
4 Estremoz ➤ 140
5 Elvas ➤ 140
6 Monsaraz ➤ 141
7 Beja ➤ 142
8 Mértola ➤ 142

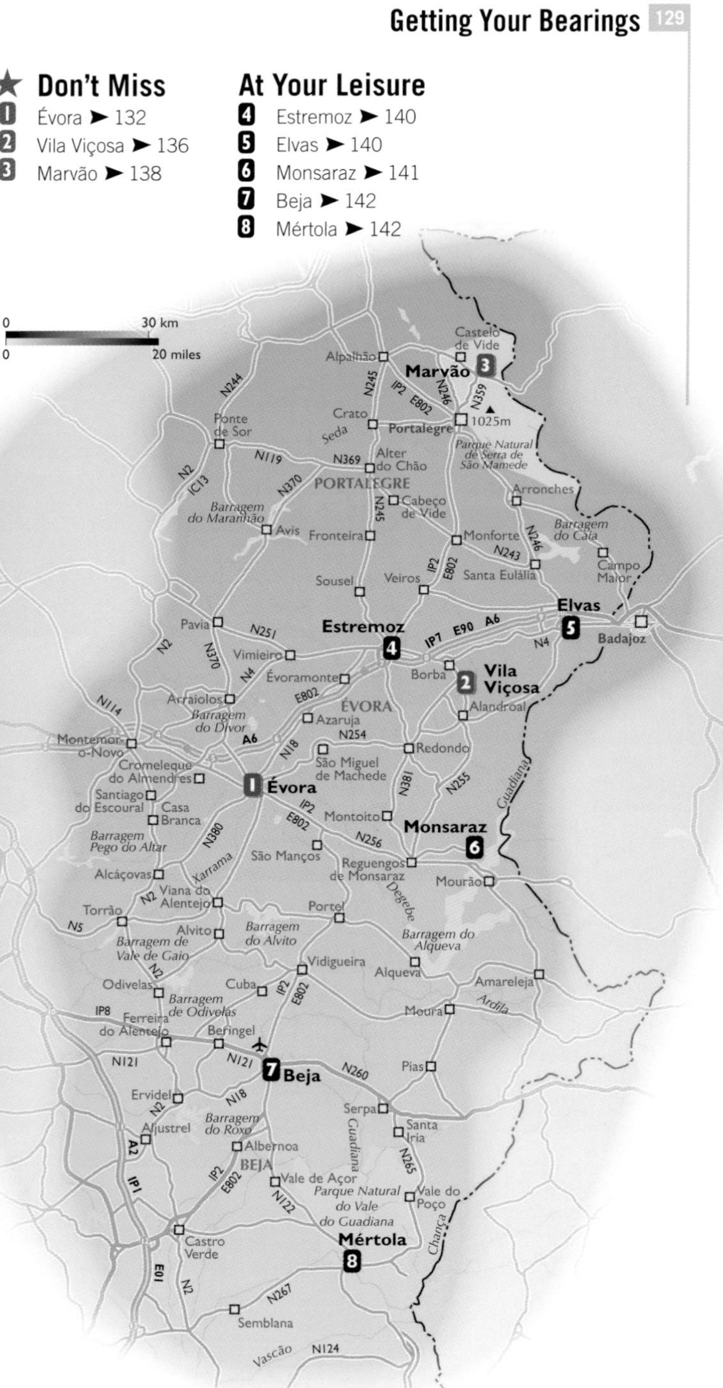

In Two Days

If you're not quite sure where to begin your travels, this itinerary recommends a practical and enjoyable two days out and about in the Alentejo, taking in some of the best places to see using the Getting your Bearings map on the previous page. For more information see the main entries.

Day 1

Morning

Walk around the walled city of 1 **Évora** (right; ➤ 132–135). Climb to the Roman temple, then visit the cathedral, museum and Capela dos Ossos (Chapel of Bones) before lunch at one of the cafés on Praça do Giraldo.

Afternoon

Leave Évora on the N18 in the direction of 7 **Beja** (➤ 142). When the road to Beja turns right, keep ahead on the N256 to Reguengos de Monsaraz. Turn left here, following signs to Monsaraz across a landscape of vineyards and olive groves. Just beyond the pottery-producing village of São Pedro de Corval, look out for Rocha dos Namorados (Lovers' Rock), a prehistoric *menhir* (stone) standing beside the road. Continue to 6 **Monsaraz** (➤ 141–142), visible on its hill across the plain.

Evening

Spend the night in quiet Monsaraz. Admire superb views from its 13th-century castle walls over the plains and the new **Alqueva Dam** (➤ 141). Book ahead for a room at **Casa Pinto** (➤ 144).

Day 2

Morning

Retrace your way to Reguengos de Monsaraz and follow signs north to Alandroal and the regal town of Vila Viçosa on the N255. Arriving in 2 **Vila Viçosa** (right, ➤ 136–137), park outside the old royal palace, once home to the Dukes of Bragança, and take a guided tour. Then wander up to the castle and down to the town centre for lunch beside the orange trees and marble fountain on Praça da República.

Afternoon

The road from Vila Viçosa to Borba leads past the quarries that are the source of the local marble. Turn right in Borba to reach the N4, passing more quarries on your way to 4 **Estremoz** (➤ 140). Drive up to the castle at the top of the town for a drink at the **Pousada da Rainha Santa Isabel** (➤ 144) and visit the municipal museum to admire the pottery. Leave Estremoz on the IP2, go north to Portalegre, bypass Portalegre and turn right towards 3 **Marvão** (➤ 138–139), whose hilltop castle (below) dominates the view as you approach. Leave your car outside the village and walk up to the castle in time to enjoy the sunset walk around its walls.

Evening

Ask at the tourist office (➤ 139) about rooms in private houses in Marvão, or stay the night at the **Pousada Santa Maria** (➤ 143) and celebrate your arrival with a hearty Alentejan meal of roast lamb or goat.

❶ Évora

With its Moorish alleys, shady squares, fountains and Renaissance mansions, the largest city in the Alentejo makes a good place for a stroll. Founded by the Romans, strengthened by the Moors and recovered from them for Afonso Henriques (➤ 80) by Geraldo Sempavor (Gerald the Fearless), Évora rose to prominence in the 15th and 16th centuries as a centre of arts and learning – a reputation that survives to this day.

The Romans built their walled city of *Ebora Cerealis* high on a hill above the Alentejo plain. At the summit of the town, they erected the temple of Diana, now the **Templo Romano** and the best-preserved Roman monument in Portugal.

Used as a slaughterhouse during the 19th century, the granite columns and marble capitals of this second-century AD temple have only recently been restored. Floodlit at night, it makes a spectacular sight.

Templo Romano illuminated at night

Carved apostles on the door of the cathedral

Convento dos Lóios

All the main sights are within the walled town, a UNESCO World Heritage Site since 1986. Directly behind the temple, the **Convento dos Lóios** is a 15th-century monastery that has been converted into an appealing *pousada* (➤ 143), where you dine in the cloisters and sleep in the monks' cells. Even if you're not staying, it's worth going in to admire the Gothic cloisters and the Manueline (➤ 14) chapter-house door.

The attached church, **Igreja dos Lóios**, was the private chapel of the dukes of Cadaval, who are buried beneath marble tombstones. The nave is lined with floor-to-ceiling *azulejos* (➤ 18–19) depicting the life of a former patriarch of Venice. You can peek through a pair of grilles in the floor to see a medieval cistern and an ossuary of human bones.

The Cathedral

The **sé** (cathedral), completed around 1250, has a fortress-like Romanesque appearance similar to the one at Coimbra (➤ 108). A Gothic portal, carved with figures of the apostles, stands between two strangely unmatched towers. Inside, there is marble everywhere, in the lectern, pulpit and high altar. The entry to the **Museu de Arte Sacra** also gives access to the Coro Alto, where the carved oak choir stalls feature scenes of rural life, such as grape-picking and pig-sticking (hunting wild boars with spears), and the **Gothic cloister**, where you can climb onto the roof for views over Évora and a close-up look at the cathedral lantern and towers. In the museum, there is an extraordinary 13th-century figure of the Virgin, whose innards open up to reveal biblical scenes.

Museu de Évora

The **Museu de Évora** is housed in the former archbishop's palace. It contains Roman bronzes and funerary inscriptions, medieval and Renaissance sculpture and 17th-century *azulejos* from Lisbon.

The Capela dos Ossos – not for the squeamish

Among the paintings on the first floor, look for *Holy Virgin with Child* by Álvaro Pires de Évora, painted around 1410. Pires is the earliest identified Portuguese artist, and although a number of his paintings are on show in Pisa and Florence, this is the first to be permanently exhibited in Portugal.

Also here is a 16th-century Flemish polyptych of 13 panels depicting the *Life of the Virgin*, which was previously the cathedral altarpiece. The museum reopened in June 2009, with enlargements carried out to the space for permanent exhibitions, as well as work on the building itself.

The Town

A staircase beside the cathedral leads down towards **Largo da Porta de Moura**, one of Évora's most attractive squares, with a Renaissance fountain and 16th-century houses with Manueline-Moorish arcades. Alternatively, take Rua 5 de Outubro (lined with souvenir and craft shops), opposite the cathedral, to reach **Praça do Giraldo**, a handsome square with arcades, a marble fountain and café terraces. During the Inquisition, this was an execution ground, but today it is a lively square that is often the scene of book fairs, music concerts or open-air theatre.

A short distance away, the Gothic-Manueline **Igreja de São Francisco** is home to one of Portugal's most macabre sights. To the right of the facade, with its unusual portico of pointed, rounded and horseshoe arches, a separate entrance leads to the cloister and the **Capela dos Ossos** (Chapel of Bones), whose walls and columns are covered with the skulls, femurs, tibias and other bones of 5,000 monks. Grinning skulls stare down from the ceiling and a grisly corpse hangs on one wall.

For something completely different, take a walk across the square to the **Jardim Público**, and the remains of a 16th-century Moorish-style palace.

A 10-minute drive west of Évora is the enigmatic **Cromlech** of the **Alimendres** megalithic site, which has some of the oldest prehistoric remains in Europe. The elliptical site consists of 95 granite menhirs (upright standing stones), and is said to date back to 3000 or 4000BC.

TAKING A BREAK

There are **outdoor cafés** on Praça do Giraldo, in the Jardim Público and the gardens by the Templo Romano. If you want a more substantial meal, there's the excellent **Taberna Tipica Quarta Feira** (➤ 145), popular with tourists, or **O Fialho** (➤ 144–145), famous for its traditional dishes.

---

201 D2 Praça do Giraldo; tel: 266 777 071; www2.cm-evora.pt/guiaturistico

Igreja dos Lóios
Largo do Conde de Vila Flor 266 704 714 Tue–Sun 10–12:30, 2–5 Moderate

Sé
Largo Marquês de Marialva 266 759 330 Jul to mid-Sep Tue–Sun 9–5; mid-Sep–May 9–12:30, 2–5 Museum: inexpensive

Museu de Évora
Largo do Conde de Vila Flor 266 702 604; http://museudevora.imc-ip.pt Tue 2:30–6, Wed–Sun 10–6

Igreja da São Francisco/Capela dos Ossos
Praça 1 de Maio 266 704 521 Daily 9–12:30, 2:30–5:30 Inexpensive

ÉVORA: INSIDE INFO

Top tips Évora's medieval appearance does not lend itself to modern transport. If you are driving, it is best to **park on the outskirts** and walk in.

- There are a number of well-signposted Ruta dos Vinhos starting from Évora. These are co-ordinated by a central office (Praça Joaquim António de Aguiar 20–21, Mon–Sat 9–1, 2–6, tel: 266 746 609).

Hidden gem A steep hill behind the cathedral and Museu de Évora leads to the **old Jesuit university**, founded by Cardinal Henrique, the future king, in 1559. The university was closed down in 1759 by the Marquês de Pombal, but is now open, so you can wander around its beautiful tiled courtyard.

In more depth Take a walk through the old Moorish quarter, **Mouraria**, with its whitewashed houses and lamplit, cobbled streets. From beneath the gardens in front of the Roman temple, Rua dos Fontes drops steeply through Mouraria to Largo do Avis, beside the only remaining medieval gateway to the walled town. From the square of Largo do Chão das Covas, Rua do Cano follows the course of the old aqueduct, parts of which can still be seen outside the walls.

2 Vila Viçosa

The power and wealth of the Portuguese kings is on display in Vila Viçosa, the seat of Portugal's last ruling dynasty, the dukes of Bragança. Built of marble, this is a prosperous town whose shining "white gold" can be seen everywhere.

Begin at **Terreiro do Paço**, the vast square in front of the Paço Ducal. A statue of João IV on horseback stands at the centre. The palace, fronted with marble, dominates the square. To one side is the royal chapel; to the other, Convento das Chagas, the mausoleum of the duchesses of Bragança, now a *pousada* (➤ 15–16). Across the square is the Mosterio dos Agostinhos, where the dukes are buried.

The **Paço Ducal** can only be visited on a guided tour, with further charges to see the armoury, treasury, Chinese porcelain and Museu dos Coches (Coach Museum). Most interesting are the private apartments of Dom Carlos (Portugal's penultimate king) and Dona Amelia, abandoned on the day of Carlos' assassination in 1908, with the table still set for dinner, family portraits and Dona Amelia's sketches on the walls. A large park outside the palace is home to deer and wild boar.

The **Museu dos Coches**, in the Royal Stables, contains beautifully maintained coaches, landaus and state carriages from the 18th–20th centuries. This is an annex to the popular coach museum in Lisbon, and exhibitions are sometimes exchanged between the two sites.

From the Terreiro do Paço, the **Avenida dos Duques de Bragança** leads towards the old walled town, dominated by a 13th-century *castelo*. This castle was the original residence

A statue of Dom João IV, the first of Bragança's kings, stands before the Paço Ducal

THE DUKES OF BRAGANÇA

Although the town was given a royal charter as early as 1270, it was the dukes of Bragança who made Vila Viçosa. The title of Bragança was created in 1442 for an illegitimate son of João I of Avis; the second duke, Dom Fernando, moved his court to Vila Viçosa, and the fourth duke, Dom Jaime, began the building of the Paço Ducal (Ducal Palace) in 1501. Vila Viçosa became the finest address in Portugal, with banquets, balls and bullfights held in the palace for the leading families of the day. All that changed in 1640 when the eighth duke, João IV, reluctantly accepted the throne, ending 60 years of Spanish rule. The Braganças ruled Portugal until the fall of the monarchy in 1910 and continued to live in the palace, though many of its treasures were taken to Lisbon and the royal palaces at Mafra (➤ 66) and Sintra (➤ 60–61).

of the dukes of Bragança (➤ left) and has a small archaeological museum, with a stash of Roman finds. It's well worth visiting to get a peek behind the scenes of the castle's chambers and tunnels.

TAKING A BREAK

Café Restauração, Praça da República, serves snacks.

201 E2 Praça da República; tel: 68 881 101; www.cm-vilavicosa.pt

Paço Ducal

Terreiro do Paço 268 980 659; http://en.museudoscoches.pt
Tue–Fri 10–1, 2:30–6, Sat–Sun 9:30–1, 2:30–6 (5 in winter). Last admission one hour before closing
Moderate (expensive with additional charges)

The main street is overlooked by the 13th-century castle

VILA VIÇOSA: INSIDE INFO

Top tip Accommodation in Vila Viçosa is not plentiful, although the tourist office should be able to help you find somewhere.

Hidden gem What looks like a pair of red garage doors at the end of a row of houses on Avenida dos Duques de Bragança opens up to reveal a **Passo**, one of a series of 16th-century Stations of the Cross remodelled in the 18th century with a marble portal and *azulejo* (➤ 18–19) tiles depicting scenes from the life of Christ.

3 Marvão

The most spectacular of all Portugal's hilltop villages perches like an eagle's nest on a rocky ridge 862m (2,827ft) up in the Serra de São Mamede. The castle and medieval walls seem to grow out of the rock, and it is clear that this must have been a near-impregnable fortress. During the 16th century, Marvão had a population of more than 1,400, but today fewer than 200 people live here.

View from the castle of the typical white dwellings of the medieval village

The Romans and then the Moors came here – the village takes its name from Ibn Maruán, the 9th-century Islamic Lord of Coimbra (Marvão comes from Maruán). After the Christian conquest, Dom Dinis, King of Portugal (1279–1325), fortified the castle here. It was to become one of a long chain of defensive outposts protecting the border with Spain.

Unless you are staying the night, it is best to park outside the village and enter on foot through the main gate, **Porta de Rodão**. From Praça do Pelourinho, with its 16th-century pillory, Rua do Espírito Santo, known for its whitewashed houses with wrought-iron balconies, leads into Rua do Castelo, which leads to the castle.

Rua do Castelo – a Living Museum

The Gothic and Renaissance architecture of Rua do Castelo has been preserved untouched during the centuries of Marvão's decline and is only now being rediscovered and restored. You can climb onto the walls, with their battlements, turrets and towers, and make a complete circuit, but it is easier to walk up to the castle along the village streets. The **castle**, originally dating from the 13th century but rebuilt almost from scratch in the 17th century, is magnificent. Held

Marvão was one of a chain of fortified towns and villages along the Portuguese border with Spain

high on a rocky crag, it is the town's most visible icon. It was built high and mighty to defend against Spanish invaders. Two fortified gates lead to a courtyard where you can climb onto the parapet for **views over the village**. Breaching a second line of defence, you come to another courtyard, which contains the armoury (a military museum) and the castle keep. The views are impressive: to the north are the snow-capped peaks of the Serra da Estrela (➤ 119–120); to the south, the mountains of the Serra de São Mamede; to the west, the Alentejo countryside; to the east, Spain.

Outside the castle walls, the **Museu Municipal**, in the 13th-century **church of Santa Maria**, displays folk costumes, religious art and Roman and medieval archaeological finds.

TAKING A BREAK

Casa do Povo in Rua de Cima, has a pretty terrace and offers well-prepared, filling Alentejan cuisine (tel: 245 993 160).

201 E4 **Largo de Santa Maria; tel: 245 909 131; www.cm-marvao.pt**

Museu Municipal
Largo de Santa Maria **245 909 132** **Daily 9:30–12:30, 2–5:30**
Inexpensive

MARVÃO: INSIDE INFO

Top tips Try to stay overnight to watch the **sunset** from the castle walls and enjoy the evening peace of the village after the day-trippers have left.

- As well as the **Pousada Santa Maria** (➤ 143), there are several **private houses** with rooms to let – ask at the tourist office.
- **Chestnut trees** thrive in this area, and a festival is held in November that sees the village come alive with music, wine and chestnut roasting.

Hidden gem Walk down the steps inside the castle entrance to see a **monumental cistern** that is capable of storing six months' water.

In more depth The surrounding **Serra de São Mamede** is a natural park with Roman and neolithic remains and wildlife including griffon vultures, red deer and Europe's largest colony of bats. Also here is the spa town of **Castelo de Vide**, with an attractive old Jewish quarter, a golf course and its own spring.

At Your Leisure

The whitewashed, red-roofed buildings of Elvas within its star-shaped fortifications

4 Estremoz

The largest of the Alentejo "marble" towns seems to have an extra sheen of white as marble from the local quarries is used as an everyday building material. Life here centres on the Rossio Marquês de Pombal, a huge square where one of Portugal's biggest markets is held on Saturdays, selling local goodies like ewe's cheese, olive oil and *chouriço* (salami).

Although now one of the most famous *pousadas* in Portugal (➤ 144), you can also visit parts of the 13th-century **castle** built by Dom Dinis for his future wife, Isabel of Aragón. As queen, Isabel became known for her devotion to the poor and she was sainted after her death. Her story is told in *azulejos* (➤ 18–19) in the Capela da Rainha Santa Isabel, including that of the Miracle of the Roses. Her husband disapproved of her giving alms, so she hid bread in the folds of her skirt where he would not see it. When he became suspicious and challenged her, she opened her skirt and the bread had miraculously turned into roses. A marble statue of the saint stands on the castle terrace, from where there are views to Évoramonte.

The **Museu Municipal** opposite features folk art in marble, cork and oak, and *bonecos* (terracotta figurines for which Estremoz is famous).

201 E2 · Rossio Marquês de Pombal; tel: 268 339 227

THREE OF THE BEST... ALENTEJAN CUISINE

- *Ensopado de borrego* – lamb stew served on slices of bread.
- *Porco à alentejana* – Alentejo pork stewed with clams.
- *Sopa alentejana* – soup with bread, garlic, coriander and poached egg.

Museu Municipal

Largo Dom Dinis · 268 333 608
Tue–Sun 9–12:30, 2–5:30 (May–Sep to 6:30)
Inexpensive

5 Elvas

Besides being famous for its Ameixa da Elvas greengage plums, Elvas is a heavily fortified frontier town, which sits just 12km (7.4 miles) from Portugal's border with Spain and 15km (9.3 miles) from the Spanish citadel at Badajoz. Captured by Afonso Henriques in 1166, retaken by the Moors, and finally seized by Christian forces in 1226, Elvas has been besieged many times but only once been taken by Spanish troops.

The star-shaped fortifications that surround the town, designed by the French military engineer, Vauban, date largely from the 17th century. They are supplemented by two fortresses, one of which, **Forte de Santa Luzia**, can sometimes be visited (check at the tourist office).

The streets of the old town radiate from Praça da República. At one end stands the **Igreja de Nossa Senhora da Assuncão**, which had cathedral status until 1882, when the town lost its bishopric. The fortified church dates back to the 16th century and ornate Manueline touches (➤ 14) can be seen on the south portal, though much of its design is a potpourri of 17th- and 18th-century styles.

Behind the church, Largo de Santa Clara is an attractive triangular "square" with a Manueline marble pillory, still with its original iron hooks to which prisoners were tied.

On one side, the **Igreja de Nossa Senhora da Consolacão** looks plain but the interior is extraordinary, an octagonal chapel with painted marble columns and blue-and-yellow *azulejos* lining the walls. Its layout was inspired by a Knights Templar church that once stood close by.

Just outside of the town, there is a large reservoir, Barragem da Caia, where you can enjoy fishing and swimming in attractive surroundings.

201 F2 Praça da República; tel: 268 622 236

BEST FOR KIDS

- **Capela dos Ossos**, Évora (for older children, ➤ 134): Grisly corpses and grinning skulls.
- **The castle at Marvão** (➤ 138–139): Fabulous views across the Serra da Estrela and magnificent fortifications.
- Europe's largest manmade reservoir at **Alqueva** has created a beach culture in lower Alentejo. From Estrela, you can organise boat trips, fishing, sailing and swimming (www.alqueva.com).

Igreja de Nossa Senhora da Consolacão

Largo de Santa Clara Tue–Sun 9–12:30, 2–5:30

6 Monsaraz

Monsaraz would be just another attractive hilltop village were it not for

The peaceful countryside around the attractive village of Monsaraz

You can climb the 40m (131ft) high walls of the castle keep at Beja

the famously fantastic views enjoyed by hordes of day trippers, and the plaques on the Porta de Vila recalling visits by Portuguese presidents Soares and Sampaio.

There are two parallel streets – Rua Direita, with a tourist office, the parish church, Igreja Matriz, and 16th-century houses, and Rua de Santiago, which has a more lived-in feel, with shops, restaurants and crafts. Rua Direita leads to the 13th-century **castle**, once a Knights Templar fortress. The ramparts have unparalleled views over the village and the Alentejo countryside. The courtyard is sometimes the bullring.

201 E2 Largo Dom Nuno Alvares Pereira; tel: 266 557 136

7 Beja

The capital of Lower Alentejo is a pleasing town of whitewashed houses, founded by Julius Caesar as *Pax Julia* to commemorate a peace *(pax)* treaty between the Romans and the Lusitani tribe. Beja Airport, opened in April 2011, has finally put this beautiful Portuguese city on the tourist map. The most striking monument is the 13th-century **castelo** (castle); you can climb the keep for views over the Alentejo wheatlands.

Beja is best known as the home of Mariana Alcoforado, the nun whose (possibly fictional) love letters to a French cavalry officer were published as *Lettres Portugaises* in France in 1669. The convent where she lived, Nossa Senhora da Conceicão, is now the **Museu Regional**, with many interesting prehistoric and Roman finds.

Of more interest are the convent buildings, especially the baroque chapel, tiled cloisters and 16th-century Hispano-Arab *azulejos* (➤ 18–19) in the chapter house.

Another convent is now the Pousada de São Francisco (➤ 144).

201 D1 Rua Capitão João Francisco de Sousa; tel: 284 311 913

Castelo

Largo do Lidador 284 311 912 Summer Tue–Sun 10–1, 2–6; winter, Tue–Sun 9–12, 1–4 Inexpensive; free Sun

Museu Regional

Largo da Conceicão 284 323 351; www.museuregionaldebeja.net Tue–Sun 9:30–12:30, 2–5:15 Inexpensive; free Sun

8 Mértola

This pretty little walled town at the confluence of the Guadiana and Oeiras rivers has a long history as a trading port at the highest navigable point on the Guadiana.

These days, Mértola promotes itself as a *vila museu* (museum town), with small museums around the town devoted to its Roman, Islamic and Portuguese history. You can visit all of them on one ticket (admission moderate), including the castle keep for views over the rooftops. Don't miss the parish church, converted from a mosque at the end of the 12th century, whose *mihrab* (niche facing east to Mecca) is visible behind the altar and the arches and columns retain a strong Islamic feel.

202 D2 Rua da Igreja 1; tel: 286 610 109; www.cm-mertola.pt Daily 9–12:30, 2–5:30 (Jul–Sep to 6pm) Museums: moderate

Where to... Stay

Prices

Expect to pay for a double room per night in high season:
€ under €60 **€€** €60–€120 **€€€** €121–€180 **€€€€** over €180

ÉVORA

Residencial Riviera €€

Well located in the centre of town, near to the cathedral square, this modern and well-priced hotel is a good base for exploring the town. The interior and public areas are functional rather than luxurious, but the 21 bedrooms are all a good size and well appointed to ensure a comfortable stay. There is an attractive dining room where a large Alentejo breakfast is served by the friendly staff.

201 D2 Rua 5 do Outubro 47–49 266 737 210; www.riviera-evora.com

Pousada dos Lóios €€€–€€€€

The fabulous 15th-century monastery of the Lóios has an excellent restaurant in the ornate cloisters, and is one of the country's leading *pousadas* (➤ 15–16, 35). The majestic rooms are furnished with antiques, in particular the "presidential" suite, which has Indo-Portuguese furniture. There is also a good-sized swimming pool. This is the perfect choice if you want to experience staying in an authentic *pousada* while enjoying plenty of modern comforts.

201 D2 Largo Conde de Vila-Flor 266 730 070; www.pousadas.pt

Convento do Espinheiro €€–€€€

Housed in a former convent, this atmospheric hotel has an excellent restaurant (open to non-residents also), and wonderful gardens with a large heated pool and tennis court. The hotel is spacious and luxurious, with whitewashed walls and good-sized, attractively furnished rooms, particularly in the new wing. The restoration work has been done with great care, and has retained enough to remind you of the former purpose of the building.

201 D2 Quinta Convento Espinheiro 266 788 200; www.conventodoespinheiro.com

VILA VIÇOSA

Casa di Colégio Velho €€–€€€

Tucked down a cobbled lane, this wonderfully B&B occupies a 16th-century mansion, commanding terrific views over landscaped gardens and the old town. The light, high-ceilinged rooms are scattered with art and antiques, some have wrought-iron bedsteads. All rooms have flat-screen TVs and marble bathrooms. Take time to relax by the pool and on the *azulejo*-tiled benches in the garden. The generous breakfasts are prepared with regional produce.

201 E2 Rua Dr Couto Jardim 34 268 889 430; www.casadocolegiovelho.com

MARVÃO

Pousada Santa Maria €€–€€€

Cool in summer and warm in the winter, like the other whitewashed houses in this pretty hilltop village, this well-appointed *pousada* is a delight inside and out. The large spacious rooms and simple dining room look across the beautiful olive trees and cork oaks of the Alentejo. Enjoy the views while sampling local specialities, including excellent cheeses and well-chosen wines.

201 E4 Rua 24 de Janeiro 7 245 993 201; www.pousadas.pt

ESTREMOZ

Pousada da Rainha Santa Isabel €€€

Generally regarded as the most prestigious *pousada*, this is housed in an austere-looking medieval castle. Four-poster beds, tapestries fit for a museum, entire walls of *azulejos* (➤ 18–19) and the long vaulted refectory earn it the epithet of "grandiose". When you are not exploring the local sights, you can relax by the swimming pool and dine on Alentejo specialities accompanied by fine wines from the extensive cellar.

201 E2 ✉ Castelo de Estremoz, Largo Dom Diniz ☎ 268 332 075; www.pousadas.pt

MONSARAZ

Casa Pinto €€

This whitewashed guesthouse combines Portuguese and oriental elements with flair. Heavy wood beams, antiques and hardwood floors blend seamlessly with filigree lanterns and mosaic-tiled sinks in rooms with names like Goa and Mombassa. The Dili room is the fairest of all, complete with four-poster bed. Enjoy breakfast on the floral patio and sip wine as the sun sets over the Alentejo countryside on the panoramic roof terrace.

201 E2 ✉ Praça D Nuno Álvares Pereira 10 ☎ 266 557 076; www.casapinto.net

BEJA

Pousada de São Francisco €€€

The cells of this ancient Franciscan monastery are now comfortable rooms. Don't be put off by the huge entrance hall and mammoth staircase – the guest areas are intimate and cheery. A cool 13th-century chapel in the complex has been carefully restored, and there is a pool in the grounds – much needed in a city where temperatures can top 40°C (104°F).

201 D1 ✉ Largo Dom Nuno Álvares Pereira ☎ 284 313 580; www.pousadas.pt

Where to... Eat and Drink

Prices

Expect to pay per person for a three-course meal, excluding drinks and tips:

€ under €12 **€€** €12–€24 **€€€** €25–€36 **€€€€** over €36

ÉVORA

Cozinha de Santo Humberto €€€

Évora probably has more reliably excellent restaurants than any other city outside Lisbon and this is one of them. When you go into the pristine white cellar (used to store wine), you'll notice a sideboard loaded with delicious starters and desserts. Another trademark of the restaurant is the row of blackened kettles hanging from the ceiling. In season, go for the game – the wild boar ragout is exceptional – or try *chispe assado* (roast pork).

201 D2 ✉ Rua da Moeda 39 ☎ 266 704 251 🕒 Fri–Wed 12–3, 7–10. Closed third week in Nov

O Fialho €€€–€€€€

Justly famous – gourmets even come especially from Lisbon to eat here – O Fialho is surprisingly simple to look at and calls itself a *cervejaria* (beer house, ➤ 37). A few hunting trophies and simple *azulejos* are the only ornaments. This is not a place to turn down the *acepipes* (➤ 38), even though the starters are fabulous. What sets the food apart is the use of herbs and spices, for example in the *bacalhau* (salt cod, ➤ 29, 37) *carpaccio*, sprinkled liberally with capers. *Lombos de javali* (medallions of wild boar) are set off with a hint of rosemary. Attentive service, outstanding wines and home-made liqueurs complete this unexpected, unpretentious experience.

201 D2 Travessa das Mascarenhas 16, near Praça Joaquim António de Aguiar 266 703 079; www.restaurantefialho.com Tue–Sun 12–12. Closed 1–21 Sep

Taberna Tipica Quarta Feira €€

Well located in the town centre, this attractive restaurant is used to serving hungry tourists but still manages to keep the emphasis on good fresh food and friendly service. The menu offers traditional Portuguese dishes based on ingredients selected from the market each day – as a result the choice isn't extensive and varies day-to-day, but you can't get fresher and more seasonal than that.

201 D2 Rua do Inverno 18 266 707 530 Daily 11–11

VILA VIÇOSA

Taverna dos Conjurados €€–€€€

Classic interior with exposed stone wall and whitewashed walls, this is a deceptively simple restaurant, which serves well-cooked, authentic cuisine. All the food is very fresh and local, and is well regarded by local residents. Expect to sit at the classic wooden tables and enjoy excellent food and hearty portions.

201 E2 Largo 25 de Abril 268 989 530 12–2:30, 7:30–11

ESTREMOZ

Adega Típica do Isaías €€

Huge, age-old amphorae tell you this has long been a wine cellar, and jugs of red are plonked onto every table. This wonderfully down-to-earth place attracts locals from every walk of life interested only in the delicious food, from *pimentos assados* (roast red peppers) to *bolo de mel* (honey cake), via *borrego no forno* (roast lamb) or *estufado de lebre* (hare stew). Meat and fish are barbecued out on the street.

201 E2 Rua do Almeida 21 268 322 318 Mon–Sat 12–2, 7–10:30. Closed 2nd and 3rd weeks in Aug

ELVAS

A Coluna €–€€

This is a discreet but popular restaurant with a whitewashed interior and white table linen. The menu is simple, and everyone swears by the *cabrito* (goat) and *bacalhau* (salt cod, ➤ 29, 37) dishes and the *cataplana* (fish stew). It's slightly hidden away from the central square, but soon fills up with locals, so get there early.

201 F2 Rua do Cabrito 11 268 623 728 Wed–Mon 12–3, 7–10

MONSARAZ

O Alcaide €€

Breathtaking views across the open plains from the picture window are a wonderful backdrop for simple home cooking. *Migas de pao con carne de porco* (pork with croutons) and *borrego* (roast lamb) are just two of the regional specialities on offer here. Recommended for an authentic dining experience.

201 E2 Rua de Santiago 18 266 557 168 Fri–Wed 12–3, 7–9. Closed 1–15 Jul and Oct

BEJA

Café Luiz da Rocha €–€€

This bustling café-bar is not a particularly beautiful place, but if you linger long enough over your coffee, you'll see an interesting cross section of the city as people pop in for a coffee or beer and a chat. Apart from the fascinating people-watching, the *queijadas* (cheese-filled cakes) are excellent.

201 D1 Rua Capitão João Francisco de Sousa 63 284 323 179; www.luizdarocha.com Dining room: daily 12–3:30, 7–10. Café: daily 8–11. Both closed Sun Jul–Sep fé

Where to... Shop

MARKETS

Visit the market in **Évora**, every second Tuesday morning. On Saturdays and Sundays, you can bargain for everything from second-hand books to antiques, bric-a-brac to art, on **Praça Primeiro de Maio**.

Estremoz has a market every Saturday on the Rossio – the cheeses are superb. Earthenware is a speciality, especially the oddly shaped *moringues* (water jars).

CRAFTS

For carpets, visit **Arraiolos**, north of Évora, where fine, local hand-knotted rugs are sold at workshops at Ilhas; or at several shops on Rua 5 Outubro, where prices are far lower than in Lisbon.

Flôr da Rosa, west of Portalegre, is renowned for its pottery, which is sold at traditional *olarias* (potteries) near the convent.

Fine crafts are sold at **Milflores** (Rua Dr Matos Magalhães 1, Marvão). Unusual goods in wood, wicker and cork are crafted by **Joaquim Canoas Vieira** (Largo de Nossa Senhora do Passo, Barbacena, near Elvas, tel: 268 662 151).

FOOD AND DRINK

This is bread country; the grain is often used as a key ingredient in soups, too. Also buy some Alentejo charcuterie. Look for the *Denominação de Origem Protegida* DOP status to be sure of quality.

Picnic provisions can be bought at Évora's covered market.

Where to... Be Entertained

FESTIVALS

The last third of June is Évora's **Feira de São João**, which combines music and crafts with food. There is also a **film festival** FIKE (www.fikeonline.net) in late October.

May is festival month for **Beja** and bullfights are held. In **Elvas**, the Festa de São Mateus features a large procession and takes place at the end of is September.

Monsaraz holds a *vacada* ("bloodless" bullfight) on the second weekend of September. During the second week of July, there's a crafts and folk festival.

SPORT AND OUTDOOR PURSUITS

The Atlantic beaches on the west coast are some of the most dramatic in the country – head for **Zambujeira** and **Odeceixe**.

One of the best places for **horse-riding** is run by **Miguel Palha** at Rua da República, Chança, near Alter do Chão.

The 18-hole **golf** course at Marvão, in the lee of the castle, has a spectacular location – **Ammaia**, Quinta do Prado, San Salvador da Aramenha 7330-330 (tel: 245 993 755, www.portugalgolf.pt).

NIGHTLIFE

Évora is about the only town in the region with any nightlife. ***Títeres*** (puppet shows) at the theatre on Praça Aguiar are worth seeing. Or check out the **Bar Casa do Vinho** (Praça 1 de Maio) or **Desassossego Bar** (Travessa do Janeiro).

The Algarve

Getting Your Bearings

Sandy beaches and sunny skies. Whitewashed villas with geraniums around the door. Fishing boats and the scent of freshly grilled sardines. These are the classic images of Portugal, and they are also the images of the Algarve.

For many people, the Algarve *is* Portugal, yet this small region at the southwest corner of Europe is, in fact, the least typical of all. The climate is more Mediterranean than Atlantic, the landscape more North African than Portuguese. This was *al-gharb*, the western outpost of Moorish Spain, which held off the Christian Reconquest for a century after the fall of Lisbon. Reminders of the Arab presence are everywhere, from latticed chimneys to the almond trees that carpet the ground with a "snowfall" of white blossom in January.

The Algarve shoreline is neatly divided in two by the provincial capital, Faro. East of here is the *sotavento* (leeward) coast, sheltered by the barrier islands and lagoons of the Ria Formosa. To the west, the *barlavento* (windward) coast is battered by the Atlantic, producing the Algarve's typical rock formations of sandstacks, grottoes, cliffs and coves. Henry the Navigator had his school at Sagres, and towns like Tavira and Lagos played a key role in the *descobrimentos* (discoveries, ➤ 12–13).

Later, the region was levelled by the 1755 earthquake, its epicentre near Lagos. But the greatest influence has been mass tourism, bringing 10 million annual visitors. High-rise resorts, golf courses and waterparks have mushroomed from Faro to Lagos, and development shows no sign of ending. To escape it, head inland to the villages of the Barrocal and the cool mountains of Monchique, or spend some time in the charming towns of Tavira, Silves and Lagos.

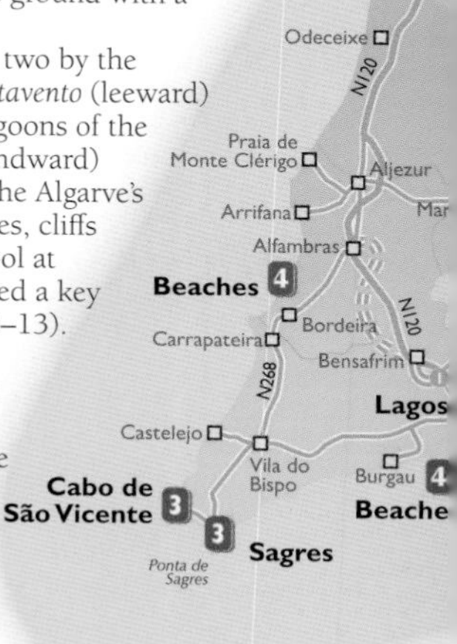

Page 147: The beach at Praia de Marinha

Left: Praia de Rocha
Right: Armaçao de Pera

★ Don't Miss

1. Tavira ➤ 152
2. Serra de Monchique ➤ 154
3. Sagres and Cabo de São Vicente ➤ 156
4. Algarve Beaches ➤ 159

At Your Leisure

5. Alcoutim ➤ 162
6. Parque Natural da Ria Formosa ➤ 162
7. Faro ➤ 162
8. Estói ➤ 163
9. Loulé ➤ 163
10. Alte ➤ 164
11. Albufeira ➤ 164
12. Silves ➤ 164
13. Lagos ➤ 165

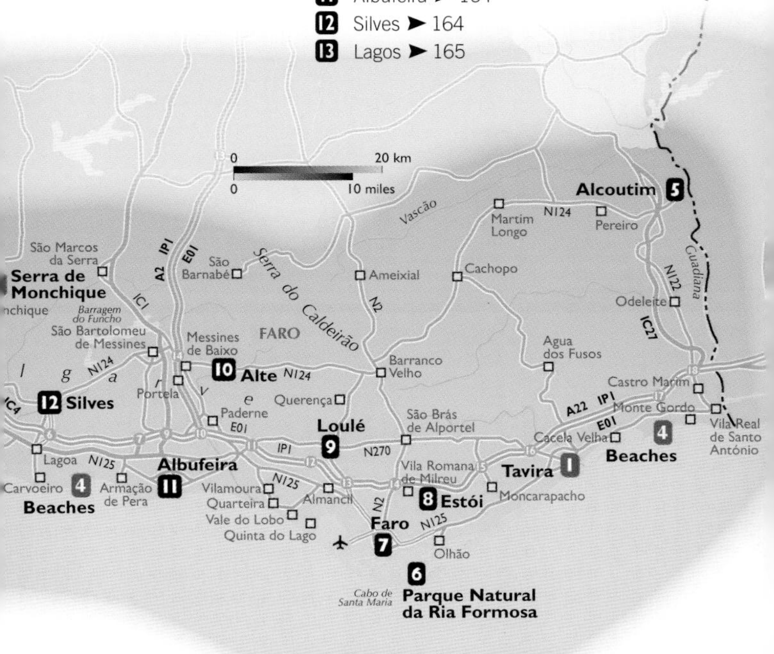

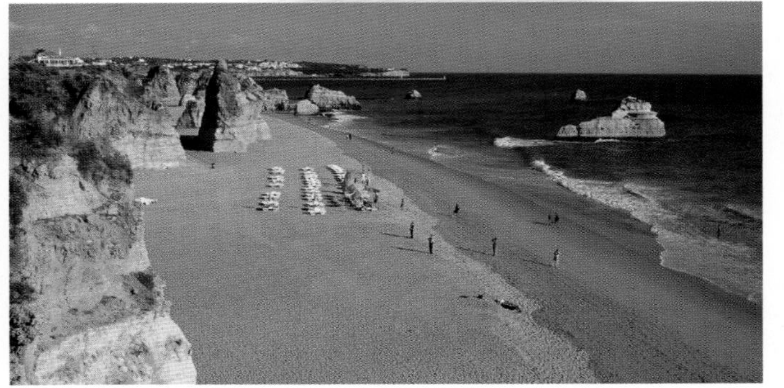

In Three Days

If you're not quite sure where to begin your travels, this itinerary recommends a practical and enjoyable three days out in the Algarve, taking in some of the best places to see using the Getting your Bearings map on the previous page. For more information see the main entries.

Day 1

Morning

Explore the elegant old town of 1 **Tavira** (➤ 152–153), with its 18th- and 19th-century town houses. Climb to the castle ruins for excellent views, then picnic in the gardens down by the riverside.

Afternoon and Evening

Catch the ferry to **Ilha de Tavira** (➤ 153, 159) from Quatro Águas, 2km (1.2 miles) east of Tavira, for the beach. The **Portas do Mar** seafood restaurant, on Quatro Águas beside the jetty, is scenic for dinner.

Day 2

Morning

Leave Tavira on the N125 towards Faro. Stop in Luz da Tavira to see its 16th-century church and *platibanda* houses, decorated with floral and geometric motifs. At Quinta de Marim, visit the bird-rich wetlands of 6 **Parque Natural da Ria Formosa** (➤ 162), then on to 7 **Faro** (➤ 162–163) to see the **Museum Municipal**, before having lunch by the harbour.

Afternoon and Evening

Continue west on the N125. Just before Almancil, pull off the road to see the astonishing church of São Lourenço, whose interior is completely covered in blue-and-white *azulejos* (➤ 18–19). Arrive at 11 **Albufeira** (left; ➤ 159 and 164) in time for a quick sea dip or a bracing walk along the cliff-flanked beach (left). Albufeira has restaurants to suit every taste and budget, but the traditional food here is salt-baked fish. If you want to splash out, book a table at **Vila Joya** (➤ 168).

Day 3

Morning

Make an early start and head inland through olive and citrus groves towards Paderne and Portela in the foothills of the Barrocal region. Take a brief diversion east on the N124 to see the pretty village of 10 **Alte** (➤ 164), renowned for its natural springs, before returning on the same road to 12 **Silves** (above, ➤ 164). Walk up to the castle and visit the Gothic cathedral before enjoying a seafood lunch at Rui Marisqueira (➤ 169).

Afternoon and Evening

Head west on the N124 and right on the N266 to climb to the lush mountains of the 2 **Serra de Monchique** (➤ 154–155). Drive up to the summit of Fóia for great views, then explore the spa village of Caldas de Monchique. Next take a scenic drive through eucalyptus and pinewoods to Aljezur, and follow the N268 south along the wild west coast. You should arrive in 3 **Sagres** (below, ➤ 156–158) in time to visit the fortress before watching the sun set from 3 **Cabo de São Vicente** (➤ 157–158).

1 Tavira

This elegant riverside town has somehow managed to escape the tourist tide sweeping the Algarve. It straddles the River Gilão and is close to some of the area's best beaches. A seven-arched bridge, dating from Roman times, joins one side of the town to the other, and its noble houses are adorned with wrought-iron balconies and latticework doors.

Grand houses with balconies line the waterfront

Tavira is the most beautiful town of the Algarve's *sotavento* (leeward) coast. It has palm-lined gardens, handsome 18th-century mansions overlooking the river and more than 35 churches. One of the most enjoyable ways to sample the many churches in Tavira is through the *Música nas Igrejas* (music in the churches) – a series of concerts that are held throughout the year in different churches.

During the Islamic era, this was one of the three biggest towns in *al-gharb* (➤ 148) and it continued to flourish up to the 16th century as a port. Tuna fishing became a major industry until it was ended by the 1755 earthquake and tsunami, which caused destruction and silted up the harbour. Today, the town thrives as a low-key, low-rise resort.

The best place to start is **Praça da República**, the arcaded square on the west bank of the River Gilão. Climb the steps to **Igreja da Misericórdia**, with its ornate 16th-century portal featuring carvings of Our Lady of Mercy flanked by saints Peter and Paul and the coats of arms of Tavira and Portugal.

A short climb to the left ends at **Castelo dos Mouros**, a ruined Moorish castle fortified by Dom Dinis, where you can walk around the ramparts for great views over Tavira and its distinctive *telhadas de tesouro* (treasure roofs), hip-gabled, pyramid shaped rooftops, which each cover a single room.

Behind the castle, the **Igreja de Santa Maria do Castelo**, built on the site of an old mosque, contains the tombs of Dom Paio Peres Correia, who captured the city in 1242.

Centro Ciência Viva de Tavira, an interactive science and technology museum offers more modern diversion, with exhibits on everything from the solar system to the internet.

From Praça da República, shady **waterfront gardens**, with an iron bandstand at the centre, lead to the **old fish market**, which has craft shops and cafés around a central courtyard.

Ilha de Tavira

From the jetty at Quatro Águas, 2km (1.2 miles) east of town, ferries depart (regularly in summer and occasionally in winter) for Ilha de Tavira, an offshore island that forms part of the **Parque Natural da Ria Formosa** (➤ 162).

Walk across the mudflats to reach the magnificent 11km (6.8-mile) **beach**, backed by sand dunes and lapped by the warmest waters in the Algarve. With beach bars and a campsite, this is a world away from the big resorts to the west.

You can also reach the island by boat from Santa Luzia, or by walking across the causeway and taking the miniature train from the nearby holiday village of Pedras d'el Rei.

Ilha de Tavira's superb sandy beach

TAKING A BREAK

Veneza, on Praça da República, has a popular pavement terrace for watching the world go by over almond-rich Portuguese sweets and strong coffee. **Portas do Mar** (➤ 167–168), a fish restaurant by the jetty at Quatro Águas, is also excellent.

202 D1 Rua da Galeria 9; tel: 81 322 511; www.tavira.pt

Centro Ciência Viva de Tavira
Convento do Carmo 9 281 326 231; www.tavira.cienciaviva.pt
Tue–Sat 10–6 Moderate

TAVIRA: INSIDE INFO

Top tip Try the local speciality, ***bife de atum em cebolada*** (tuna steak with onions) at one of the riverside restaurants.

- Try **tuna** straight off the boat at the nearby fishing village of Cabanas.

Hidden gem **Cacela Velha**, 10km (6 miles) east of Tavira, is a tiny village with a fort, church and houses perched on a cliff overlooking a sandy beach on the edge of the Ria Formosa. It is one of the few unspoiled Algarve coastal spots.

2 Serra de Monchique

The green hills of the volcanic Monchique mountain range provide a welcome respite from the summer heat of the Algarve coast. A trip into the mountains offers the chance to experience a different Algarve, far removed from the overcrowded beaches and busy resorts of the south.

The mountains provide a natural barrier between the Alentejo and the Algarve, sheltering the coastal region and helping to ensure its famous mild climate. Cork oaks, chestnut and eucalyptus trees grow on wooded hillsides, and the meadows are alive with wild flowers in spring.

A Spa Village and a Monastery

The easiest approach to the mountains is to drive north from **Portimão**, one of the Algarve's largest towns. After 20km (12.5 miles) you reach **Caldas de Monchique**, which has been a spa village since Roman times. Climb up to the vantage point for views of the spa nestling in the valley. This is a delightful spot, made more attractive by the recent renovation of the 19th-century spa buildings and neo-Moorish casino.

You can taste the water at **Fonte dos Amores** (Lovers' Spring), then walk up through the woods to a picnic area by a stream. Bear in mind that the most famous visitor to the spa,

A vast view out over the countryside of the Algarve from the vantage point of the summit of Mount Foia

The restored spa buildings at Caldas de Monchique

King João II, died after taking the waters in 1495.

The road continues for 6km (3.7 miles) to **Monchique**, the region's main town. Climb steps in the old town to reach the 16th-century parish church, Igreja Matriz, with Manueline portal columns carved into knotted ropes.

Keep going to eventually reach the **Nossa Senhora do Desterro**, a Franciscan monastery, destroyed in the 1771 earthquake, with gardens of lemon and magnolia trees and views to the peak of Picota (773m/2,535ft).

A short drive from Monchique is the highest summit in the Algarve, **Pico da Fóia** (902m/2,960ft), topped by a radio transmitter, café and gift shop. Often shrouded in mist, on clear days the views stretch to Portimão, Lagos (► 165) and Cabo de São Vicente (► 157–158). A few hours' hike away, the Algarve's second-highest peak, **Picota** (774m/2,538ft) offers less crowded views. Return to Portimão, the same way you came, or follow the N267 on a scenic mountain road to Aljezur and the **beaches of the west coast** (► 159–161).

TAKING A BREAK

There are several **inns** on the road to Fóia offering rustic mountain cuisine or tuck into hearty local fare like *feijao* (bean stew) with local sausages and chestnuts at country-style **A Charrette** (Rua Dr Samora Gil 30–34, tel: 282 912 142) in the centre of the old town.

---

202 B2 | Largo de São Sebastião, Monchique; tel: 282 911 189

Villa Termal das Caldas de Monchique – Spa Resort
Caldas de Monchique | 282 910 910; www.monchiquetermas.com
The pools are for guests only

SERRA DE MONCHIQUE: INSIDE INFO

Top tips Look out for ***medronho***, a local firewater spirit made from the fruit of the arbutus (wild strawberry) tree.

- Skirting Monchique on the road back down to the coast, stop to look at the handmade **folding wooden chairs**, a design brought to Monchique by the Romans and kept alive by the "Chair Man of Monchique" at a workshop halfway down the hill. Each chair is individually signed.

In more depth Ask at the tourist information office in Monchique for information about **walking in the mountains**. A popular walk is the climb to the summit of Picota, the second highest in the range, which takes around 1.5 hours from Monchique.

3 Sagres and Cabo de São Vicente

This wild and windswept cape at the southwest tip of Europe was once known as *O Fim do Mundo* (The End of the World). Standing on the headland and gazing out into the ocean as the waves crash against the cliffs, it is difficult not to feel the excitement of the medieval explorers who set off from Sagres into the great unknown, wondering what perils lay ahead and whether they would ever return.

School of Navigation

It was here that Prince Henry the Navigator founded his School of Navigation in the 15th century, gathering together the greatest cartographers, astronomers, mariners and shipbuilders in Europe. Huge advances were made, including a new design for a ship, the caravel, a lateen-rigged sailing vessel that was later used by Christopher Columbus for his Atlantic crossings. It was the invention of the caravel that paved the way for Portugal's era of maritime discovery (➤ 12–14). Among the explorers who studied at Sagres were Vasco da Gama, Pedro Álvares Cabral and Ferdinand Magellan.

Henry's school was pillaged in 1587 by the British buccaneer Sir Francis Drake, and his precious library was burned to the ground. It probably stood on the site of the **Fortaleza de Sagres**, a late 18th-century fortress on a windy promontory on the edge of town. All that remains from an earlier age are the simple chapel of **Nossa Senhora da Graça** and the huge **Rosa dos Ventos** (Wind Compass), 43m (47 yards) in diameter, possibly dating from Henry's time. Today, there is a visitor centre, shop and café.

The Town

Sagres is an end-of-the-road sort of town, attracting surfers and backpackers in summer, with a wide range of accomodation.

However, the real attraction is its **beaches**, which are some of the best in the Algarve – although the water is cold, and there are strong waves and ocean winds. There are more sheltered beaches east of the fortress.

Praia da Mareta is the most accessible, just below the main square. From **Praia da Baleeira**, by the harbour, it is a short walk to

View across the water to Fortaleza

the windsurfing beach of **Praia da Martinhal**.

Cabo de São Vicente

From the *fortaleza*, the road continues for 6km (3.7 miles) across the headland to Cabo de São Vicente, named *Promontorium Sacrum* (Sacred Promontory) by the Romans, who thought the sun sank into the water here every night. Later, it became a Christian shrine, based on the legend that the body of St Vincent had been washed ashore here in the fourth century AD. Later still, in the 12th century, the relics were said to have been transferred to Lisbon in a boat piloted by ravens, and St Vincent is now the patron saint of the capital.

Henry the Navigator is thought to have built his palace on the headland, roughly where the lighthouse now stands. This is one of the most powerful lighthouses in Europe, its 3,000-watt bulb visible up to 100km (62 miles) out at sea. The waters around the cape have been the site of numerous naval battles, but these days there is not much to disturb the peace, although it is still one of the world's busiest shipping routes.. The gusts up on the 60m (197ft) cliffs can be fierce, and fishermen risk their lives by dangling oversize

The rugged cliffs on the peninsula of Sagres

rods into the sea from the edge of the rock face. Come up here at sunset for magical views.

The huge wind compass at Sagres is thought to date from the 15th century

TAKING A BREAK

The best places are the **Pousada do Infante** (tel: 282 620 240), or anywhere on the Praça da República in Sagres. Alternatively, head to **A Pau de Pita**, a relaxed surfers' haunt, on Rua Comandante Matoso. Just out of town, on Praia da Mareta, **Mar a Vista** (tel: 282 624 247) has superb sea views.

202 B1 Rua Comandante Matoso, Sagres; tel: 282 624 873

Fortaleza de Sagres
Ponta de Sagres 282 620 140 May–Sep daily 9:30–9:30; Oct–Apr 9:30–5:30 Moderate

SAGRES AND CABO DE SÃO VICENTE: INSIDE INFO

Top tips Take a **sweater** to the cape even in summer. If you forget, stalls by the lighthouse sell chunky cardigans and rugs.

- You can walk from Sagres to Cabo de São Vicente along a **clifftop path**. It's a good way of admiring the wild flowers that burst into life on the rocky cape in spring.

Hidden gem **Praia do Beliche** is a secluded, sheltered cove beneath the cliffs on the way from Sagres to Cabo de São Vicente.

In more depth If Sagres has given you a taste for wild Atlantic beaches, continue up the west coast on the **Costa Vicentina** (➤ 160–161).

4 Algarve Beaches

Stretching for 200km (124 miles), the Algarve has some of the finest beaches in Europe. You could spend your entire holiday searching for your favourite: from crescents of soft golden sand to tiny coves hidden beneath grottoes and ochre cliffs. There are beaches for families, watersports or for an away-from-it-all feeling – just take your pick.

The beach at Albufeira is popular with fishermen

Family Beaches

Aptly named **Praia Verde** (Green Beach) is reached by crossing a valley of pine trees and walking down through the dunes. The sea here is calm and warm – perfect for small children. This is one of a chain of beaches that stretches from Cacela Velha to Monte Gordo, 2km (1.2 miles) east.

In Tavira, take the ferry to reach **Ilha de Tavira** (► 153), a popular island beach. The main beach is suitable for families, but be warned that there are some nudist sections further along. Praia do Barril, 4km (2.5 miles) away at the island's western end, is usually less crowded.

Albufeira is another classic beach. Walk through the rock tunnel or take the elevator to reach the beach, with sandstacks beneath the cliffs. West of Albufeira is a series of attractive cove beaches, such as Praia de São Rafael and Praia da Galé.

The biggest and possibly most famous beach in the Algarve is **Armação de Pêra.** This superb beach has sandstacks at one end and flat sands stretching towards Albufeira. The resort is popular with Portuguese families.

Praia da Rocha was the first tourist town in the Algarve, giving it a certain time-worn appeal, although a new paved beachside walk has smartened up the resort. From the old fortress, there are views over the wide beach of sand, with eroded rocks sheltering beneath 70m (230ft) cliffs.

Sheltered Coves

Praia da Marinha is the largest of the cove beaches around the fishing village of Carvoeiro, now a growing resort. In summer, you can take boat trips from Carvoeiro to other nearby cove beaches, including Praia do Benagil and Praia Senhora da Rocha. Another perfect cove beach is **Praia de Dona Ana,** located just outside Lagos, which means it gets crowded on summer weekends. You can take a boat trip to see the grottoes and caves of Ponte da Piedade (➤ 185).

Perfect for Watersports

Many beaches are popular for watersports. One of the best is **Meia Praia,** on the east side of Lagos, which has a long crescent-shaped beach stretching for 4km (2.5 miles). Popular with windsurfers, children like this beach too, as there are lots of shells washed up on the sand. Watch the strong currents.

The largest resort to the west is **Praia da Luz**. This beach has windsurfing and diving schools and a splendid beach backed by cliffs at its eastern end. A clifftop path leads past Ponte da Piedade to Lagos (➤ 185). The sheltered, dark sandy cove of **Praia de Odeceixe** on the borders of the Alentejo and the Algarve is also popular with surfers. It sits at the mouth of the Seixe estuary 4km (2.5 miles) from the nearest village.

Off-the-beaten-track

If you have your own transport, then it is worthwhile heading to some of the more remote beaches, such as **Boca do Rio**, located halfway between Burgau and Salema on the edge of the Budens wetland reserve. This small beach is situated at a river mouth inside the **Costa Vicentina** natural park. You can walk along the cliffs to the beach at Cabanas Velhas.

Alternatively, boats depart from the fishing port of Olhão for the attractive holiday island of **Ilha da Armona**. There are sand dunes on the sheltered, landward side, or you can escape the crowds by walking across to the other side of the island to a fine white-sand beach. You can also camp on the island.

The wave-thrashed west coast has a string of spectacular beaches, including the remote **Praia da Cordoama,** which

The sheltered cove beach at Praia da Marinha

The superb beach at Boca do Rio is located on the edge of a wetland reserve

is reached by following a dirt track beneath grey slate cliffs. Popular with surfers, the nearby beach of **Praia do Castelejo** is slightly more accessible and surrounded by black schist rocks with gold-red sand. Alternatively, head for the huge, curving beach of **Praia da Bordeira**, backed by sand dunes, and situated around a lagoon at the mouth of the Bordeira River near Carrapateira. Huge Atlantic rollers attract surfers to dune-flanked **Praia do Amado**, 4km (2.5 miles) south on the other side of the headland.

Praia da Arrifana is another beautiful crescent of sand, 10km (6 miles) outside Aljezur. There are sweeping views along the coastline from the ruined fortress above the beach. The long, sheltered sandy beach of **Praia de Monte Clérigo**, 8km (5 miles) from Aljezur, is a great choice for families.

TAKING A BREAK

Most of these beaches have **summer restaurants and bars**. If you are visiting remote beaches like Cordoama and Odeceixe out of season, take a **picnic**.

Praia Verde 202 D1
Ilha da Armona 202 D1
Ilha de Tavira 202 D1
Albufeira 202 C1
Armação de Pêra 202 C1
Praia da Marinha 202 C1
Praia de Dona Ana 202 B1
Meia Praia 202 B1
Praia da Luz 202 B1
Praia de Odeceixe 202 B2
Boca do Rio 202 B1
Praia da Rocha 202 B1
Praia do Castelejo 202 B1
Praia da Bordeira 202 B1
Praia do Amado 202 B1
Praia da Arrifana 202 B1
Praia de Monte Clérigo 202 B1
Praia da Cordoama 202 A1

ALGARVE BEACHES: INSIDE INFO

Top tips Beware of **dangerous currents** on the west coast beaches (Arrifana, Amado, Bordeira, Castelejo, Cordoama and Odeceixe). On calm days the sea can seem almost benevolent, but only experienced swimmers should go in.

- The easiest **access** to the west coast beaches is from Lagos to Arrifana or Sagres to Bordeira.

At Your Leisure

The impressive remains of the castle walls at Alcoutim

5 Alcoutim

A giant casuarina tree stands by the harbour in the sleepy village of Alcoutim, looking across the River Guadiana to the Spanish village of Sanlúcar de Guadiana. Here you are close enough to Spain to hear dogs barking, children playing and the church clock chiming the hour on the far bank. Local fishermen will ferry you across, and in summer you can take river trips as far south as Vila Real. Climb to the 14th-century castle at the top of the village for the best views. Take the time to explore the little archaeological museum in the castle, and then follow the beautiful drive along the valley on a twisting road to Foz de Odeleite.

202 D2 Rua 1º de Maio; tel: 281 546 179

6 Parque Natural da Ria Formosa

The Ria Formosa nature reserve covers 60km (37 miles) of coastline, sheltered from the ocean by partly submerged sand dunes and a network of salt marshes and lagoons.

The best introduction to the park's ecology and history is to follow the 3km (2-mile) **self-guided trail** at the Quinta de Marim Environmental Education Centre near Olhão, which leads through pinewoods and along the shore, passing a working tide mill on the way to a freshwater lake. The watery lagoon landscape makes for great birdwatching. Bring binoculars and you might spot herons, storks, purple gallinule (a relative of the moorhen) and migratory flamingoes taking advantage of the rich pickings on the marshes. Keep an eye out for fiddler crabs scuttling across the shore, too. You can pick up a map at the reception gate.

202 C1 3km (2 miles) east of Olhão, signposted off the N125 289 700 210; www.icn.pt Daily 10–7 Inexpensive

7 Faro

The capital of the Algarve is one of the most underrated cities in Portugal, known mainly for its airport through which millions pass on their way to the south coast beaches.

Starting at the marina, you enter the old town through **Arco da Vila**, a handsome gateway – just inside the gateway, an 11th-century horseshoe arch is all that remains of the Moorish walls. Climb to the cathedral square, cobbled and lined with orange trees, then make your way to the **Museu Municipal**, housed in a former convent. Besides the Renaissance cloisters, the chief attraction here is a third-century Roman mosaic depicting the head of Neptune surrounded by the four winds.

It's worth making the short stroll through the new town to the Igreja do Carmo, best known for its chilling **Capela dos Ossos** (Chapel of Bones), whose walls are covered with more than 1,200 skulls and body parts – though this is not as impressive as the similar chapel in Évora (➤ 134).

202 C1 Rua da Misericórdia 8–12; tel: 289 803 604; www.cm-faro.pt

Museu Municipal

Praça Dom Afonso III 289 897 400 Jun–Sep Tue–Fri 10–7, Sat–Sun 11:30–6; Oct–May Tue–Fri 10–6, Sat–Sun 10:30–5 (last entry 30 mins before closing) Inexpensive; free Sun 10:30–2

Capela dos Ossos

Largo do Carmo 289 824 490 Apr–Oct Mon–Fri 10–1, 3–5, Sat 10–1; Nov–Mar Mon–Fri 10–1, 3–6, Sat 10–1 Inexpensive

8 Estói

The pink, neo-rococo palace that dominates the village was begun in 1840 for the Conde de Cavalhal. It has been restored and opened as a glamorous *pousada* (you can visit the gardens and some rooms) with a very good restaurant. Just down the hill from the village are the Roman ruins at **Milreu**, which include some well-preserved mosaics depicting leaping dolphins and fish.

The handsome Arco da Villa, which marks the entrance to the old town at Faro

A statue in the palace grounds of Estoi

202 D1

Milreu

289 997 823 May–Sep Tue–Sun 9:30–12:30, 2–6; Oct–Apr Tue–Sun 9:30–12:30, 2–5 Inexpensive

9 Loulé

The Algarve's second city is also a thriving crafts centre and market town. Saturday is the best time to come, when the busy market sells local produce and pottery in and around a neo-Moorish market hall. In the streets below the castle, you can watch craftspeople at work, carving wood, weaving baskets and making lace in tiny workshops. Loulé is known across Portugal for its Carnival celebrations, which take place just before Lent and are the biggest in the country. Look out for two contrasting churches – the parish church of **São Clemente**, its bell tower housed in a 12th-century minaret, and the space-age **Nossa Senhora da Piedade**, beside an 18th-century chapel on a hill overlooking the town.

202 C1 Avenida 25 de Abril 9; tel: 289 463 900

10 Alte

This charming village of whitewashed houses is in the foothills of the Barrocal, a fertile region north of Loulé, which produces figs, almonds, and oranges. You could easily spend an hour or two in the village, admiring the parish church with its Manueline (➤ 14) portal and 16th-century *azulejos* (➤ 18–19) and walking up to the Fonte Pequena and Fonte Grande to cool down by the springs at this well-known beauty spot by the River Alte. While you're there, don't miss the stunning Queda do Vigario waterfall.

202 C1

11 Albufeira

What was once a quiet fishing village has been transformed over the last 50 years into Portugal's biggest seaside resort. Yet, the old town has also survived. Here is a maze of medieval alleyways on a cliff overlooking the beach, its Moorish archway and whitewashed houses lit by lanterns at night. A tunnel carved through the cliff face and a new elevator lead to the main beach, with its magnificent sandstacks; a second beach, Praia dos Barcos, has fishing boats on the sand. Beyond here is the raucous nightlife area known as "the Strip", which is packed with British-focused pubs, karaoke bars, restaurants and clubs.

202 C1 **Rua 5 de Outubro; tel: 289 585 279**

12 Silves

The Moorish capital of *al-gharb* (➤ 148) was once a magnificent city, a place of poets, princes and splendid bazaars described in Islamic chronicles as a place of "shining brightness", 10 times greater than Lisbon. Rising dramatically above the town is the ruined Moorish **castle**, once the centrepiece of the medina, which affords far-reaching views across the town to the River Arade and countryside dotted with citrus groves, cork-oak woods and carob trees. Nearby is the 13th-century **cathedral**, the pink granite columns of its Gothic nave uncluttered by the baroque decoration of so many Portuguese churches. The tombstones are those of medieval crusaders who helped capture the town in 1242.

Take the steep path down from the cathedral to the **Museu Municipal de Arqueologia**, which showcases regional history through Moorish, Roman and Phoenician times.

202 B1

Castelo
282 445 624 **Jul–Aug daily 9–9; Sep–Jun daily 9–5:30** **Inexpensive**

Museu Municipal de Arqueologia
Rua das Portas de Loulé **282 444 832**
Mon–Sat 9–5:30 **Inexpensive**

Silves, the former Moorish capital, makes a good day out from the Algarve beaches

The detailed gilded woodwork in the tiny chapel of São Antonio in Lagos

13 Lagos

Partly enclosed by medieval walls and bordered by cliff-backed beaches, Lagos is a very visually appealing and historically interesting town. Ships sailed to Africa from here during the Age of Discovery. A **statue of Henry the Navigator** (➤ 12) stands on Praça Infante Dom Henrique, facing the harbour. More ominously, on a corner of the same square is the site of the first European *mercado de esclavos* (slave market), now an art gallery. In the backstreets, the **Museu Municipal** gives access to the gilded chapel of São Antonio and also has a collection of Bronze Age menhirs (standing stones), Roman mosaics, African artefacts, fishing nets, pickled animals, weapons and coins.

202 B1 Rua Belchoir Moreira de Barbudo; tel: 282 763 031

Museu Municipal

Rua General Alberto da Silveira 282 762 301 Tue–Sun 9:30–12:30, 2–5 Inexpensive

BEST FOR KIDS

If your children are bored with the beaches, here are some suggestions to keep them busy:

- Karting Algarve (www.kartingalgarve.com), Almancil, offers karting with junior carts, and other activities.
- Museu Municipal (➤ left) Lagos, with a collection of oddities from mosaics to pickled animals.
- Zoomarine (on N125 near Guia, open Mar–Oct, www.zoomarine.com), an aquarium with dolphin and parrot shows.
- Slide and Splash (on N125 near Lagoa, open Easter–Oct, www.slidesplash.com), the Algarve's biggest waterpark.
- Aqualand (on N125 near Porches, open Jun to mid-Sep), has an array of thrilling waterslides and flumes, a wave pool and a Mini Park splash area for young children.
- Lagos Zoo (Barão de São João, Apr–Sep daily 10–7, Oct–Mar 10–5, www.zoolagos.com), features birds, primates and a kid's farm.

Where to... Stay

Prices
Expect to pay for a double room per night in high season:
€ under €60 **€€** €60–€120 **€€€** €121–€180 **€€€€** over €180

TAVIRA

Pousada Convento da Graça €€€

This romantic and blissfully peaceful *pousada* (➤ 35) is housed in a converted convent, founded in the 16th century by Augustinian nuns. The centrepiece is a beautiful Renaissance cloister, which lends the place an air of grandeur. High-ceilinged spaces lead to rooms that are decorated in warm hues with Moorish elements. All have cable TV, air conditioning and WiFi, and the best have private balconies. The swimming pool is great for cooling off on hot days. Activities, including golf, can be arranged.

202 D1 Rua Dom Paio Peres Correia
281 329 040; www.pousadas.pt

FARO AND AROUND

Hotel Eva €€–€€€

Attractively positioned on the edge of the marina, you can enjoy superb views from the rooftop pool over the Ria Formosa and the boats in the harbour – the hotel can even arrange boat trips out to sea. Some of the more expensive rooms also share this stunning view. Sleek and contemporary in feel throughout, the main areas are light and airy. The service is excellent and all rooms have WiFi.

202 C1 F1 Avenida da República
289 001 000; www.tdhotels.pt

Hotel Quinta do Lago €€€€

Thirty minutes by car from Faro, the Quinta do Lago sits in verdant luxury, overlooking the lagoon and the sea. Arguably justified in calling itself "the finest hotel in the Algarve", its first-rate facilities include a spa with a gym and a jacuzzi overlooking the Ria Formosa, a private beach club, tennis courts and kids club. Sports enthusiasts are spoiled for choice, and it is particularly popular with golfers who can choose from four different championship courses (➤ 170). Guests can dine on Portuguese gourmet fare while watching the sun set in the Brisa do Mar, or feast on Italian cuisine in the intimate Cá d'Oro restaurant. Stylish and comfortable rooms come with spacious terraces and little luxuries, such as chocolates, a carafe of port and flowers.

202 C1 Quinta do Lago, Almancil
289 350 350; www.quintadolagohotel.com

ESTÓI

Monte do Casal €€€–€€€€

This small and exclusive English-run hotel is tucked away in the gentle hills above Faro, with fine views down to the sea. Surrounded by botanical gardens and terraces, it has its own spa, bar and a first-class restaurant. The individually designed rooms are exquisitely decorated in warm colours, rich fabrics and mahogany furnishings, and have marble bathrooms, DVD players (with free DVDs and CDs available from reception) and terraces. The restaurant is a converted coach house that specializes in sophisticated French cuisine. In summer, guests can dine on the terrace under the palms; in cooler months, open log fires and candlelit tables provide guests with

a warm and cosy welcome.
202 D1 Cerro do Lobo 289 990 140; www.montedocasal.pt Closed late-Nov to early Feb

PORCHES

Casa Bela Moura €€–€€€

A modern house decorated in Moorish style, this is a family-run guesthouse with rooms divided between the main house and a nearby annexe. The bar, breakfast room and reception are welcoming, and the 13 rooms are very clean. It has its own pool and is only 1.5km (1 mile) from the pretty cove of Nossa Senhora da Rocha.
202 C1 Estrada de Porches 530, Alporchinhos 282 313 422; www.casabelamoura.com Closed Nov–Feb

SILVES

Casa das Oliveiras €€

Peace and quiet reigns at this comfortable guest house, which is not far outside of Silves and surrounded by orange groves and olive trees. There is no restaurant, but breakfast is substantial and the friendly owners will point you in the direction of a number of good local places to eat. This makes a very good base for exploring both the beautiful inland towns and villages, and heading off to the nearby coast.
202 C1 Montes da Vala 282 342 115; www.casa-das-oliveiras.com

LAGOS

Casa Grande €–€€

The Casa Grande is a delightful, rambling guesthouse furnished with antiques and curiosities. The house is a short walk from the beach. The attractively furnished rooms, all with en-suite bathrooms, are large, comfortable and good value for money. Upstairs rooms have their own balconies. There's also a restaurant.
202 B1 Burgau, Lagos 282 697 416; www.casagrandeportugal.com

Where to... Eat and Drink

Prices
Expect to pay per person for a three-course meal, excluding drinks and tips:
€ under €12 **€€** €12–24 **€€€** €25–36 **€€€€** over €36

TAVIRA

Mesa do Cume €€

The road is long and winding, but you won't regret the uphill drive from Tavira to Mesa do Cume (take the N397 towards Cachopo). Set dramatically above wooded hills tumbling down to the Atlantic, the panorama from the terrace here is breathtaking. The food, prepared with fresh, seasonal ingredients is creative. Starters such as creamy fish soup with garlic toast are followed by dishes that might include Alentejo black port with home-made pesto and desserts like chocolate-coated fig bonbons. This is a magical spot for a light lunch or a romantic evening meal.
202 D1 Alcaria do Cume 281 326 144; www.mesadocume.net Wed–Sun 10– 5:30, 6:30–10

Portas do Mar €€

Located on the waterfront where the River Gilão meets the Rio Formosa estuary, this is one of a cluster of fish restaurants downstream from Tavira. It's a modern building with a pretty blue-and-white interior and a terrace for views of the estuary. The choice of fish, the freshest of which is hauled ashore at the nearby port,

ranges from lobster and crayfish to monkfish or shellfish *cataplana* (a hearty seafood stew, ➤ 28).
202 D1 ✉ Sítio das Quatro Águas ☎ 281 321 255 Jul–Sep Wed–Mon 12:30–3, 7–11; Oct–Jun 12:30–3, 6:30–10:30

MONCHIQUE

A Rampa €–€€
Perched high above Monchique on the road to Foia, this laid-back rustic restaurant is famous for one thing: chicken piri-piri. It doesn't disappoint. Portions are generous, the chicken is tender and the piri-piri is spicy but not overpowering. The views are just as good, reaching over forested hills and patchwork fields to the glittering Atlantic.
202 B1 ✉ Caminho Foia ☎ 282 912 620 Wed–Mon 12–2:30, 7–10

FARO

Adega Nova €
The prices are modest, the welcome warm and the food second to none at this bustling, unpretentious restaurant near the station. Pull up a chair at one of the communal tables for some of the best value Portuguese fare in the Algarve. Fish is the speciality – try the catch of the day or the seafood kebabs – and pairs nicely with the crisp house white. The *tarta de alfarroba* (carob cake) is the star of the dessert menu.
202 C1 ✉ Rua Francisco Barreto 24 ☎ 289 813 433 Daily 12-11:30

LOULÉ

A Quinta €€–€€€
Tucked away but well worth the effort to find, A Quinta is a rustically elegant restaurant on the old Loulé-Almancil road. Warm colours, candlelight and wood beams create an inviting backdrop for French-inspired cuisine – expertly cooked and beautifully presented. Try the butter-soft fillet steak or seared turbot with truffle mash. The service is polished and the coastal views from the terrace are breathtaking.
202 C1 ✉ Rua Vale Formosa, Almancil ☎ 289 393357 Daily 12–2:30, 7–10. Closed Dec and Jan

ALBUFEIRA

Cabana Fresca €€
The pick of the restaurants on the seafront promenade fringing Praia do Pescador (Fisherman's Beach), Cabana Fresca ticks all the boxes with its buzzy ambiance, friendly service and excellent fresh fish. Dishes like king prawns in garlic and seafood risotto are matched with reasonably priced Portuguese wines. Be sure to save room for dessert – the chocolate lasagne is delicious. It's worth booking ahead in summer.
202 C1 ✉ Praia do Pescador ☎ 289 585 456 Daily 9–11

Vila Joya €€€€
Considered by many to be one of the Algarve's best restaurants, Vila Joya is worth seeking out for an extra special dinner, with local ingredients that are given an imaginative twist by the very talented chef, Dieter Koschina. The food not only uses freshly sourced Portuguese ingredients, but also the best ingredients from international cuisine, from Wagyu beef to Italian white truffles. There are rooms here also if you can't bear the thought of driving home. Book well ahead.
202 C1 ✉ Praia da Gale ☎ 289 591 795; www.vilajoya.com Daily 12–2.30, 7–11

LAGOS

Don Sebastião €€
The central location on the main pedestrian street and a warm welcome here ensures a steady stream of visitors. It's not the cheapest place in town, but there are fine appetisers, the fish and seafood are excellent and there are home-made desserts. Choose from prawns, crayfish or lobster,

or the fish risotto. There is also an extensive wine list.

202 B1 ✉ Rua 25 de Abril 20 ☎ 282 762 795; www.restaurantedonsebastiao.com ⌚ Daily 12–11

SILVES

Rui Marisqueira €€–€€€

This is one of the Algarve's best-known fish restaurants, with a great choice of shellfish on the menu and understandably popular with locals and tourists. The décor is nothing very special, it is fairly noisy inside and the service can be offhand, but all is forgiven when the generous-sized seafood platters arrive at your table overflowing with fresh lobster and juicy crab, prawns and oysters. Main courses range from grilled fresh fish to clams, *cataplana* and fish risotto. Fish dishes are priced by the kilo, so ask the price before you order that fat bass or bream.

202 C1 ✉ Rua Commendador Vilarinho 27 ☎ 282 442 682 ⌚ Wed–Mon 12–3:30, 6:30–10:30

Where to... Shop

MARKETS

Olhão has the Algarve's best fish market (Mon–Sat), which is held by the fruit and vegetable market.

Loulé's lively market on Saturday mornings offers goods from olives and sausages to poultry and pottery.

The covered food market in **Lagos** (Rua das Portas de Portugal, Mon–Sat 8–1) has splendid fresh fish, fruit and vegetables, and there's a very colourful "gypsy market" on the first Saturday of every month.

Monchique's market is held every second Friday of the month and there is a daily market in **Tavira**.

CLOTHING AND CRAFTS

For good, hand-painted Portuguese pottery, visit the roadside studios on the N125 in Porches. You can see artists at work at the **Olaria de Porches**. Close by, **Olaria Pequena** (www.olariapequena.com) presents the bold, colourful designs of Scottish artist, Ian Fitzpatrick.

Faro's main shopping street is **Rua de Santo António**. The **Casa Verde** (Rua Dr. Francisco Gomes, tel: 289 825 153) has excellent lace, pottery and leather. **Loulé** is one of the best towns to see Algarvio craft workers in action: old liquor stills and copper *cataplana* pots are sold along Rue de Barbacá. For hand-painted pottery and decorative *azulejos*, try **O Arco** (Rua dos Almadas 4, tel: 289 415 06) or **Casa Louart** (Largo Dom Pedro I, tel: 289 110 485) by the castle.

Monchique is renowned for wooden handicrafts, cork and basketry. For the best handmade Roman-style *cadeiras de tesoura* (scissor chairs), visit **Casa dos Arcos** (Estrada Velha, tel: 282 911 071). Nearby, Leonel Telo creates beautiful ceramics at his studio, **Casa da Nogueira** (Rua do Córro 2, tel: 282 911377).

FOOD AND DRINK

For ports, wines, liqueurs and olive paté, try **Garrafeira Vital** (Praça da República 9) in Tavira. The **Adega Cooperativa** between Portimão and Lagoa holds guided tours, including tastings (tel: 282 342 181).

Despensa Algarvia in Faro (Rua Conselheiro Bivar 19–21, tel: 289 813 195, http://despensaalgarvia.com) stocks goodies like fig cakes, marzipan, honey with rosemary, oils, vinegars, wines and liqueurs.

Caldas de Monchique, 7km (4.3 miles) south of Monchique, is famous for *medronho*, a firewater made from local arbutus berries – taste it at the craft centre.

Where to... Be Entertained

WATERSPORTS

Watersports in the Algarve are excellent. Try the **Watersports Centre** near Albufeira (tel: 289 394 929) for surfing, windsurfing, parasailing, diving and boat trips.

WATERPARKS

In Lagoa, **Slide & Splash** (along the N125, Vale de Deus, Estômbar, tel: 282 340 800) is a huge complex.

GOLF

There are 33 excellent golf courses in the region (www.portugalgolf.pt). The luxury resorts of **Quinta do Lago** (tel: 289 390 7056, www.quintadolagogolf.com) and **Vale do Lobo** have six scenic courses between them. One of Vilamoura's top ranking courses is the **Oceanico Millennium** (tel: 289 310 333); the **Sir Henry Cotton Championship Course** (outside Portimão on the N125, tel: 282 420 200, www.lemeridienpenina.com) is an 18-hole course. There is also **Alto Golf** between Alvor and Portimão (tel: 282 460 870, www.altoclub.com).

TENNIS

Portugal's leading academies are **Vale do Lobo** (tel: 289 357 850), with 14 courts, pool and gym, and **Barrington's** (tel: 289 351 940).

MUSIC AND NIGHTLIFE

Although **Albufeira** has plenty of nightlife venues, the best clubs are out of town. Recommended is industrial-chic **Le Club** (www.leclubsantaeulalia.com), with a stunning sea-facing location on Praia de Santa Eulália. Another is mammoth **Kadoç** (www.kadoc.pt) on the Albufeira-Vilamoura road where top DJs such as David Guetta play to up to 7,000 clubbers.

More intimate is the **St James' Club** in Almancil, an exclusive bar-disco (with enforced dress code) that offers a drive-home service.

In Silves, the bohemian **Café Ingles** (Rua do Castelo 11, tel: 282 442585) is a relaxed venue for weekend jazz and *fado* (➤ 20–21) concerts. In Lagos, **Stevie Ray's** (Rua da Senhora da Graça 9, tel: 282 768 086, www.stevie-rays.com) hosts live jazz, soul, blues and funk.

Other venues for live music are **Harry's Bar** and **Central Station** on Largo Duarte Pacheco, Albufeira.

Faro's nightlife is concentrated on **Rua do Prior** and **Rua Conselheiro Bivar,** where DJ bars and late-night cafés attract a young crowd. Try **Bar Columbus** (Arcadas Jardim Manuel Bivar 13, www.barcolumbus.com), under the arcades near the harbour.

In **Lagos** and **Almancil**, the **Centro Cultural** (Rua Lançarote de Freitas, tel: 282 770 450) and the **Centro Cultural de São Lourenço** (tel: 289 395 475) both host concerts and recitals featuring international musicians.

In Tavira, *fado* is played (Sat and Tue) at converted wine cellar **Adega do Papagaio** (tel: 282 789 423).

BOAT TRIPS AND FISHING

Riosul arranges boat trips along the River Guadiana from Vila Real de Santo António, some of the Algarve's least spoiled scenery (Rua Tristão Vaz Teixeira, Monte Gordo, tel: 281 510 200, www.riosultravel.com).

Portitours (tel: 282 470 063, www.portitours.pt) among others, offer half-day cruises from Portimão, visiting caves, grottoes and beaches – they will arrange transport from your hotel.

Walks and Tours

1 LISBON

Walk

DISTANCE 4km (2.5 miles) walking plus tram and funicular rides **TIME** 2–2.5 hours
START/END POINT Praça do Comércio 196 C1

This walk introduces you to four very different districts – Alfama, Baixa, Chiado and Bairro Alto – which together make up the rich and diverse historic core of Lisbon. The journey includes a tram ride and a climb on a funicular, which are not only enjoyable in themselves, but also a convenient way of getting up the hills. Although the walk can be done in as little as two hours, it is best to allow at least half a day, giving some time for window shopping, cafés and visits to churches and museums along the way.

1–2

Start in **Praça do Comércio**, the large open square on the waterfront, with your back to the river. The square is still known as Terreiro do Paço, after the royal palace that once stood on this site. At the centre is a statue of Dom José I, king of Portugal at the time of the 1755 earthquake and the subsequent rebuilding of Lisbon. Walk straight ahead through the triumphal arch, the symbolic gateway to the city from the river. This brings you into **Rua Augusta**, the principal shopping street of the Baixa (lower town). On sunny days the promenade comes alive with buskers, street traders, busy news stands and café terraces. The shops along here are an eclectic mix of high street fashion chains and quirky local stores such as **Casa Macário** (No 272–274), an old-fashioned coffee shop where bottles of vintage port gather dust on the shelves. Approaching the top of the street, glance to your left to see the **Elevador de Santa Justa**, a much-loved iron lift designed by a pupil of Gustave Eiffel; it opened in 1902 to connect Baixa with Chiado. If you have a bus pass, it will be valid on the *elevador,* too. Although the escalators inside the Baixa-Chiado metro station now do a more efficient

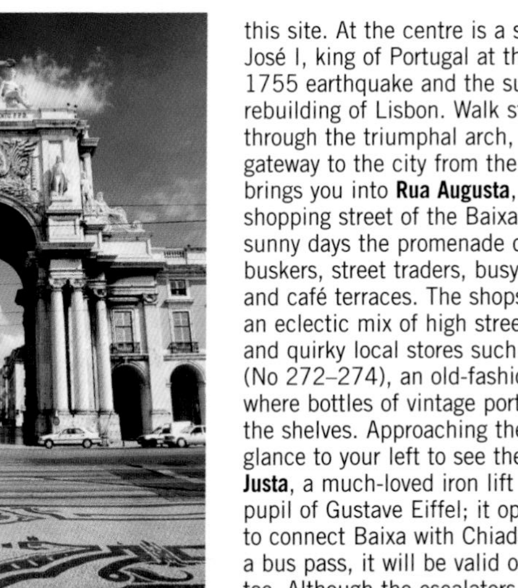

Page 171: People walking through the beautiful Praça do Comércio in Baixa

Right: The grand Arco da Rua Augusta, Praça do Comércio, in the Baixa area

job, the ride on the *elevador* is still an exhilarating experience and the views across Lisbon from the top are breathtaking.

2–3
Rua Augusta ends in the **Rossio**, the nearest thing in Lisbon to a central square, with its fountains, flower stalls and a wavy mosaic pavement. The square is officially named Praça Dom Pedro IV after the statue of the king at its centre – though the statue was initially designed as a likeness of Emperor

Maximilian of Mexico, who was executed before it could be completed. Café Nicola and Pastelaria Suiça, facing each other across the Rossio, offer a choice of terraces for people watching, and there are good views of the ruined **Igreja do Carmo** (➤ 175), high on the hill above the western side of the square. Leave the square by the far left corner and you find yourself in front of Rossio station, with its imposing neo-Manueline facade. Built as Lisbon's central station in 1892, it is the departure point for trains to Sintra (➤ 60–62).

Continue onwards into **Praça dos Restauradores**, a large square with an obelisk at the centre commemorating Portugal's independence from Spain. On your left is **Palácio Foz**, a former nightclub and Ministry of Propaganda building now housing the city tourist office.

3–4

Just beyond the palace, the **Elevador da Glória** funicular trundles up to the Bairro Alto on what must be one of the world's steepest, and most enjoyable, public transport rides, emerging opposite the **Solar do Vinho do Porto** (➤ 70). Turn right at the upper terminus to reach the garden and **Miradouro of São Pedro de Alcântara**, with magnificent views of the cathedral, castle and Tagus estuary. Now you can head into the intriguing warren of medieval streets that make up the **Bairro Alto** (➤ 64).

This area rewards random exploration, but one possible route is to follow Travessa de São Pedro from opposite the fountain, take the second left along Rua dos Mouros (Street of the Moors), then turn left and immediately right along Rua do Diário de Notícias. As you reach Travessa da Queimada, turn left, passing Café Luso, one of Lisbon's famous *fado* (➤ 20–21) houses, which has *fado* and folk dancing on most nights.

Dom Pedro IV statue and in front of the Dona Maria National Theatre in Rossio Square

TAKING A BREAK

A Brasileira €
196 B3 Rua Garrett 120–122 213 469 547 Daily 8am–2am

Café Nicola €
196 C4 Praca Dom Pedro IV (Rossio) 24–25 Mon–Fri 8–10, Sat 9–10, Sun 10–7

Pastelaria Suiça €
196 C4 Praca Dom Pedro IV (Rossio) 96–104 213 214 090 Daily 7–10 (9 in winter)

Porta d'Alfama €
197 F3 Rua São João da Praça 17 218 864 536 Daily 12–3, 7:30–10

This brings you out opposite Largo Trinidade Coelho, known as Largo da Misericórdia, dominated by the Jesuit **Igreja de São Roque**. This is the headquarters of the Misericórdia charity, beneficiaries of Portugal's national lottery – hence the bronze statue of a ticket seller in front of the church. Leave this square by the Calçada do Duque steps and take the second right along Rua da Condessa to reach **Largo do Carmo**, a pretty square located at the heart of the Chiado district. The ruined convent here, an empty shell following the 1755 earthquake, is now an interesting archaeological museum.

4–5

Leave the square by Rua da Trinidade. When you see a house with a *azulejo*-tiled facade on your right, turn left along Rua Serpa Pinto. This brings you out onto Rua Garrett, Chiado's most fashionable shopping street, restored after a disastrous fire in 1988. Treat yourself to a *bica* (espresso) and pastry on the terrace or in the grand wood-panelled interior of **Pastelaria Bernard** or **A Brasileira** (➤ 70). The poet Fernando Pessoa used to meet his friends at A Brasileira and his statue on the pavement acts as a magnet for tourists.

5–6

Cross Rua Garrett to reach Rua António Maria Cardoso, where you can get tram 28, dropping back down to Baixa and passing the **sé** (cathedral, ➤ 54–55) on the way up to Largo das Portas do Sol. Get off the tram opposite the **Museu de Artes Decorativas** (➤ 55).

From the *miradouro* (viewpoint), there are views over the Alfama rooftops to the churches of São Vicente de Fora and Santa Engrácia. From here you descend to explore **Alfama** (➤ 54–57).

6–7

Take the staircase beside **Santa Luzia church** to a secret world of cobbled lanes, washing hanging from balconies, fountains, patios and hidden courtyards of orange trees. Turn left down more steps to Largo de São Miguel, where a palm tree stands guarding the church. Turn left along Rua de São Miguel. At the end of this street, turn right and right again to reach Largo do Chafariz de Dentro, an open square facing the **Museu do Fado** (➤ 56–57).

7–8

Leave this square by the far corner along Rua de São Pedro, where women sell sardines from their doorways on weekday mornings. Continue along Rua de São Pedro, passing a rare surviving section of Moorish wall. The road widens and becomes Rua de São João da Praça, where several of the apartment blocks and shopfronts are decorated with *azulejo* tiles. Continue on this street, passing the sé, then follow the tramlines down to Rua da Conceição and turn left along Rua Augusta to return to Praça do Comércio.

2 PORT COUNTRY

Drive

This spectacular drive takes you through the steeply terraced vineyards of the Douro Valley, where the grapes in port wine are grown. The scenery is magnificent at any time of year but at its best in summer when the grapes are ripening on the vines, or in September and October when the harvest is taking place. Some of the roads are twisting and narrow, so allow plenty of time.

DISTANCE 130km (80.5 miles) **TIME** 4 hours
START/END POINT Vila Real 198 C3

1–2

Start in **Vila Real** (➤ 87) and follow signs for the IP4 in the direction of Porto and Amarante. Take care as this motorway climbs steeply and it is a notorious spot for accidents. After 24km (15 miles), turn off at the sign for "pousada" and cross the bridge to reach the **Pousada do Marão in São Gonçalo.**

Turn right, follow the minor N15 for around 12km (7.4 miles) as it snakes down through the pine forests of the Ovelha Valley in the foothills of the Serra de Marão.

The fountain at Nossa Senhora dos Remédios, Lamego

LAMEGO

A short detour south from Peso da Régua on the new IP3 motorway leads to Lamego, an attractive town of Renaissance and baroque mansions overlooked by two hills. On one hill stands a ruined 12th-century castle; on the other is the sanctuary of Nossa Senhora dos Remédios, reached by a magnificent baroque stairway similar to that at Bom Jesus near Braga (➤ 89–90). The chapel is the focus for a major pilgrimage, which takes place on 8 September each year. Lamego was the setting for the first Cortes (National Assembly), a meeting of the nobility, clergy and townspeople, which proclaimed Afonso Henriques first king of Portugal in 1143. These days it is better known as the centre of production for Raposeira, Portuguese sparkling wine. For a tour, visit Quinta da Pacheca to see the process of port and still wine making (tel: 254 313 228, tours daily). For sparkling wine, try Caves da Raposeira (tel: 254 655 003, http://cavesdaraposeira.com).

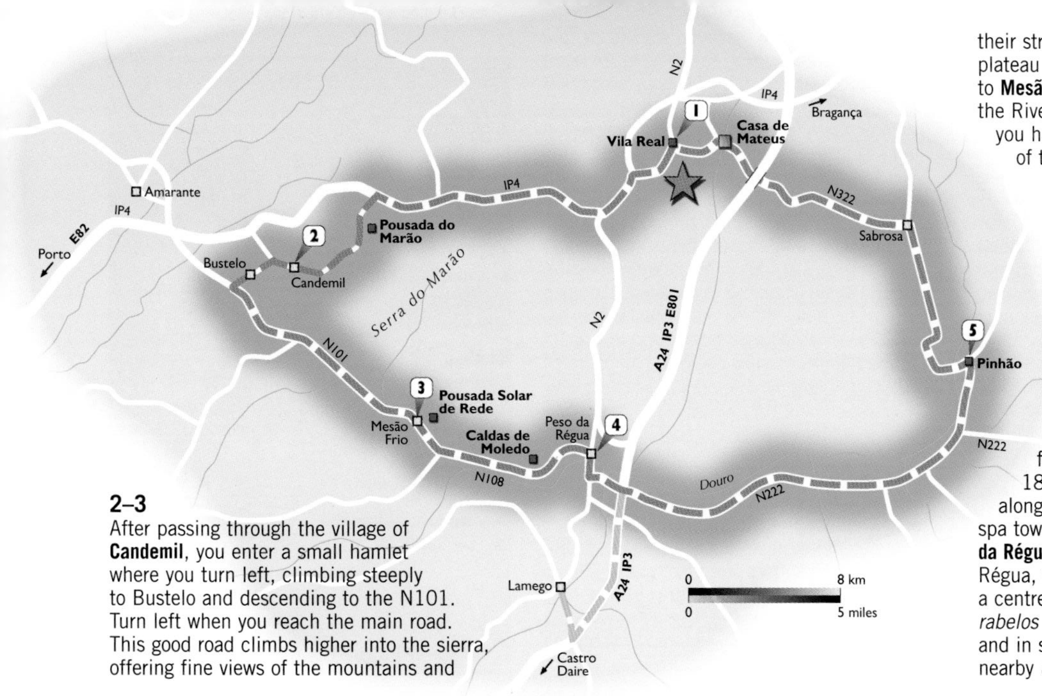

2–3

After passing through the village of **Candemil**, you enter a small hamlet where you turn left, climbing steeply to Bustelo and descending to the N101. Turn left when you reach the main road. This good road climbs higher into the sierra, offering fine views of the mountains and their strange granite boulders, then reaches a plateau and drops down through the vineyards to **Mesão Frio**. Cross the stone bridge across the River Teixeira to enter the town and soon you have your first view of the great sweep of the River Douro down below.

3–4

Now you are in the heart of port wine country, surrounded by the steep slopes of the vineyards, carved into terraces by generations of farmers. As a local saying has it: "God created Earth, but man created the Douro." The road narrows, twisting and turning as it drops to the river, passing the Pousada Solar da Rede, one of the finest *pousadas* (➤ 15–16), set on an 18th-century wine estate. Follow the river along its north bank (N108) through the spa town of **Caldas de Moledo** as far as **Peso da Régua.** This busy town, usually known as Régua, was built to serve the port trade and is a centre for transporting wine to Porto. *Barcos rabelos* (➤ 84) are moored on the riverbank and in summer you can take a cruise to the nearby *quintas* (wine estates). **Quinta de São**

The town of Lamego, set in hilly, fertile countryside

Domingos (Peso da Régua, tel: 254 320 260, Mon–Fri 9–12:30, 2–5, Sat–Sun 9–6, tours take about 20 minutes, free), in the town centre, offers tours and tastings throughout the year. There are plenty of restaurants and cafés along the waterfront at Peso da Régua or try O Malheiro, set just back from the river on the main street. (For a detour to **Lamego** ➤ 176.)

4–5

Take the lower of the two bridges across the River Douro and keep right to swing back under the bridge and emerge beside the river. Now follow the N222 along the south bank of the Douro to Pinhão. This is a lovely drive, clinging close to the river with views of vineyards, olive groves, dry-stone walls and white-painted *quintas* with the names of the famous port houses emblazoned on the hillsides. Several of the *quintas* are open to visitors – **Quinta do Panascal** (on the slopes above the River Távora, tel: 254 732 321, http://quintadopanascalvisitorscentre.wordpress.com, Mon–Fri 10–6, also weekends Apr–Oct, to 8pm Jul-Oct) has audio tours in nine languages, vineyard walks and a stone *lagar*, where the grapes are crushed by foot.

TAKING A BREAK
O Malheiro €
198 C4 Rua dos Camilos, Regua
254 313 684 Daily 9:30–midnight

About 23km (14 miles) from Régua, turn left to enter **Pinhão**, crossing an iron bridge over the Douro to return to the north bank. Drive along the main street; don't miss the station building with its *azulejo* tiles depicting vineyards and rural scenes. This small town is one of the main centres of quality port production, and several of the leading houses have *quintas* here. For a glass of port, drop into the **CS Vintage House Hotel** (Lugar da Ponte, Pinhão, tel: 254 730 230), in a beautiful setting on the riverbank.

5–6

Leaving Pinhão, fork left where the road divides, following signs for Sabrosa and Vila Real. The road climbs through terraced vineyards. At **Sabrosa**, birthplace of the great navigator Ferdinand Magellan (➤ 13), turn left towards Vila Real. You pass the Roman site of **Panóias** on your way to **Casa de Mateus**

LEAVING THE CAR BEHIND

The dramatic landscapes of the Douro Valley can also be explored on scenic train and boat journeys from Porto (➤ 80–83). River trips run from Porto and Vila Nova de Gaia (➤ 84–85) between March and October, typically travelling upstream as far as Peso da Régua and returning to Porto by train. Several trains a day leave Porto's São Bento station on the Douro Valley train line, which joins the river about 60km (37 miles) from Porto and follows its banks as far as Peso da Régua (2.5 hours), Pinhão (3 hours), Tua and Pocinho. Tickets are inexpensive and can be bought in advance or at the time of travel from São Bento station in Porto, or from the stations at Peso da Régua or Pinhão. There are also two scenic narrow-gauge branch lines along tributaries of the River Douro – the Corgo line running from Régua to Vila Real, and the Tua Valley line from Tua to Mirandela.

(➤ 86–87), the impressive Portuguese manor house that you can see from a bend in the road as you approach. Turn right immediately after Mateus to return to Vila Real.

One of several *quintas* (wine estates) in Pinhão

3 LOWER ALENTEJO

Drive

DISTANCE 222km (138 miles) **TIME** 4 hours
START/END POINT Beja ✚ 201 D1

This enjoyable drive takes you into Lower Alentejo, a region ignored by most visitors in the dash from Lisbon to the Algarve. Few people live here and there are few must-see sights – the pleasures of this region are to be found driving along empty roads and pottering around small towns. Despite, or perhaps because of, the absence of other visitors, it is in places like Serpa and Moura that you can really feel the soul of southern Portugal and the influence of its Moorish past.

1–2

Start in **Beja** (➤ 142) and leave the city by following the IP2 in the direction of Faro. The road crosses a wide open landscape of wheat fields and cork oak trees, many with numbers painted on the stripped bark to indicate the date of the harvest. After 15km (9.3 miles), turn left on the N122 towards Mértola, on a quiet road with more cork oaks and the occasional isolated farmhouse or roadside hamlet. Turn right at the roundabout to enter **Mértola** (➤ 142) and park beneath the castle in the centre of town.

The convent at Beja, where the love letters of a Portuguese nun are said to have been written

2–3

Once you have explored Mértola, leave by the same way you entered and take the bridge across the River Guadiana, following signs to Serpa – be sure to glance back as you cross the bridge for a lovely view of the town. The road climbs steeply at first, then levels out, with avenues of eucalyptus trees to either side. After 17km (10.5 miles), you reach **Mina de São Domingos**, an old copper-mining town first discovered by the Romans and still mined until the 1960s. The mines are now being turned into a tourist attraction with people visiting to see the effects of 2,000 years of mining on the landscape (free access at any time). There is also a large reservoir here, with a picnic area and a small beach.

3–4
Continue driving across typical Alentejo countryside, with its cork oaks, wheat fields and sheep. The road is long and straight and the absence of traffic is remarkable – this is one of the most sparsely populated regions in Portugal. Shortly after passing through the olive- and orange-growing village of **Santa Iria**, you reach a main road where you turn left and immediately left again to **Serpa**. Before entering the town, follow the signs to your left to climb the hill to the *pousada*, where

Nossa Senhora de Guadalupe, Serpa

THE STORY OF SALÚQUIA
Look at the coat of arms on the town hall in **Moura** (➤ 183) and you will see a young girl lying dead at the foot of a tower. This is Salúquia, a Moorish princess, who lived in Moura at the time of the Christian conquest of the town in 1233. The story goes that on her wedding day her fiancé and his entourage were murdered by Christian knights on their way to the wedding ceremony. The Christians put on their victims' clothes and masqueraded as the wedding party in order to gain access to Moura. In this way they were able to capture the castle, and Salúquia threw herself from the tower in despair. There are many similar folk legends in Portugal, but this one is unusual as it casts Christians in the role of villains and Moors as their unfortunate victims.

TAKING A BREAK

Pousada de São Francisco €€€

202 D3 Beja 284 313 580 Daily lunch and dinner 12–3, 7:30–10:30

there is a small whitewashed Moorish-looking chapel, **Nossa Senhora da Guadalupe,** and sweeping views over the plain.

4–5

Serpa is known as *vila branca* (white town) because of the typically Portuguese whitewashed houses lining its narrow cobbled streets. Like the other towns on this route, it makes a pleasant place to while away a couple of hours. It has a watch museum, a folk museum, a botanical garden and a small archaeological museum housed within the castle walls. From the town's square, Praça da República, you can climb the steps past the tourist office to reach the parish church, with its separate bell-tower standing opposite. Cafés on the main

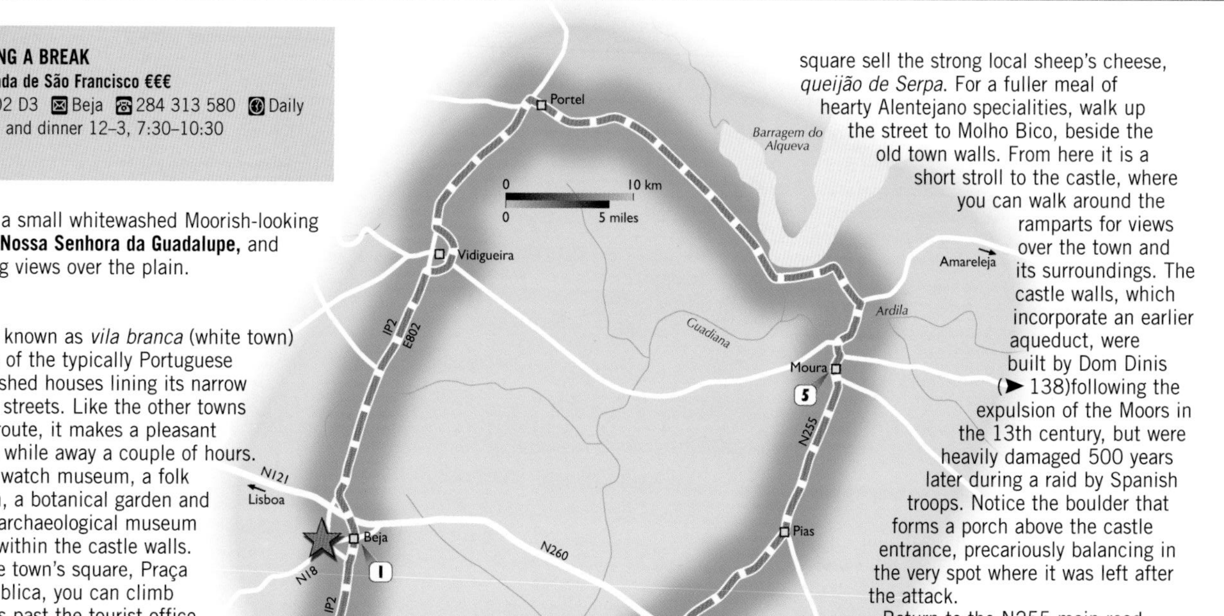

square sell the strong local sheep's cheese, *queijão de Serpa*. For a fuller meal of hearty Alentejano specialities, walk up the street to Molho Bico, beside the old town walls. From here it is a short stroll to the castle, where you can walk around the ramparts for views over the town and its surroundings. The castle walls, which incorporate an earlier aqueduct, were built by Dom Dinis (➤ 138)following the expulsion of the Moors in the 13th century, but were heavily damaged 500 years later during a raid by Spanish troops. Notice the boulder that forms a porch above the castle entrance, precariously balancing in the very spot where it was left after the attack.

Return to the N255 main road (signposted "Espanha" – Spain) and turn left, then take the next right towards Moura. Soon you reach the village of

Pias, known for its strong red wines and the frescoes in the Santa Luzia church. Turn left to pass through the centre of the village then continue on this road through the vineyards and olive groves to the spa town of **Moura**.

5–6

Moura means "Moorish Maiden" and the town takes its name from the legend of Princess Salúquia (➤ 181). This is another town with a ruined castle, cobbled streets and a long history. The Moorish quarter, called Mouraria, has whitewashed houses, ornamental chimneys and is particularly atmospheric.

Follow signs to the castle and park your car near the parish church of São João Baptista, with its rich Manueline (➤ 14) portal. There are also some fine Sevillian *azulejo* (➤ 18–19) tiles adorning the high altar, the side chapels and the niche in the facade of the bell-tower. Across the street, storks can sometimes be seen nesting in the castle tower. Nearby are the peaceful public gardens of the old spa, where people come for an evening stroll and to enjoy sunset views over the hills.

The thermal spa town of Moura has its own castle, grand mansions and pretty houses

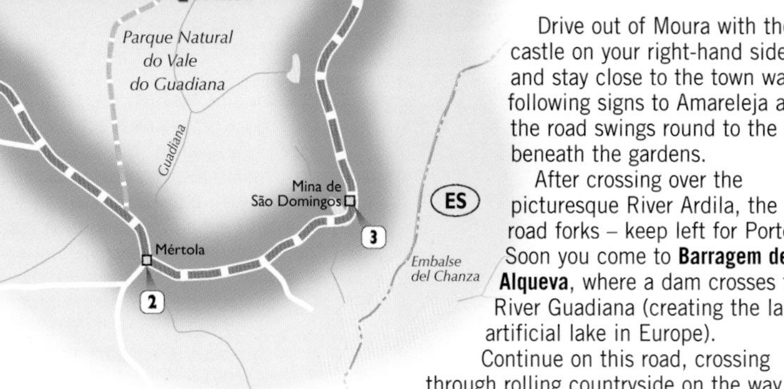

Drive out of Moura with the castle on your right-hand side and stay close to the town walls, following signs to Amareleja as the road swings round to the right beneath the gardens.

After crossing over the picturesque River Ardila, the road forks – keep left for Portel. Soon you come to **Barragem de Alqueva**, where a dam crosses the River Guadiana (creating the largest artificial lake in Europe).

Continue on this road, crossing through rolling countryside on the way to **Portel**, whose castle is visible from afar. Follow signs to Beja and return on the IP2.

PULO DO LOBO

The Pulo do Lobo (Wolf's Leap) waterfall is a place of rapids and weird rock formations in a deep gorge carved out by the River Guadiana between Mértola and Serpa. Although it is signposted from the Mértola to Serpa road, the easier approach is from a minor road 3km (2 miles) out of Mértola on the way to Beja.

4 LAGOS TO PRAIA DA LUZ

Walk

DISTANCE 6km (3.7 miles) **TIME** 3.5–4 hours
START POINT Lagos A202 B1 **END POINT** Praia da Luz 202 B1

The cliffs of western Algarve offer some superb walking, with sweeping views over the Atlantic and the bizarre rock formations that characterize this stretch of coast. Although you are hardly likely to find yourself alone, walking on the cliffs can be a good way of escaping the crowded beaches in summer. This walk is best done in the late afternoon or early evening, when the heat of the day has relented and the sunlight casts a softer glow of ever-changing colours on the ocean. If you are lucky, you might catch one of the famous Atlantic sunsets from the cliffs above Praia da Luz.

1–2

Begin on the riverfront at **Lagos** (➤ 165), opposite the **fishing harbour**, and follow **Avenida dos Descobrimentos** towards the sea. Across the road is the municipal market, which opened in 1924. Fresh fish is sold downstairs, and there is a produce market upstairs selling fruit, flowers and jars of honey and *piri-piri* (hot pepper sauce).

Beside the market, **Praça Gil Eanes** contains an extraordinary statue of the boy-king Sebastião, a national hero who died in 1578 during a disastrous naval expedition from Lagos to Morocco. Have a coffee or snack at a pavement café here, as there will be few other opportunities for refreshment on this walk.

Continue walking along the riverside promenade, lined with palm trees. This place has a powerful feel of the great Age of Discovery, when Henry the Navigator's (➤ 12, 156) caravels sailed from here. There is a statue of Prince Henry across the road in **Praça Infante Dom Henrique** and a statue of the explorer Gil Eanes outside the nearby castle. To your left, beyond the harbour walls, ocean waves wash the shore of Meia Praia, Lagos' long and windswept **town beach**. Walk past the **Ponte da Bandeira fortress**, which contains a small museum devoted to the discoveries. Alongside the fort is the pretty cove beach of Praia da Batata. Now climb the main road out of town, passing a *miradouro* (viewpoint) with a monument to São Gonçalo, a local fisherman's son who became a monk and is now the patron saint of Lagos.

Praça Gil Eanes, with the statue of King Sebastião in the centre of Lagos

2–3

At the top of the hill, leave the road and take the path to the left, signposted to Praia do Pinhão, following it as it leads along the cliffs to **Praia de Dona Ana**, one of the Algarve's most attractive beaches, with typical rock formations and sandstacks. Cross the car park above the beach and climb back on to the cliffs, taking care on the partly eroded track. From here, just keep the sea to your left as you continue across the cliffs towards **Ponte da Piedade** (Bridge of Piety), a well-known beauty spot where the red rock has been sculpted by the wind and sea into a series of dramatic boulders, arches and caves. Walk out past the **lighthouse** on to a spit for the best views along the coast. In summer, fishermen offer boat trips into the grottoes from a small landing stage at the foot of the cliffs.

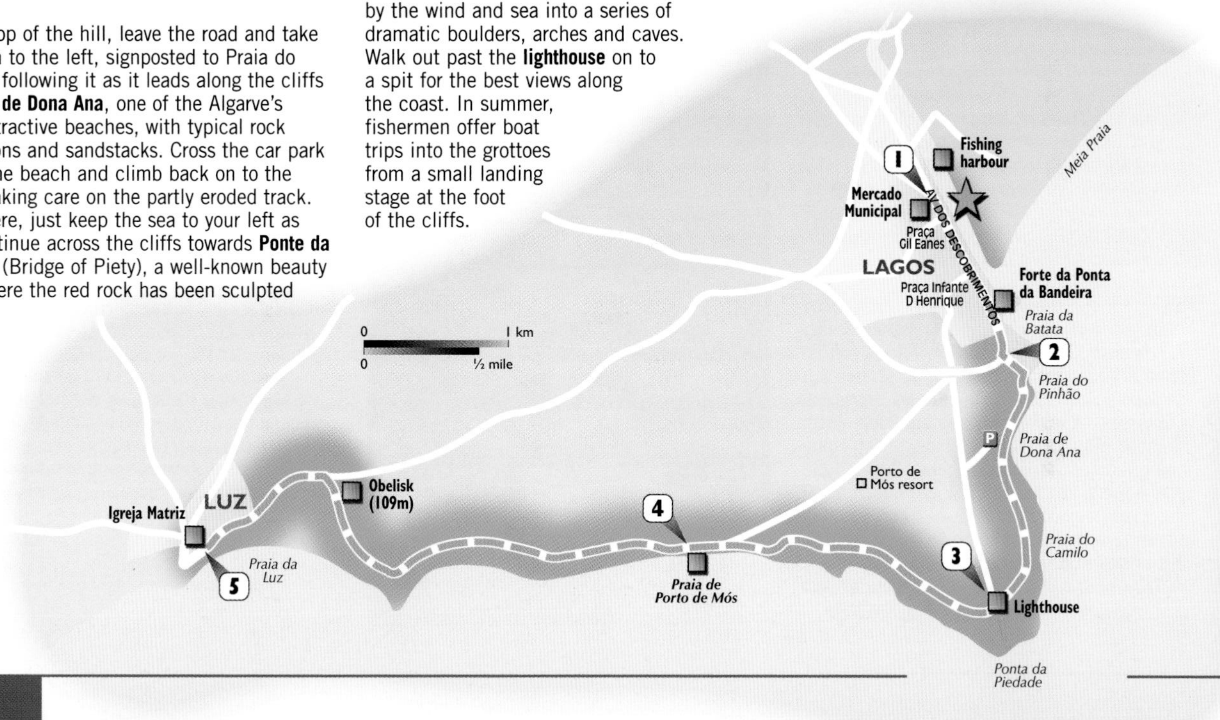

3–4

Leaving the lighthouse, head west along the clifftop path. You need to stay close to the sea to avoid being forced into the resort development at Porto de Mós. Instead, drop straight down to the **beach** (watch your step here, although as building work is completed, this descent will get easier), where there are a couple of decent restaurants. If you feel you've done enough walking by now, there are occasional buses from here back to Lagos.

4–5

The next stretch of the walk is the hardest as it involves a long (but steady) climb to the highest point of the cliffs. The path is clear and offers spectacular views over the Atlantic, as far as **Cabo de São Vicente** (➤ 157–158) on a clear day.

ESCAPE ROUTE

The coastal footpath between Praia de Dona Ana and Ponte da Piedade also gives access to Praia do Camilo, a classic cove beach that is usually quieter than the others on this walk.

Stop to admire the stunning views over the coves and grottoes of Ponte da Piedade

After about 45 minutes you reach an **obelisk** marking the summit (109m/358ft). Just beyond the obelisk, look for a gap in the bushes to your left and scramble down towards **Praia da Luz**, emerging on a cobbled path that leads to the beach. Praia da Luz is a low-key but growing resort of whitewashed apartments and villas climbing above a splendid beach. Stroll along the beachfront promenade, with its mosaic pavement, to reach the balcony at the end. Near here is the restaurant Fortaleza da Luz (➤ below), inside an old fortress, facing the parish church. Regular buses to Lagos stop beside the church.

TAKING A BREAK

Bora Café €

202 B1 · Rua Conselheiro Joaquim Machado 17, Lagos · 282 768 520 · Jun–Sep Mon–Fri 8:30am–midnight, Sat 9am–midnight, Sun 10am–midnight, Jul–Aug daily until 2am; shorter hours in winter; closed Sun Nov–Feb

Fortaleza da Luz €€€

202 B1 · Rua da Igreja 3, Praia da Luz · 282 789 926 · Daily lunch and dinner (closed mid-Nov to mid-Dec)

Practicalities

BEFORE YOU GO

WHAT YOU NEED

● Required
○ Suggested
▲ Not required
△ Not applicable

Some countries require a passport to remain valid for a minimum period (usually at least six months) beyond the date of entry – check beforehand.

	UK	Germany	USA	Canada	Australia	Ireland	Netherlands	Spain
Passport	●	●	●	●	●	●	●	●
Visa (regulations can change – check before booking)	▲	▲	▲	▲	▲	▲	▲	▲
Onward or Return Ticket	○	○	○	○	○	○	○	○
Health Inoculations	▲	▲	▲	▲	▲	▲	▲	▲
Health Documentation	▲	▲	▲	▲	▲	▲	▲	▲
Travel Insurance (➤ 192, Health)	○	○	○	○	○	○	○	○
Driver's Licence (national)	●	●	●	●	●	●	●	●
Car Insurance Certificate	●	●	●	●	●	●	●	●
Car Registration Document	●	●	●	●	●	●	●	●

WHEN TO GO

High season: APR–OCT. Low season: JAN–MAR, NOV–DEC.

	JAN	FEB	MAR	APR	MAY	JUN	JUL	AUG	SEP	OCT	NOV	DEC
°C	15°C	16°C	18°C	21°C	24°C	30°C	35°C	37°C	33°C	28°C	19°C	17°C
°F	59°F	61°F	64°F	70°F	75°F	86°F	95°F	99°F	91°F	82°F	66°F	63°F
Weather	Sunshine and showers	Sunshine and showers	Sunshine and showers	Sunshine and showers	Sun	Sun	Sun	Sun	Sun	Sun	Sunshine and showers	Sunshine and showers

Sun — Sunshine and showers

Temperatures are the **average daily maximum** for each month in the Algarve. Spring (April to June) and autumn (September to October) are the best times to visit Portugal as the summer months can be unbearably hot and crowded. Added attractions are wild flowers in spring and the Douro Valley grape harvest in autumn. Summer is hot and dry inland, and mild on the coast, where sea temperatures vary from 16°C (61°F) on the west coast to 23°C (73°F) in the Algarve. Winters are cool and wet in the north, but pleasantly mild in the Algarve, where walking and golf are year-round activities and swimming is possible from March to November, although you will probably need a wetsuit – the sea temperature can be quite chilly. Hotel rates tend to be much lower in January and February, making this a good time to visit Lisbon and the Algarve.

GETTING ADVANCE INFORMATION

Websites

- Welcome to Portugal: www.portugal.org
- Portugal National Tourist Office: www.visitportugal.com
- Algarve Net: www.visitalgarve.pt
- Pousadas de Portugal: www.pousadas.pt
- Solares de Portugal: www.solaresdeportugal.pt

In the UK

Portuguese National Tourist Office
11 Belgrave Square
London SW1X 8PP
☎ 020 7201 6666

GETTING THERE

By Air There are international airports at Lisbon, Porto and Faro. **British Airways** and the Portuguese national airline **TAP Portugal** and discount airline easyJet operate scheduled flights from London to all three cities, with a flight time of around two and a half hours. Ryanair flies to Porto and Faro from several UK and European cities. There is also a wide selection of charter flights, especially to Faro in summer, from British, Irish and European airports. Most seats on charter flights are sold by tour operators as part of a package holiday, but it is usually possible to buy a flight-only deal through travel agents or on the internet. The disadvantage of charter flights is that you are sometimes restricted to periods of 7 or 14 days.
From the USA TAP has scheduled flights to Lisbon from New York (6.5 hours), with connections to other North American cities.

By Car There are several entry points along the border with Spain, with few or no border controls. The main roads into Portugal are from Vigo to Porto, Zamora to Bragança, Salamanca to Guarda, Badajoz to Elvas and the motorway from Seville to the Algarve. From Britain, take a car ferry to Bilbao or Santander in northern Spain, from where it is a drive of about 800km (500 miles) to Porto and 1,000km (620 miles) to Lisbon.

By Rail There are regular trains to Lisbon from Madrid (10 hours) and Paris (24 hours). A train line from Vigo in Spain crosses the border at Valença do Minho to Porto and Lisbon.

TIME

Portugal is on Greenwich Mean Time (GMT), and one hour behind most of continental Europe. But between the last Sundays in March and October, it is GMT plus one hour (GMT+1).

CURRENCY AND FOREIGN EXCHANGE

Currency The euro (€) is the official currency of Portugal. Euro coins are issued in denominations of 1, 2, 5, 10, 20 and 50 euro cents and €1 and €2. Notes are issued in denominations of €5, €10, €20, €50, €100, €200 and €500. Note: €200 and €500 notes are not issued in Portugal, but those issued elsewhere are valid.

Foreign Currency and Traveller's Cheques can be changed at banks and exchange bureaux, as well as in many hotels. Exchange bureaux generally offer the best deal, but it pays to shop around and compare commission charges. You will need to show your passport when cashing traveller's cheques.

You can also withdraw cash from ATM machines using your credit or debit card and a PIN (personal identification number). Your bank will usually charge for this service.

Major Credit Cards, including Visa, Cirrus and Maestro, are accepted in most major resorts and cities. That said, Portugal is not always plastic-friendly and some shops, restaurants and even hotels only accept cash. In the countryside, keep small denomination notes to hand. It is easier and no more expensive (depending on your credit card charges) to rely solely on plastic, rather than taking travellers' cheques or buying cash in advance.

In Ireland
Portuguese National Tourist Office
54 Dawson Street
Dublin 2
☎ 01 670 9133

In the USA
Portuguese National Tourist Office
590 Fifth Avenue
4th Floor
New York NY 10036-9702
☎ 646/723 0200

In Canada
Portuguese National Tourist Office
60 Bloor Street West
Suite 1005
Toronto, Ontario M4W 3B8
☎ (416) 921 7376

WHEN YOU ARE THERE

NATIONAL HOLIDAYS

1 Jan	New Year's Day
Feb/Mar	Shrove Tuesday
Mar/Apr	Good Friday/Easter Monday
25 Apr	Day of the Revolution
1 May	Labour Day
May/Jun	Corpus Christi
10 Jun	National Day
15 Aug	Feast of the Assumption
5 Oct	Republic Day
1 Nov	All Saints' Day
1 Dec	Independence Day
8 Dec	Feast of the Immaculate Conception
25 Dec	Christmas Day

ELECTRICITY

The power supply is 220 volts AC. Sockets take two-pronged round continental plugs. Visitors from the UK will need an adaptor, and visitors from the USA will need a transformer for 100–120 volt devices.

OPENING HOURS

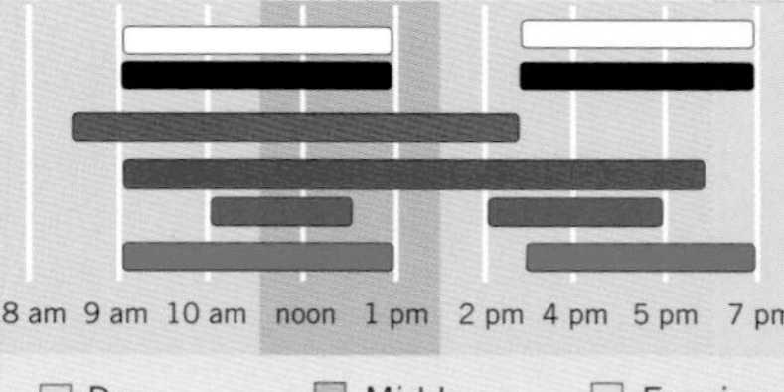

Shops Usually 9–1, 3–7. Large stores and supermarkets open 9–7 or 10 (5 on Sundays).
Banks Banks are open 8:30–3.
Post Offices Mon–Fri 9–6, Sat 9–12 in cities, shorter hours in provincial areas.
Museums and Churches Usually 10–12:30, 2–5, but check before visiting.
Pharmacies Usually 9–12:30, 2–7, but duty chemists will be open longer (➤ 192).

TIPS/GRATUITIES

Tipping is not expected for all services and rates are lower than elsewhere in Europe.
As a general guide:

Restaurant bill	(service not included) 10%
Taxis	10%
Tour Guides	half day €3 full day €5
Porters	€1 per bag
Chambermaids	€2 per night
Toilet attendants	small change

DRINKING LAWS

There is no minimum age for drinking in Portugal, although the minimum age to purchase alcohol is 16. Drinking and driving laws, however, are very strict, and the alcohol limit is 0.5g per litre of blood, with hefty fines imposed if found in breach of this limit.

TIME DIFFERENCES

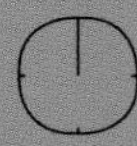
GMT 12 noon

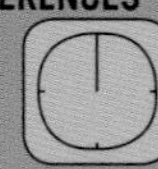
Portugal 12 noon

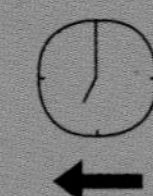
USA (New York) 7am

USA (Los Angeles) 4am

Spain 1pm

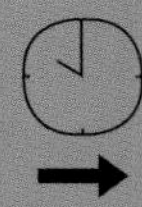
Sydney 10pm

STAYING IN TOUCH

Post Stamps *(selos)* can be bought at post offices, kiosks and tobacconists. Letters to European Union (EU) countries should arrive within five to seven days, and to the USA within 10 days. Send urgent mail by *correio azul* and ensure that you post it in a blue postbox. Other postboxes are red.

Telephones There are public telephones on almost every street corner. They take coins, credit cards or phonecards, available from post offices, kiosks and shops displaying the PT (Portugal Telecom) logo. International calls are cheaper between 9pm and 9am and at weekends. Calls from hotel rooms will invariably attract a heavy premium.

International Dialling Codes
Dial 00 followed by

UK:	**44**
USA/Canada:	**1**
Irish Republic:	**353**
Australia:	**61**
Spain:	**34**

Mobile Providers and Services The coverage for mobile phones across Portugal is fairly extensive, and your mobile should pick up the local network automatically – although US cell phones may have more difficulty. Call charges will vary according to your contract. Check with your service provider before travelling.

WiFi and Internet There is high-speed internet access across Portugal, but WiFi service is sporadic. You will find WiFi, however, in most good hotels, particularly in Lisbon, Porto and the Algarve, and in some cafés and libraries, although this is still unusual. Most WiFi is offered through the mobile phone networks, and you pay for usage per minute or hour. There are internet cafes in most beach resorts on the Algarve (expect them to be busy), and some in Lisbon.

PERSONAL SAFETY

Violence against tourists is unusual in Portugal. Theft from cars is the most common form of crime.

- Do not leave valuables on the beach or poolside.
- Always lock valuables in hotel safety deposit boxes
- Never leave anything inside your car. If you have to, lock valuables in the boot.
- Beware of pickpockets in crowded markets, around train stations and on crowded buses in Lisbon and Porto.
- Do not leave bags unattended while standing at a car hire desk or loading suitcases onto a bus.

Police Assistance:
☎ 112 from any phone

There are police stations *(esquadra da policia)* in all towns and villages across Portugal. If your lose your passport, credit cards or any personal items, you will need to fill out a crime report at a police station for insurance or replacement purposes. In 2001, Portugal decriminalized drugs for personal use.

EMERGENCY NUMBERS

POLICE 112

FIRE 112

AMBULANCE 112

HEALTH

Insurance Citizens of EU countries receive reduced-cost emergency health care with relevant documentation (European Health Insurance Card – EHIC), but private medical insurance is still advised and essential for all other visitors.

Dental Services The standard of dental care is generally excellent. Dental practices advertise in the free English-language magazines and newspapers at hotels. You have to pay for treatment, but your insurance should cover the costs.

Weather The sun is intense at all times of year and it is possible to burn very quickly, even on cloudy days. Cover up with high-factor sunscreen, wear a hat and drink plenty of water, especially if walking in the hills or along the coast.

Drugs Chemists *(farmâcia)* are open Mon–Fri 9–1 and 2:30–7, and Sat 9–12.30. Some open through lunch and the late-night duty chemist is posted in pharmacy windows. Pharmacists are highly trained and can sell some drugs that require prescriptions in other countries. However, take adequate supplies of any drugs you take regularly as they may not be available.

Safe Water Tap water is safe but its mineral content may make it taste unpleasant. Ask for sparkling *(água com gás)* or still *(água sem gás)* bottled water.

CONCESSIONS

Young People Most museums have lower admission rates for students (and entry is generally free for children) on production of a passport or valid student identity card.

Senior Citizens Senior citizens from many European countries come to the Algarve for its year-round warmth and long-stay low-season rates. Travellers over 65 are usually entitled to discounted admission at museums and reduced fares on public transport (proof of age needed). If mobility is a problem getting around can be a bit of a trial (➤ Travelling with a Disability, above).

TRAVELLING WITH A DISABILITY

Facilities in Portugal for disabled travellers are slowly improving, but many older hotels and public buildings are still inaccessible, especially in cities where hotels are often on the upper floors of apartment blocks. Cobbled streets are a problem for wheelchair users. There are "blue badge" car parking spaces in most town centres, and adapted toilets at airports and railway stations.

It is best to discuss your particular needs with your tour operator or hotel before booking a holiday.

CHILDREN

Hotels and restaurants tend to be child-friendly, and many coastal hotels have playgrounds and children's pools. Facilities are improving.

TOILETS

There are public toilets in shopping centres and by some of the larger beaches.

CUSTOMS

Duty-free allowances when travelling from Portugal to the UK are 3,200 cigarettes, 3kg tobacco, 10L spirits, 90L wine and 20L fortified wine. For details and information for non-EU residents, see www.taxfreetravel.com.

CONSULATES AND EMBASSIES

UK ☎ 213 924 000

USA ☎ 217 273 300

Ireland ☎ 213 929 440

Australia ☎ 213 101 500

Canada ☎ 213 164 600

USEFUL WORDS AND PHRASES

There are two distinctive Portuguese sounds: firstly, the nasalised vowels written with a til (~, like the tilde on Spanish *ñ*): (so "bread", *pão*, is pronounced "pow!" with a strong nasal twang; secondly, "s" and "z" are often pronounced as a slushy "sh" (so "banknotes", *notas*, is pronounced "not-ash").

GREETINGS AND COMMON WORDS

Yes/No **Sim/Não**
Please **Se faz favor**
Thank you **Obrigado** *(male speaker)/* **Obrigada** *(female speaker)*
You're welcome **De nada/Foi um prazer**
Hello/Goodbye **Olá/Adeus**
Welcome **Bem vindo/a**
Good morning **Bom dia**
Good evening/night **Boa noite**
How are you? **Como está?**
Fine, thank you **Bem, obrigado/a**
Sorry **Perdão**
Excuse me, could you help me? **Desculpe, podia-me ajudar?**
My name is... **Chamo-me...**
Do you speak English? **Fala inglês?**
I don't understand **Não percebo**
I don't speak any Portuguese **Não falo português**

EMERGENCY! URGÊNCIA!

Help! **Socorro!**
Stop! **Pare!**
Stop that thief! **Apanhe o ladrão!**
Police! **Polícia!**
Fire! **Fogo!**
Go away, or I'll scream! **Se não se for embora, começo a gritar!**
Leave me alone! **Deixe-me em paz!**
I've lost my purse/wallet **Perdi o meu porta-moedas/a minha carteira**
My passport has been stolen **Roubaram-me o passaporte**
Could you call a doctor? **Podia chamar um médico depressa?**

DIRECTIONS AND TRAVELLING

Airport **Aeroporto**
Boat **Barco**
Bus station **Estação de camionetas**
Bus/coach **Autocarro**
Car **Automóvel**
Church **Igreja**
Hospital **Hospital**
Market **Mercado**
Museum **Museu**
Square **Praça**
Street **Rua**
Taxi rank **Praça de táxis**
Train **Comboio**
Ticket **Bilhete**
  Return **Ida e volta**
  Single **Bilhete de ida**
Station **Estação**
I'm lost **Estou perdida**
How many kilometres to...? **Quantos quilómetros faltam ainda parachegar a...?**
Here/There **Aqui/Ali**
Left/right **À esquerda/À direita**
Straight on **Em frente**

NUMBERS

0 **zero**
1 **um**
2 **dois**
3 **três**
4 **quatro**
5 **cinco**
6 **seis**
7 **sete**
8 **oito**
9 **nove**
10 **dez**
11 **onze**
12 **doze**
13 **treze**
14 **catorze**
15 **quinze**
16 **dezasseis**
17 **dezassete**
18 **dezoito**
19 **dezanove**
20 **vinte**
21 **vinte e um**
30 **trinta**
40 **quarenta**
50 **cinquenta**
60 **sessenta**
70 **setenta**
80 **oitenta**
90 **noventa**
100 **cem**
101 **cento e um**
500 **quinhentos**

DAYS

Today **Hoje**
Tomorrow **Amanhã**
Yesterday **Ontem**
Tonight **Esta noite**
Last night **Ontem à noite**
In the morning **De manhã**
In the afternoon **De tarde**
Later **Logo/Mais tarde**
This week **Esta semana**
Monday **Segunda-feira**
Tuesday **Terça-feira**
Wednesday **Quarta-feira**
Thursday **Quinta-feira**
Friday **Sexta-feira**
Saturday **Sábado**
Sunday **Domingo**

MONEY: DINHEIRO

Bank **Banco**
Banknote **Notas**
Cash desk **Caixa**
Change **Troco**
Cheque **Cheque**
Coin **Moeda**
Credit card **Cartão de crédito**
Exchange office **Casa de cámbio**
Exchange rate **Cámbio**
Foreign **Estrangeiro**
Mail **Correio**
Post office **Agência do correios**
Traveller's cheque **Cheque de viagem**
Could you give me some small change, please? **Podia-me dar também dinheiro trocado, se faz favor?**

ACCOMMODATION

Are there any...? **Há...?**
I'd like a room with a view of the sea **Queria um quarto com vista para o mar**
Where's the emergency exit/fire escape? **Onde fica a saída de emergência/ escada de salvação?**
Does that include breakfast? **Está incluido o pequeno almoço?**
Do you have room service? **O hotel tem serviço de quarto?**
I've made a reservation **Reservei um lugar**
Air conditioning **Ar condicionado**
Balcony **Varanda**
Bathroom **Casa de banho**
Chambermaid **Camareira**
Hot water **Água quente**
Hotel **Hotel**
Key **Chave**
Lift **Elevador**
Night **Noite**
Room **Quarto**
Room service **Serviço de quarto**
Shower **Duche**
Telephone **Telefone**
Towel **Toalha**
Water **Água**

RESTAURANT: RESTAURANTE

Could we see a menu, please? **Poderia**
I'd like to book a table **Posso reservar uma mesa?**
A table for two, please **Uma mesa para duas pessoas, se faz favor**
dar nos a ementa, se faz favor
What's this? **O que é isto?**
A bottle of... **Uma garrafa de...**
Alcohol **Álcool**
Beer **Cerveja**
Bill **Conta**
Bread **Pão**
Breakfast **Pequeno almoço**
Café **Café**
Coffee **Café**
Dinner **Jantar**
Lunch **Almoço**
Menu **Menú/ementa**
Milk **Leite**
Mineral water **Água mineral**
Pepper **Pimenta**
Salt **Sal**
Table **Mesa**
Tea **Chá**
Waiter **Empregado/a**

SHOPPING

Shop **Loja**
Where can I get....? **Em que loja posso arranjar...?**
Could you help me please? **Pode-me atendar, se faz favor?**
I'm looking for... **Estou a procura de...**
I would like... **Queria...**
I'm just looking **Só estou a ver**
How much? **Quanto custa?**
It's too expensive **Acho demasiado caro**
I'll take this one/these **Levo este(s)/ esta(s)**
Good/Bad **Bom/Mau**
Bigger **Maior**
Smaller **Mais pequeno**
Open/Closed **Aberto/Fechado**
I'm a size... in the UK **Na Grã Bretanha o meu número é...**
Have you got a bag please? **Tem um saco, se faz favor?**

TOWN PRONUNCIATION GUIDE

Braga **brag-uh**
Bragança **bra-gan-suh**
Coimbra **queem-bruh**
Évora **e-vor-uh**
Faro **far-ooh**
Fátima **fa-tee-muh**
Lagos **lah-goosh**
Lisboa **leezh-boh-ah**
Marvão **mar-vow**
Porto **port-ooh**
Sagres **sar-gresh**
Tavira **ta-veer-ah**
Vila Viçosa **vee-lah-vee-soh-sah**

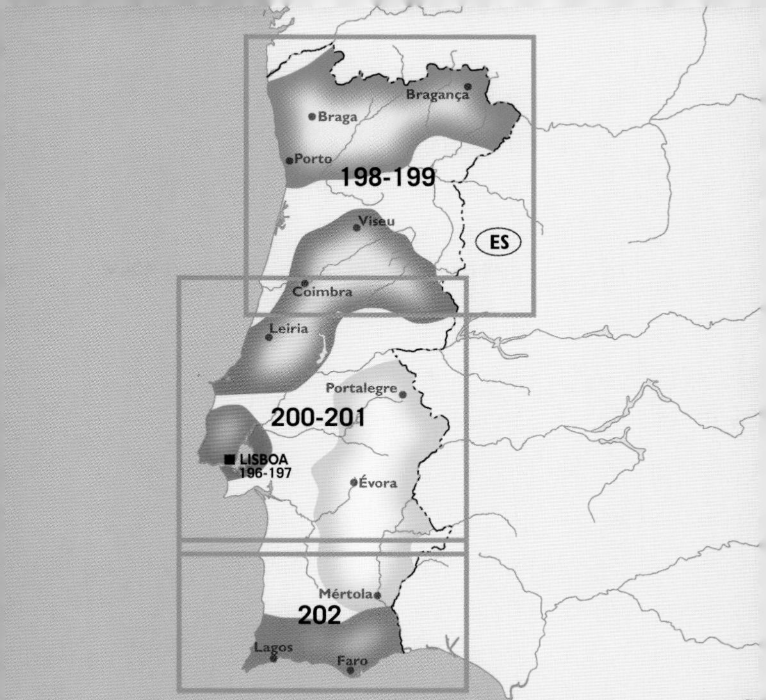

Bragança
Braga
Porto
198-199
Viseu
ES
Coimbra
Leiria
Portalegre
200-201
LISBOA
196-197
Évora
Mértola
202
Lagos
Faro

To identify the regions, see the map on the inside of the front cover

Streetplan

Main/other road	Featured place of interest
Minor road	Metro station
Railway	Tourist information
Funicular railway	Church
Important building	Post Office
Park/garden	Miradouro/viewpiont

Regional Maps

International boundary	City
Regional boundary	Town/village
Major route	Airport
Motorway/toll motorway	Built up area
National road	National/Natural park
Regional road	Featured place of interest
Other road	Place of interest
Railway	Height in metres

196/197 0 150 metres 0 150 yards

198-202 0 25 km 0 15 miles

Museu Calouste Gulbenkian, Parque Eduardo VII
AVENIDA DA LIBERDADE
Rua de São José
C do Lavra
Largo d Anunciada
Rua d Portas d Santo Antão
Hospital de São José
Rua Lázaro
Praça da Alegria
Rua da Glória
Rua St António Glória
Rua das Taipas
Coliseu
Praça dos Restauradores
Palácio Foz
Restauradores
Rua M Vaz
Rua do A da Graça
RUA DA PALMA
Rato
Miradouro de São Pedro de Alcântara
R D PEDRO V
Elevador da Glória
C da Glória
ESTAÇAO CENTRAL DO ROSSIO
Teatro Maria II
Largo São Domingos
Rua do Teixeira
RUA SÃO PEDRO ALCÂNTARA
Museu de Arte Sacra
Largo D Cadaval
Rossio
R D DUARTE
Travessa da Boa Hora
Igreja de São Roque
Rossio (Praça Dom Pedro IV)
Praça da Figueira
C do Duque
Largo Trindade Coelho
Rua da Atalaia
Travessa da Queimada
Rua d Condessa
Rua da Oliveira
Rua do Carmo
RUA DA BETESGA
BAIRRO ALTO
Rua das Gáveas
RUA D MISERICÓRDIA
Rua Nova d Trindade
Museu Arqueológio do Carmo
Elevador de Santa Justa
Rua dos Douradores
Travessa dos Fiéis de Deus
Rua da Trindade
Rua dos Correeiros
RUA DA PRATA
T do Carmo
C do Sacramento
Baixa-Chiado
Rua da Assunção
Rua Augusta
Rua dos Sapateiros
RUA AUREA
Estrêla
Rua das Salgadeiras
CHIADO
Rua d Vitória
Rua d Loreto
Largo do Chiado
Praça L de Camões
Rua Garrett
Rua do Crucifixo
R d H Seca
Rua N do Almada
Largo S Carlos
Rua Capelo
Rua Ivens
BAIXA
Rua da Emenda
Rua d Flores
RUA DO ALECRIM
Rua A Maria Cardoso
Rua D de Bragança
Teatro S Carlos
Rua Serpa Pinto
Largo da Biblioteca Pública
Rua da Conceição
Rua de São Julião
Rua do Comércio
Ministérios
Museu do Chiado
Rua Vitor Cordon
Praça do Município
Rua d S Paulo
Lapa
Rua Nova do Carvalho
Rua do Arsenal
Praça do Comércio
Belém, Museu Nacional de Arte Antiga
Cais do Sodré
Praça D da Terceira
Ministério
Welcome Center
AVENIDA DA RIBEIRA DAS NAUS
CAIS DO SODRÉ
Cais do Sodré
Gare Fluvial
A
B
C
1
2
3
4
5

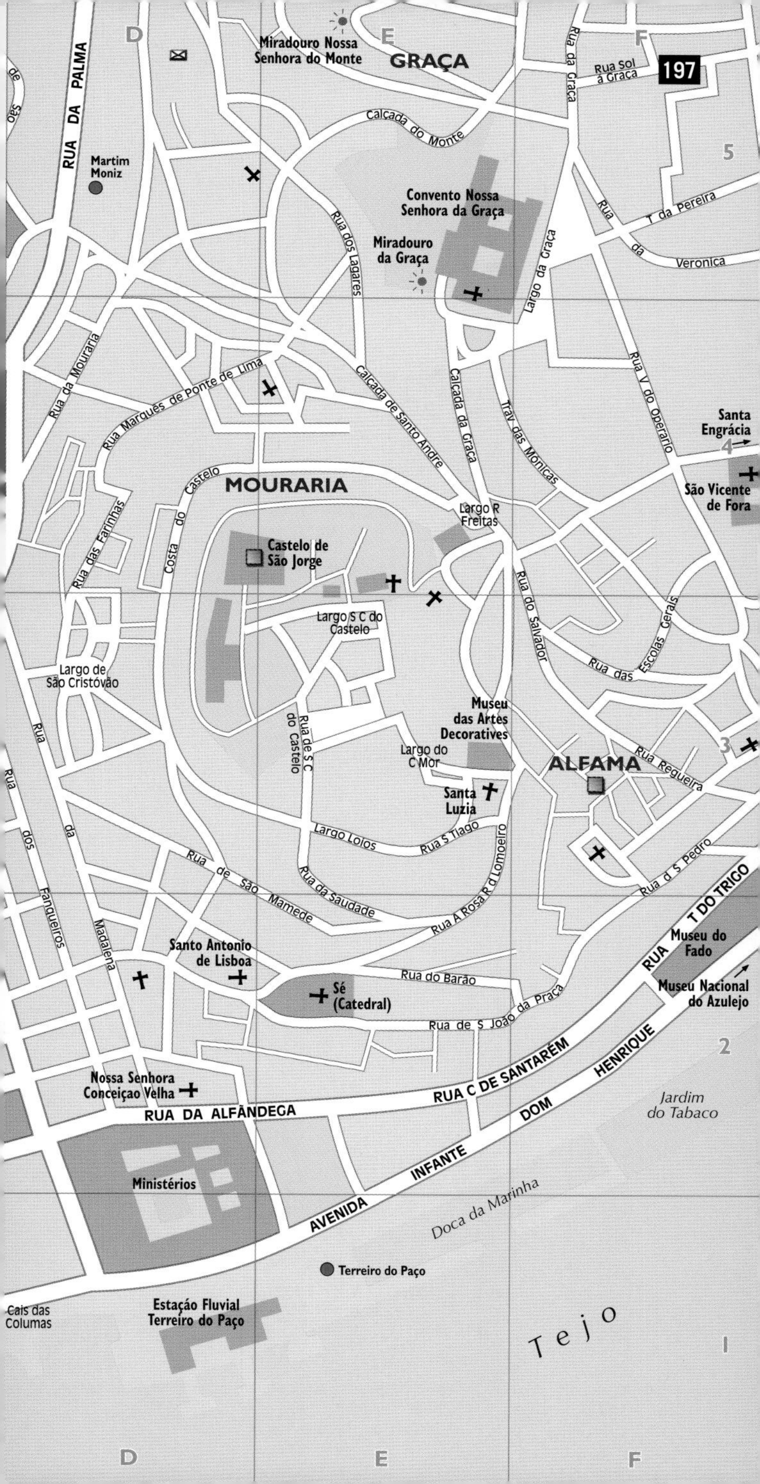

D
E
F
Miradouro Nossa Senhora do Monte
GRAÇA
Rua da Graça
Rua Sol à Graça
Calçada do Monte
RUA DA PALMA
Martim Moniz
Convento Nossa Senhora da Graça
Miradouro da Graça
Rua dos Lagares
Rua T da Pereira
Rua da Veronica
Largo da Graça
Rua da Mouraria
Rua Marquês de Ponte de Lima
Calçada de Santo Andre
Calçada da Graça
Trav das Mónicas
Rua V do Operario
Santa Engrácia
São Vicente de Fora
MOURARIA
Costa do Castelo
Rua das Farinhas
Largo R Freitas
Castelo de São Jorge
Rua do Salvador
Largo S C do Castelo
Rua das Escolas Gerais
Largo de São Cristóvão
Museu das Artes Decoratives
Rua de S C do Castelo
Largo do C Mor
ALFAMA
Rua Regueira
Santa Luzia
Rua dos Fanqueiros
Rua da Madalena
Largo Loios
Rua S Tiago
Rua R d Lomoeiro
Rua d S Pedro
Rua de São Mamede
Rua da Saudade
Rua A Rosa
RUA T DO TRIGO
Museu do Fado
Santo Antonio de Lisboa
Rua do Barão
Sé (Catedral)
Rua de S João da Praça
Museu Nacional do Azulejo
Nossa Senhora Conceiçao Velha
RUA C DE SANTARÉM
RUA DA ALFÂNDEGA
AVENIDA INFANTE DOM HENRIQUE
Jardim do Tabaco
Ministérios
Doca da Marinha
Terreiro do Paço
Cais das Columas
Estaçáo Fluvial Terreiro do Paço
Tejo
5
4
3
2
1

A
B
C
5
4
3
2
1
Nigrán
Cabo Silleiro
O Porriño
Ramallosa
Salvaterra de Miño
Tui
Melgaço
São Gregório
Padrenda
Celanova
Sandias
Verea
Xinzo de Limia/ Ginzo de Limia
Bande
Arrabal/ Oia
Valença do Minho
Monção
Extremo
Serra da Peneda
Cualedro
A Guarda/ La Guardia
Vila Nova de Cerveira
Paredes de Coura
1416m
Entrimo
Muiños
Baltar
Caminha
Lanhelas
Soajo
Lobios
Randín
Moledo
VIANA DE CASTELO
Arcos de Valdevez
Lindoso
Vila Praia de Âncora
Afife
Parque Nacional da Peneda-Gerês
Vale do Rio Cávado
Montalegre
Ponte da Barca
Barragem de Paradela
Gralhos
Viana do Castelo
Ponte de Lima
Serra do Gerês
Paradela
Deão
Caldas do Gerês
Barragem de Venda Nova
Barragem do Alto Rabagão
Darque
Costa Verde
Vila Verde
Balugães
Louredo
Venda Nova
Boticas
Castelo do Neiva
Barragem da Caniçada
Serra do Barroso
VILA REAL
Feitos
Bom Jesus do Monte
Póvoa de Lanhoso
Esposende
BRAGA
Barcelos
Citânia de Breiteros
Ribeira de Pena
Ofir
Arco de Baúlhe
Estela
Guimarães
Fafe
Rio Mau
Póvoa do Varzim
Vila Nova de Famalicão
Nespereira
Mondim de Basto
Vila de Conde
Santo Tirso
Caldas de Vizela
Felgueiras
Celorico de Basto
Casa de Mateus
Paços de Ferreira
Lixa
Vila Real
Porto
Amarante
Perafita
Maia
Alfena
Lousada
PORTO
1415m
Sabros
Matosinhos
Paredes
Penafiel
Santa Marta de Penaguião
PORTO
Vila Nova de Gaia
Valongo
Gondomar
Paço de Sousa
Baiao
Mesão Frio
Serra do Marão
Peso da Régua
Douro
Entre Ambos-os-Rios
Francelos
Granja
Espinho
Cinfães
Lamego
Castelo de Paiva
Tarouca
Santa Maria da Feira
Moimenta da Beira
Arouca
Rossas
VISEU
Furadouro
São João da Madeira
Castro Daire
Ovar
Válega
Vale de Cambra
Serra da Gralheira
1120m
Vila Nova de Paiva
Oliveira de Azeméis
Bestida
Estarreja
AVEIRO
São João da Serra
São Pedro do Sul
Lordosa
Torreira
Murtosa
Albergaria-a-Velha
Sever do Vouga
Oliveira de Frades
Vouga
Vouzela
Sátão
Angeja
São Jacinto
Viseu
Penalva do Castelo
Gafanha da Nazaré
Aveiro
Lamas do Vouga
Alcofra
Costa Nova do Prado
Ílhavo
Águeda
Serra do Caramulo
Caramulo
Mangualde
Vagos
Oiã
Oliveira do Bairro
Bolfiar
Nelas
Mondego
1074m
Boialvo
Tondela
Rio Torto
Praia de Mira
Mamarrosa
Anadia
Carregal do Sal
Canas de Senhorim
Parque Natural da Serra da Estrela
Mira
Tamengos
Santa Comba Dão
Seia
Luso
Rojão Grande
Cantanhede
Mealhada
Buçaco
Oliveira do Hospital
Tocha
Tábua
Serra da Estrela
COIMBRA
Gândara
Vide
1993m
Torre
Vendas de Galizes
Arazede
Penacova
São Martinho
Quiaios
Arganil
Tortosendo
COIMBRA
Rio Mondego
Vila Nova de Poiares
Figueira da Foz
Montemor-o-Velho
Ceira
Serpins
Góis
Cepos
1418m
Silvares
Condeixa-a-Nova
Lavos
Lousã
Soure
Leirosa
Conimbriga
Miranda do Corvo
Pampilhosa da Serra
Orvalho
Serra da Guardunha
Louriçal
Penela
Castanheira de Pera
Carriço
Zêzere
Foz Giraldo
Pedrógão
Pedrógão
200
201
AG57
AP9
A3
IP1
IC28
A28
IP9
A27
E01
A11
IC14
A7
IC5
IC1
A42
IC25
E82
IP4
A4
A24
IP3
A29
A1
IP5
E80
A25
A17
IC2
A14
E801
IC12
N202
N203
N101
N13
N103
N205
N206
N204
N105
N104
N14
N106
N15
N222
N322
N323
N227
N229
N327
N109
N234
N231
N17
N230
N342
N112
N110
N237
N540
C531
N2
N1

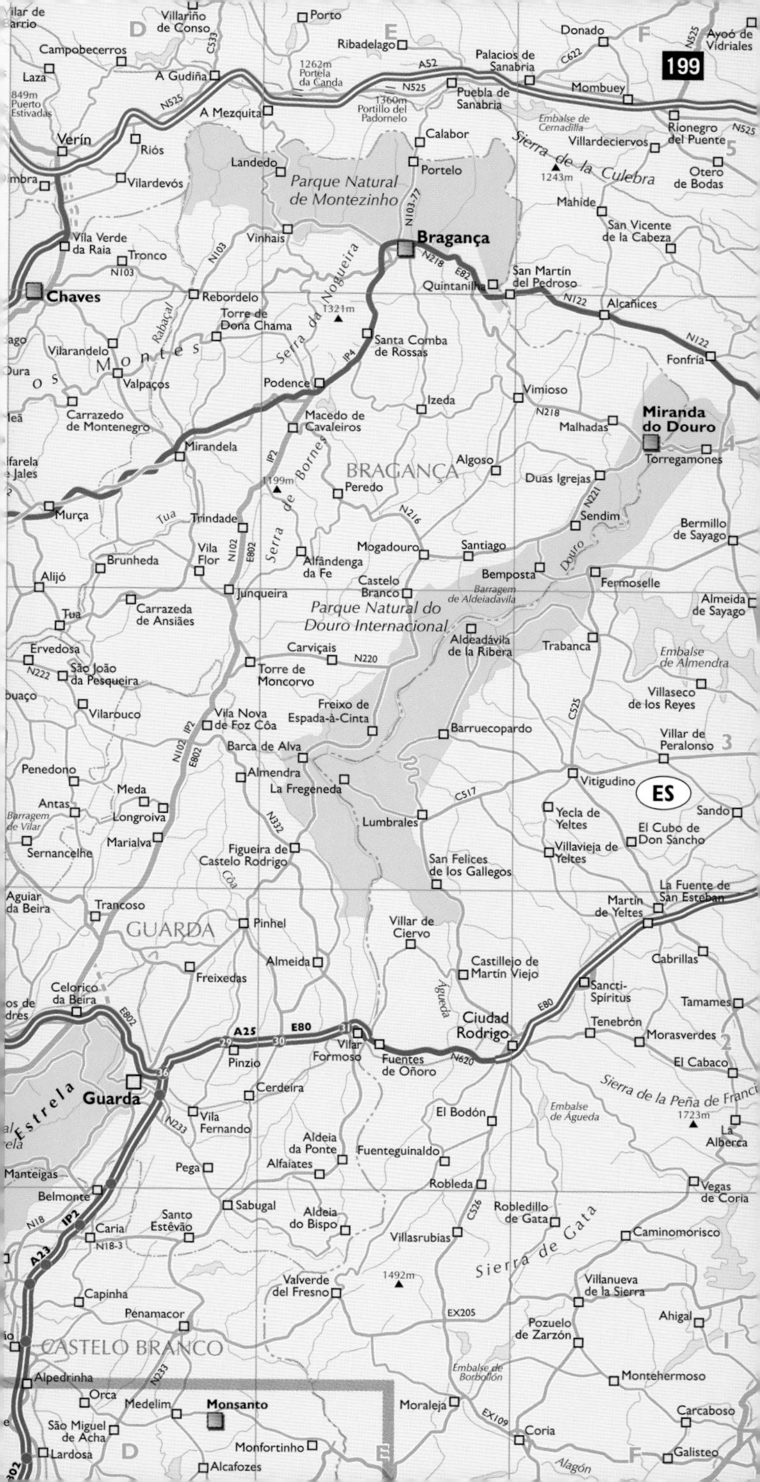
199
Villariño de Conso
Porto
Ribadelago
Donado
Ayoó de Vidriales
Campobecerros
Laza
A Gudiña
Palacios de Sanabria
Mombuey
1262m Portela da Canda
1360m Portillo del Padornelo
Puebla de Sanabria
849m Puerto Estivadas
A Mezquita
Embalse de Cernadilla
Rionegro del Puente
Verín
Riós
Calabor
Villardeciervos
Sierra de la Culebra
1243m
Otero de Bodas
Landedo
Portelo
Vilardevós
Parque Natural de Montezinho
Mahide
San Vicente de la Cabeza
Vila Verde da Raia
Tronco
Vinhais
Bragança
Chaves
Rebordelo
Quintanilha
San Martín del Pedroso
Alcañices
Torre de Dona Chama
1321m
Serra da Nogueira
Santa Comba de Rossas
Fonfría
Vilarandelo
Montes
Valpaços
Podence
Vimioso
Izeda
Miranda do Douro
Carrazedo de Montenegro
Macedo de Cavaleiros
Malhadas
Mirandela
Torregamones
Algoso
BRAGANÇA
Duas Igrejas
1199m
Serra de Bornes
Peredo
Murça
Trindade
Sendim
Bermillo de Sayago
Vila Flor
Serra de Bornes
Mogadouro
Santiago
Brunheda
Alfândenga da Fe
Bemposta
Douro
Alijó
Fermoselle
Junqueira
Castelo Branco
Barragem de Aldeiadavila
Almeida de Sayago
Carrazeda de Ansiães
Tua
Parque Natural do Douro Internacional
Aldeadávila de la Ribera
Trabanca
Ervedosa
Carviçais
Embalse de Almendra
São João da Pesqueira
Torre de Moncorvo
Villaseco de los Reyes
Vilarouco
Freixo de Espada-à-Cinta
Vila Nova de Foz Côa
Barruecopardo
Villar de Peralonso
Barca de Alva
Penedono
Almendra
Vitigudino
ES
La Fregeneda
Meda
Antas
Longroiva
Lumbrales
Yecla de Yeltes
Sando
Barragem de Vilar
El Cubo de Don Sancho
Marialva
Sernancelhe
Figueira de Castelo Rodrigo
Villavieja de Yeltes
San Felices de los Gallegos
Côa
Aguiar da Beira
La Fuente de San Esteban
Trancoso
Martín de Yeltes
GUARDA
Pinhel
Villar de Ciervo
Almeida
Castillejo de Martín Viejo
Cabrillas
Freixedas
Agueda
Sancti-Spíritus
Celorico da Beira
Tamames
Ciudad Rodrigo
Tenebrón
A25
E80
Vilar Formoso
Morasverdes
Pinzio
Fuentes de Oñoro
El Cabaco
Guarda
Cerdeira
Sierra de la Peña de Francia
Estrela
Vila Fernando
El Bodón
Embalse de Águeda
1723m
La Alberca
Aldeia da Ponte
Fuenteguinaldo
Alfaiates
Pega
Manteigas
Robleda
Vegas de Coria
Belmonte
Sabugal
Robledillo de Gata
Santo Estêvão
Aldeia do Bispo
Caria
Villasrubias
Caminomorisco
Sierra de Gata
1492m
Valverde del Fresno
Villanueva de la Sierra
Capinha
Penamacor
Ahigal
Pozuelo de Zarzón
CASTELO BRANCO
Embalse de Borbollón
Alpedrinha
Montehermoso
Orca
Medelim
Monsanto
Moraleja
Carcaboso
São Miguel de Acha
Coria
Monfortinho
Lardosa
Galisteo
Alcafozes
Alagón

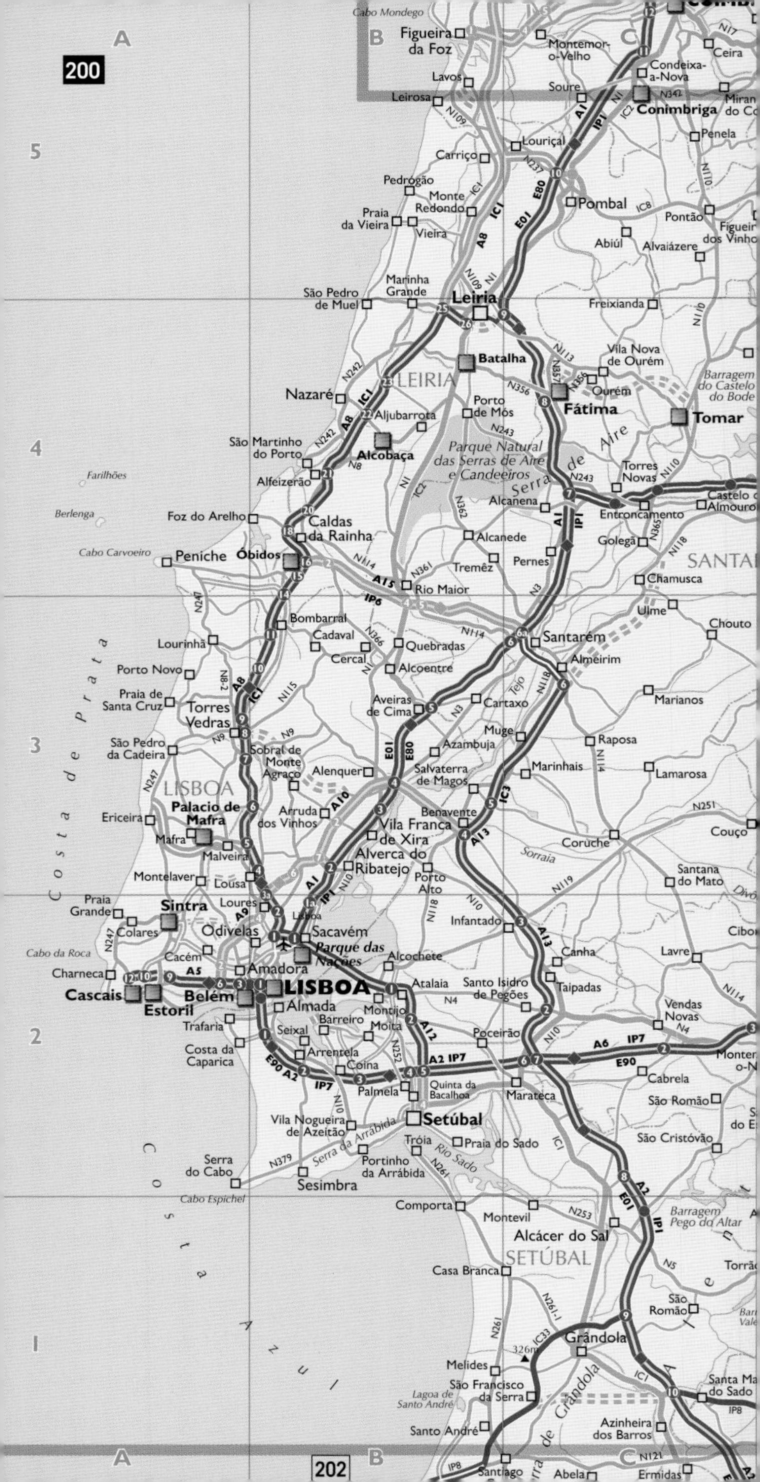
200
A
B
C
5
4
3
2
1
202
Cabo Mondego
Figueira da Foz
Montemor-o-Velho
Condeixa-a-Nova
Ceira
Lavos
Soure
Leirosa
Conimbriga
Penela
Louriçal
Carriço
Pedrogão
Monte Redondo
Pombal
Praia da Vieira
Vieira
Pontão
Abiúl
Alvaiázere
Marinha Grande
São Pedro de Muel
Leiria
Freixianda
Batalha
Vila Nova de Ourém
Ourém
Barragem do Castelo do Bode
LEIRIA
Nazaré
Porto de Mós
Fátima
Tomar
Aljubarrota
Alcobaça
São Martinho do Porto
Parque Natural das Serras de Aire e Candeeiros
Serra de Aire
Torres Novas
Farilhões
Alfeizerão
Alcanena
Entroncamento
Castelo de Almourol
Berlenga
Foz do Arelho
Caldas da Rainha
Alcanede
Golegã
Cabo Carvoeiro
Peniche
Óbidos
Tremêz
Pernes
SANTAR
Rio Maior
Chamusca
Ulme
Chouto
Bombarral
Cadaval
Quebradas
Santarém
Lourinhã
Cercal
Alcoentre
Almeirim
Porto Novo
Praia de Santa Cruz
Torres Vedras
Aveiras de Cima
Cartaxo
Marianos
Costa de Prata
São Pedro da Cadeira
Sobral de Monte Agraço
Muge
Azambuja
Raposa
Alenquer
Salvaterra de Magos
Marinhais
Lamarosa
LISBOA
Palacio de Mafra
Ericeira
Arruda dos Vinhos
Benavente
Vila Franca de Xira
Mafra
Malveira
Alverca do Ribatejo
Coruche
Couço
Sorraia
Montelavar
Lousa
Porto Alto
Santana do Mato
Praia Grande
Sintra
Loures
Colares
Odivelas
Sacavém
Infantado
Cabo da Roca
Cacém
Parque das Nações
Alcochete
Canha
Lavre
Charneca
Amadora
Atalaia
Santo Isidro de Pegões
Taipadas
Cascais
Estoril
Belém
LISBOA
Almada
Montijo
Vendas Novas
Trafaria
Barreiro
Seixal
Moita
Poceirão
Costa da Caparica
Arrentela
Coina
Cabrela
Palmela
Quinta da Bacalhoa
Marateca
São Romão
Vila Nogueira de Azeitão
Setúbal
São Cristóvão
Serra da Arrábida
Tróia
Praia do Sado
Rio Sado
Serra do Cabo
Portinho da Arrábida
Sesimbra
Cabo Espichel
Costa Azul
Comporta
Montevil
Barragem Pego do Altar
Alcácer do Sal
SETÚBAL
Casa Branca
Torrão
São Romão
Grândola
326m
Melides
São Francisco da Serra
Lagoa de Santo André
Santa Margarida do Sado
Azinheira dos Barros
Santo André
Serra de Grândola
Santiago
Abela
Ermidas
A1
A2
A5
A6
A8
A9
A10
A12
A13
A15
IP1
IP6
IP7
IP8
IC1
IC2
IC3
IC8
IC33
E01
E80
E90
N1
N3
N4
N5
N8
N9
N10
N109
N110
N113
N114
N115
N118
N119
N121
N237
N242
N243
N247
N251
N252
N253
N261
N261-1
N342
N356
N357
N361
N362
N365
N366
N379
N8-2

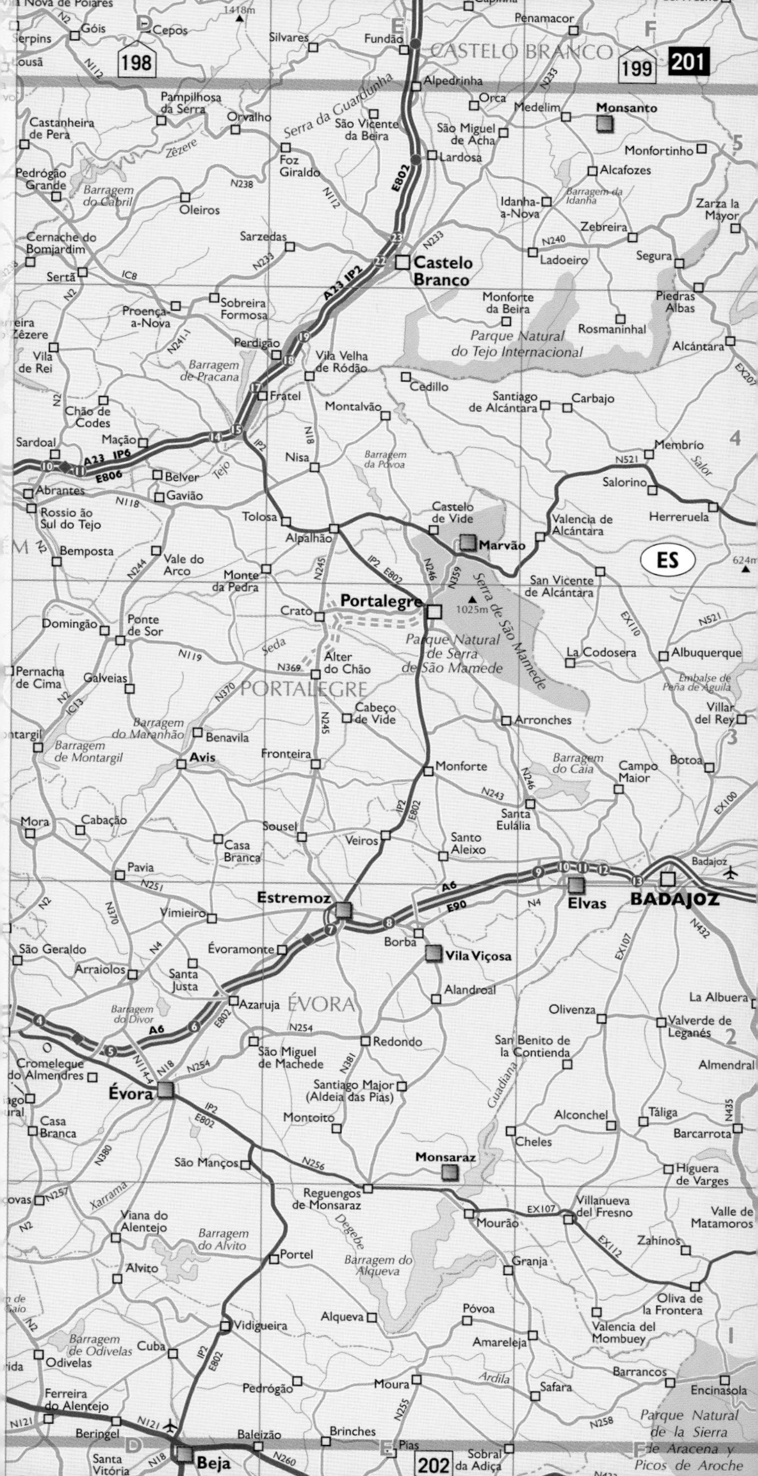
198
199
202
CASTELO BRANCO
PORTALEGRE
ÉVORA
ES
Góis
Cepos
Serpins
Lousã
Silvares
Fundão
Penamacor
Alpedrinha
Orca
Medelim
Monsanto
Pampilhosa da Serra
Orvalho
Serra da Guardunha
São Vicente da Beira
São Miguel de Acha
Castanheira de Pera
Zêzere
Foz Giraldo
Lardosa
Monfortinho
Alcafozes
Pedrógão Grande
Barragem do Cabril
Oleiros
Idanha-a-Nova
Barragem da Idanha
Zarza la Mayor
Cernache do Bomjardim
Sarzedas
Zebreira
Castelo Branco
Ladoeiro
Segura
Sertã
Sobreira Formosa
Monforte da Beira
Piedras Albas
Proença-a-Nova
Parque Natural do Tejo Internacional
Rosmaninhal
Alcántara
Perdigão
Vila de Rei
Barragem de Pracana
Vila Velha de Ródão
Cedillo
Fratel
Montalvão
Santiago de Alcántara
Carbajo
Chão de Codes
Sardoal
Mação
Barragem da Póvoa
Membrío
Nisa
Salor
Belver
Tejo
Abrantes
Gavião
Salorino
Rossio ão Sul do Tejo
Tolosa
Castelo de Vide
Herreruela
Alpalhão
Valencia de Alcántara
Marvão
Bemposta
Vale do Arco
Monte da Pedra
San Vicente de Alcántara
Portalegre
Crato
Serra de São Mamede
1025m
624m
1418m
Domingão
Ponte de Sor
Seda
Parque Natural de Serra de São Mamede
La Codosera
Albuquerque
Alter do Chão
Pernacha de Cima
Galveias
Embalse de Peña de Águila
Cabeço de Vide
Villar del Rey
Arronches
Barragem do Maranhão
Benavila
Barragem de Montargil
Avis
Fronteira
Barragem do Caia
Campo Maior
Botoa
Monforte
Mora
Cabação
Santa Eulália
Sousel
Casa Branca
Veiros
Santo Aleixo
Badajoz
Pavia
Estremoz
Elvas
BADAJOZ
Vimieiro
São Geraldo
Évoramonte
Borba
Vila Viçosa
Arraiolos
Santa Justa
Alandroal
La Albuera
Barragem do Divor
Azaruja
Olivenza
Valverde de Leganés
Redondo
San Benito de la Contienda
Cromeleque do Almendres
São Miguel de Machede
Almendral
Évora
Santiago Major (Aldeia das Pias)
Casa Branca
Montoito
Alconchel
Táliga
Guadiana
Cheles
Barcarrota
São Manços
Monsaraz
Higuera de Varges
Xarrama
Reguengos de Monsaraz
Viana do Alentejo
Degebe
Villanueva del Fresno
Mourão
Valle de Matamoros
Barragem do Alvito
Portel
Zahínos
Alvito
Barragem do Alqueva
Granja
Oliva de la Frontera
Alqueva
Póvoa
Vidigueira
Valencia del Mombuey
Barragem de Odivelas
Cuba
Amareleja
Odivelas
Ardila
Barrancos
Pedrógão
Moura
Safara
Encinasola
Ferreira do Alentejo
Parque Natural de la Sierra de Aracena y Picos de Aroche
Beringel
Baleizão
Brinches
Pias
Sobral da Adiça
Santa Vitória
Beja
A23 IP2
E802
A23 IP6
E806
A6
E90
IP2
N2
N18
N112
N118
N119
N233
N238
N240
N244
N245
N246
N251
N254
N256
N257
N258
N260
N121
N359
N369
N370
N380
N381
N4
N243
N255
N432
N435
N521
N114-4
N241-1
IC8
IC13
EX107
EX110
EX112
EX100
EX207

200
201
202
A
B
C
D
E
1
2
3
ES
Beja
Faro
Lagos
Portimão
Silves
Albufeira
Loulé
Tavira
Estói
Olhão
Sagres
Cabo de São Vicente
Ponta de Sagres
Sines
Cabo de Sines
Santiago do Cacém
Santo André
Vila Nova de Milfontes
Odemira
Aljezur
Mértola
Alcoutim
Castro Verde
Ourique
Almodôvar
Serpa
Moura
Huelva
Ayamonte
Vila Real de Santo António
Serra de Monchique
Monchique
902m
Fóia
Serra do Caldeirão
Parque Natural do Vale do Guadiana
Sierra de Aracena
de la Sierra de Aracena y Picos de Aroche
Costa de la Luz
Guadiana
Alte
Carvoeiro
Alvor
Praia da Rocha
Praia de Dona Ana
Praia da Luz
Praia de Odeceixe
Praia de Monte Clérigo
Praia da Arrifana
Praia da Bordeira
Praia do Amado
Praia da Cordoama
Praia do Castelejo
Praia da Marinha
Armação de Pera
Ilha de Tavira
Ilha da Armona
Quinta do Lago
Vale do Lobo
Vilamoura
Quarteira
Almancil
Vila Romana de Milreu
São Brás de Alportel
Moncarapacho
Fuseta
Cacela Velha
Praia Verde
Monte Gordo
Castro Marim
Odeleite
Cachopo
Martim Longo
Pereiro
Espírito Santo
Santana de Cambas
Mina de São Domingos
Vale do Poço
Aldeia Nova de São Bento
Rosal de la Frontera
Aroche
Cortegana
A22
A2
IP1
E01
IC27
A49
N120
N125
N2
N122
N124

Picture credits

The Automobile Association would like to thank the following photographers, companies and picture libraries for their assistance in the preparation of this book.

Abbreviations for the picture credits are: (t) top; (b) bottom; (c) centre; (l) left; (r) right; (AA) AA World Travel Library

2i AA/J Edmanson; **2**ii AA/C Jones; **2**iii AA/M Wells; **2**iv AA/T Harris; **3**i AA/A Mockford and N Bonetti; **3**ii www.photolibrary.com; **3**iii AA/C Jones; **3**iv AA/M Wells; **5**l AA/J Edmanson; **5**c AA/M Wells; **5**r AA/M Wells; **6/7** AA/M Wells; **9** AA/A Mockford and N Bonetti; **11** AA/A Mockford and N Bonetti; **12** AA/C Jones; **13** AA/A Mockford and N Bonetti; **14** AA/T Harris; **15** AA/A Mockford and N Bonetti; **16** AA/A Mockford and N Bonetti; **17** AA/A Mockford and N Bonetti; **18** AA/A Mockford and N Bonetti; **19**t AA/A Kouprianoff; **19**c AA/M Wells; **21** AA/M Wells; **22-23** www.photolibrary.com; **24** AA/A Mockford and N Bonetti; **25**l www.photolibrary.com; **25**r AA/P Wilson; **26**l Getty Images/Sean Gallup; **26**r www.photolibrary.com; **27** AA/P Wilson; **28** AA/C Jones; **30** AA/C Jones; **31**l AA/C Jones; **31**c AA/M Wells; **31**r AA/M Wells; **41**l AA/M Wells; **41**c AA/M Wells; **41**r AA/M Wells; **43** AA/M Wells; **44** AA/M Wells; **45**t AA/M Wells; **45**b AA/A Mockford and N Bonetti; **46** AA/M Wells; **47** AA/T Harris; **48** AA/M Wells; **49** AA/M Wells; **50** The Mirror of Venus, **1870-76** (oil on canvas), Burne-Jones, Sir Edward (**1833-98**)/Museu Calouste Gulbenkian, Lisbon, Portugal/The Bridgeman Art Library; **51** AA/A Kouprianoff; **52** AA/M Wells; **53** AA/M Wells; **54** AA/M Wells; **55** AA/A Kouprianoff; **56** AA/A Kouprianoff; **57** AA/M Wells; **58** AA/M Wells; **59**t AA/A Mockford and N Bonetti; **59**b AA/M Wells; **60/61** AA/A Mockford and N Bonetti; **61** AA/T Harris; **62** AA/A Mockford and N Bonetti; **63** AA/A Kouprianoff; **64** AA/M Wells; **65**t AA/M Wells; **65**b AA/A Mockford and N Bonetti; **66** AA/A Kouprianoff; **75**l AA/T Harris; **75**c AA/T Harris; **75**r AA/T Harris; **76** AA/T Harris; **77** AA/P Wilson; **78** AA/T Harris; **79**t AA/A Mockford and N Bonetti; **79**b AA/A Mockford and N Bonetti; **80** AA/T Harris; **80/81** AA/P Wilson; **82**t AA/T Harris; **82**b AA/A Mockford and N Bonetti; **83** AA/A Kouprianoff; **84** AA/A Mockford and N Bonetti; **85** AA/T Harris; **86/87** AA/T Harris; **88** AA/A Mockford and N Bonetti; **89**t AA/A Mockford and N Bonetti; **89**b AA/A Kouprianoff; **90** AA/A Mockford and N Bonetti; **91** AA/A Mockford and N Bonetti; **92** AA/T Harris; **93** AA/P Wilson; **94**t AA/C Jones; **94**b AA/A Kouprianoff; **95** AA/A Kouprianoff; **101**l AA/A Mockford and N Bonetti; **101**c AA/A Kouprianoff; **101**r AA/A Mockford and N Bonetti; **103** AA/A Kouprianoff; **104** AA/A Kouprianoff; **105** AA/A Mockford and N Bonetti; **106** www.photolibrary.com; **107** AA/A Kouprianoff; **108** AA/A Kouprianoff; **109** www.photolibrary.com; **110** AA/A Kouprianoff; **111** AA/A Kouprianoff; **112** AA/P Wilson; **113** AA/A Kouprianoff; **114** AA/A Kouprianoff; **115** AA/A Mockford and N Bonetti; **116**c AA/A Kouprianoff; **116**b AA/A Kouprianoff; **117** AA/T Harris; **118** AA/T Harris; **119** AA/A Mockford and N Bonetti; **120** AA/T Harris; **121** AA/A Mockford and N Bonetti; **122** AA/A Kouprianoff; **127**l www.photolibrary.com; **127**c AA/A Mockford and N Bonetti; **127**r AA/A Kouprianoff; **128** AA/J Edmanson; **130** AA/A Kouprianoff; **131**t AA/A Mockford and N Bonetti; **131**b AA/A Kouprianoff; **132** AA/A Mockford and N Bonetti; **133** AA/A Kouprianoff; **134** AA/P Wilson; **136** AA/A Mockford and N Bonetti; **137** www.photolibrary.com; **138** AA/A Kouprianoff; **139** AA/A Kouprianoff; **140** AA/J Edmanson; **141** AA/A Kouprianoff; **142** AA/A Kouprianoff; **147**l AA/C Jones; **147**c AA/C Jones; **147**r AA/C Jones; **148** AA/C Jones; **149** AA/C Jones; **150** AA/C Jones; **151**t AA/M Chaplow; **151**b AA/C Jones; **152** AA/M Chaplow; **153** AA/C Jones; **154** AA/M Chaplow; **155** AA/M Chaplow; **156/157** AA/A Mockford and N Bonetti; **157** AA/A Kouprianoff; **158** AA/J Edmanson; **159** AA/C Jones; **160** AA/C Jones; **161** AA/A Mockford and N Bonetti; **162** AA/M Chaplow; **163**t AA/M Birkitt; **163**b AA/C Jones; **164** AA/M Chaplow; **165** AA/A Kouprianoff; **171**l AA/M Wells; **171**c AA/J Edmanson; **171**r AA/S Day; **172** AA/A Mockford and N Bonetti; **174** AA/M Wells; **176** AA/A Kouprianoff; **178** AA/A Kouprianoff; **179** AA/T Harris; **180** AA/M Birkitt; **181** AA/P Wilson; **183** AA/J Edmanson; **184** AA/C Jones; **186** AA/M Chaplow; **187**l AA/A Mockford and N Bonetti; **187**c AA/A Kouprianoff; **187**r AA/M Jourdan; **191**t AA/M Chaplow; **191**c AA/A Mockford and N Bonetti; **191**b AA/C Jones

Every effort has been made to trace the copyright holders, and we apologise in advance for any unintentional omissions or errors. We would be pleased to apply any corrections in a following edition of this publication.

Questionnaire

Dear Traveler

Your comments, opinions and recommendations are very important to us. So please help us to improve our travel guides by taking a few minutes to complete this simple questionnaire.

Send to: Spiral Guides, MailStop 64, 1000 AAA Drive, Heathrow, FL 32746–5063

Your recommendations...

We always encourage readers' recommendations for restaurants, nightlife or shopping – if your recommendation is added to the next edition of the guide, we will send you a FREE AAA Spiral Guide of your choice. Please state below the establishment name, location and your reasons for recommending it.

____

____

____

____

____

Please send me AAA Spiral ______________________________
(see list of titles inside the back cover)

About this guide...

Which title did you buy?

______________________________ AAA Spiral

Where did you buy it? ______________________________

When? m m / y y

Why did you choose a AAA Spiral Guide? ______________________________

____

____

____

____

Did this guide meet your expectations?

Exceeded ☐ Met all ☐ Met most ☐ Fell below ☐

Please give your reasons ______________________________

____

____

____

____

continued on next page...

Were there any aspects of this guide that you particularly liked?

Is there anything we could have done better?

About you...

Name (Mr/Mrs/Ms)

Address

Zip

Daytime tel nos.

Which age group are you in?

Under 25 ☐ 25–34 ☐ 35–44 ☐ 45–54 ☐ 55–64 ☐ 65+ ☐

How many trips do you make a year?

Less than one ☐ One ☐ Two ☐ Three or more ☐

Are you a AAA member? Yes ☐ No ☐

Name of AAA club

About your trip...

When did you book? m m / y y When did you travel? m m / y y

How long did you stay?

Was it for business or leisure?

Did you buy any other travel guides for your trip? Yes ☐ No ☐

If yes, which ones?

Thank you for taking the time to complete this questionnaire.